JOAN HAMBURG'S
# Most-for-Your-Money
## NEW YORK SHOPPING, FOOD AND SERVICES GUIDE

Books by Joan Hamburg

*New York on $25 a Day* (originally *New York on $5 a Day*)
*The New York Lunch Book*

# JOAN HAMBURG'S
# Most-for-Your-Money
## NEW YORK SHOPPING, FOOD AND SERVICES GUIDE

**RAWSON ASSOCIATES**
*New York*

Library of Congress Cataloging in Publication Data

Hamburg, Joan.
  Joan Hamburg's Most-for-your-money New York shopping, food and services guide.

  Includes index.
  1. Shopping—New York (N.Y.)—Directories.    2. New York (N.Y.)—Stores, shopping centers, etc.—Directories.
I. Title.   II. Title: Most-for-your-money New York shopping, food and services guide.
TX335.H343   1983        380.1′029′47471       81-42698
ISBN 0-89256-241-2
ISBN 0-89256-242-0 (pbk.)

Copyright © 1983 by Maplehill Communications, Inc.
All rights reserved
Published simultaneously in Canada by McClelland & Stewart, Ltd.
Composition by Westchester Book Composition Inc.
Yorktown Heights, New York
Printed and bound by Fairfield Graphics,
Fairfield, Pennsylvania
Designed by Jacques Chazaud
First Edition

For Skip, Liz and John

# Contents

*Acknowledgments xiii*
*Before you begin this book xv*

## I. SHOPPING AND FOOD GUIDE

Appliances *4*
   The Lower East Side *4*
   Appliances by Phone *5*
Art Prints and Posters *5*
Art Supplies and Related Items *6*
   Beads, Buttons, Notions and Trimmings *6*
   Ceramic and Sculpture Supplies *7*
   Dyes and Theatrical Paints *7*
   Miniatures, Models and Hobby Supplies *8*
   Needlework Supplies *9*
   Stained-Glass Supplies *10*
   Stencil Supplies *10*
Auctions *11*
   Unclaimed Merchandise *12*

Bathroom Accessories *13*
Beer- and Winemaking Supplies *14*
Bicycles *14*
Bookstores *15*
Bottles *17*
Buttons and Zippers *18*
Candles and Talismans *19*
Cigars *20*
Clothing and Accessories *20*
   Antique Clothing *20*
   Children's Clothing *22*
   Clothing for Women by Location *25*
      The Lower East Side *25*
      Seventh Avenue and Around Manhattan *26*
      Out of Manhattan and Out of Town *28*

Clothing in Extra-Small and
    Extra-Large Sizes for
    Men and Women  30
Costumes  32
Custom-made Shirts  33
Furs  34
Handbags, Hats and
    Gloves  35
Hip Chic  37
Lingerie and Hosiery  39
Maternity Clothes  41
Men's Clothing  42
Men, Women and
    Children's Clothing  45
Resale and Thrift Shops  48
Shoes  50
    Athletic Shoes  50
    Children's Shoes  50
    Men's Shoes  50
    Shoes for Men and
        Women  51
    Shoes for Men, Women
        and Children  52
    Women's Shoes  52
Sporting Goods and
    Clothing  53
    Billiard and Gaming
        Tables  55
    Dancewear  55
    Fishing and Boating
        Gear  56
    Riding and Western Wear
        and Gear  56
    Wedding Dresses  58
Closeout Stores  59
Drugstores and
    Pharmacies  60

Electronics Equipment  62
Eyeglasses  62
Fabrics  63
Feathers and Flowers  65
Fireplace Accessories  66
Firewood  67
Flea Markets  67
Flowers  70
Food  70
    Caviar  71
    Cheese  71
    Chinatown Shopping  72
    Chocolates  73
    Coffee and Tea  74
    Dried Fruits and Nuts  74
    Farmers' Markets  75
    Gourmet Emporia  75
    Meats  79
    Pasta  80
    Poultry Market  80
    Sausages  81
    Scandinavian Specialties  81
    Spanish Foods  81
    Wholesale Markets  82
    Wine and Liquor  83
Furniture  84
    Architectural Salvage  84
    Brass  84
    Butcher Blocks  85
    Canvas—That Casual
        Look  85
    Children's Furniture  86
    Furniture by Phone  86
    Pillow Furniture  87
    Plastics  87

CONTENTS ix

Hot Tubs 89
Housewares 89
International Handicrafts 91
Jewelry 92
Kitchenware and Cutlery 93
Lamps and Lighting 94
Linens, Beds and Bedding 96
Luggage 98
Magic 98
Millinery Supplies 99
Music Boxes 99
Musical Instruments 100
Newspapers and Magazines 101
Office Equipment 102
Paint, Wallpaper and Window Shades 102
Perfumes 104
Pets 105
Photographic Equipment 108
Picture Framing 109
Records and Tapes 110
Rugs and Carpets 110
Scientific Equipment 111
Seashells 112
Stamps, Coins and Antiquities 112
Stone and Tile 113
Toys 113
Umbrellas 116
Videocassettes and Discs 116

## II. SERVICES GUIDE

Adult Education—A Smorgasbord of Courses 121
Beauty Services 125
    Beauty Bargains 125
    Beauty on the House 126
    Days of Beauty 127
    Face-lifts Without Surgery 129
    Make-over Magic—Getting It/Keeping It 129
    Nail Salons 131
    Trichologists/Hair Care 131
Brief Vacations 132
    Art Tours 132
    Atlantic City—The Luxury Bus 133
Bed and Breakfast Accommodations 133
The Best Bus Tours 134
Brass Rubbings and English Tea 134
Cut Your Own Christmas Tree 135
Folk Dancing 135
Fossil Tours 136
Home Exchange Vacations 136
Learning Vacations 137
Lincoln Center Tours 137
Living Luxuriously Abroad 138
Pick Your Own Fruits and Vegetables 138

Unusual Outings  139
Walking Tours  140
City Gardening  140
Dry Cleaners, Laundries,
  Tailors and Dyers  143
  Dry Cleaning  143
  Dyeing  144
  Hand Laundering  145
  Leather and Suede Cleaning,
    Repairing and
    Restoring  145
  Mending and Tailoring  146
Experts and Consultants  146
  Antique Appraisals  146
  Contractors  147
  Image Consultants  147
  Interior Designers  148
  Moving Consultants  148
  Shoppers, Gift Brokers and
    People Who Will Do
    Anything at All  149
  Writers and Researchers  152
  Miscellaneous Services  153
    Baby-sitters  153
    Dating Service  154
    Diet Food Delivery  154
    Divorce and Will Kits—Do
      It Yourself  155
    Fireplace and Heating
      Stove Installation and
      Renovation  156
    Flagmakers  156
    Florists  157
    Homework Help  157
    Knife Sharpening  158
    Marriage Counseling  158
    Massage  159
    Office and Office Personnel
      Rental  159
    Postal Services  160
    Realistic Environmental
      Portraiture  160
    Sanding Machines—
      Rental  161
    Seltzer Delivery  161
    Singing Telegrams,
      etc.  162
    Stretcher Makers  163
    Tuxedo Rental  163
    Wine by Wire  163
    Women's Sports Hot
      Line  164
Getting a Job—Employment
  Services and
  Counseling  164
  For Young Adults  166
  For the Over-Forty Exec  167
Health  167
  Dentistry  168
  Headaches  168
  Heart Trouble  169
  Help for Stutterers  169
  Lifelines and Emergency
    Care  170
  Losing Weight and Learning
    to Eat Correctly  171
  Medical and Health
    Information  172
  Medical Help Abroad  173
  Medical Massage  173
  Stop Smoking  174
Household Cleaning and
  Help  174

## CONTENTS xi

Disaster Specialists *174*
Fabrics and Upholstered Furniture *175*
Mixed Bags *176*
Rugs and Carpets—Cleaning and Reweaving *177*
Window Plus *177*
International New York *177*
   Arab Atlantic Avenue *178*
   Athens in Astoria *181*
   Brooklyn's Little Scandinavia *184*
   Little India *187*
   Ukrainian East Village *190*
Money *194*
   Buying Art for Investment *194*
   Contests *195*
   The Debt Dilemma *195*
   Foundation Grants *196*
   Fund Raising *196*
   Measuring the Risk of Your Stock Market Investments *197*
   Setting Up Business After You Relocate *197*
   Tracing Old Stock Certificates *198*
Parties *199*
   Bartenders *199*
   Especially for Children *199*
   The Food *201*
      Caterers, Picnics and Platters *201*
      Chinese Banquets *204*
      Gourmet Shops *205*
      Picnics Only *207*
      Where to Get the Cake *207*
   Party Entertainers *208*
   Party Places/Party Ideas *210*
   Party Planners *212*
   Party Poems *213*
   Party Supplies and Favors *213*
   Teen Party Ideas *214*
   White House Greetings *215*
Photographic Services *215*
   Camera Rental *215*
   Color Printing and Developing *216*
   Damaged Movie Film Repair *216*
   Darkroom Rental *216*
Psyche and Spirit *217*
   Choose a Therapist *221*
   Handwriting Analysis *224*
Repairers, Restylers and Restorers *224*
   Antiques *225*
   Appliances, Household *225*
   Brass Renewal *225*
   Camping Wear and Gear and Outdoor Equipment *226*
   Cane and Wicker Furniture *227*
   China, Crystal and Glassware *227*
      How to Find Discontinued Patterns—China, Crystal and Silver *228*
   Dolls *229*

Furniture Stripping and Restyling 229
Handbags 230
Jewelry 230
Lamps 231
Leather Goods 231
Pianos 232
Sewing Machines 233
Shoes and Boots 233
Tin and Copperware 234
Upholsterers 235
Anything Missing? 236
Shopping for a Neighborhood You Can Afford— Renaissance Neighborhoods 236
Avenues B and C: The Far East 237
Brooklyn Brownstoning— Sunset Park and Greenpoint 237

The Fifth Outer Borough: Washington Heights-Inwood 239
The Kosher Bronx—Pelham Parkway 240
Ridgewood—Living in Two Boroughs 240
Staten Island: The Forgotten Borough—St. George, Tompkinsville and Stapleton 241
Shopping for Sports 242
Belly Dancing 242
Dancing, Roller Skating and Dancing on Skates 243
Gymnastics 243
Running 245
Theater 245

## Acknowledgments

I would like to give special thanks to my wonderful listeners, who were instrumental in urging me to prepare such a book. Also special thanks to Rina Bulkin for her expert research assistance, great sense of adventure and willingness to explore untapped areas of New York.

Special thanks to my publisher, Eleanor Rawson, whose enthusiasm, suggestions and love affair with Manhattan added to every page.

## Before You Begin This Book

I love this town. It's been good to me and my family—a source of constant stimulation and excitement, an ever-changing and always provocative kaleidoscopic environment, where life is lived with more intensity than any other place on earth.

In New York everything is possible and the improbable happens every day. Like Lewis Carroll's White Queen, New Yorkers have all learned to believe "six impossible things before breakfast." Just walk down any street and you'll likely see impromptu flea markets, bizarrely attired punk rockers with rainbow-hued hair, three-card monte games with a lookout keeping an anxious eye peeled for the cops, businesspeople wheeling and dealing in front of office buildings, joggers and roller skaters, at least ten people whose behavior would get them certified anywhere else, Hare Krishnas, food carts selling everything from crepes to Japanese dumplings, petitioners for half a dozen political causes... and nine out of ten people rushing by without noticing any of it.

The streets can be tough, but so are New Yorkers, who pride themselves on their "street smarts," survival ability and possession of endless tidbits of information that make the difference between just existing and relishing the urban experience. I've discovered it's inside information that counts, and the more of it you have, the easier it is to relate to what makes this city tick.

The truly savvy urbanite doesn't even have to live here. There are legions of suburbanites and country cousins who, fortified with fresh air, make frequent forays into town, seeking out the best restaurants, shopping bargains, theater, music, art—seeking out all that makes life richer.

As consumer director and broadcaster for WOR radio, with many years of television and journalism behind me, I've spent just about my whole adult life tracking down the kinds of data that are so essential to all of us who deal with this very complex city. For years I've responded to thousands of letters and calls each week requesting information about shopping, services, educational opportunities, health problems, finance, vacations—just about anything and everything that has to do with basic survival, life enhancement and, of course, saving money. The information kept piling up. When it reached the point of no return—files bursting, notebooks overflowing, bookshelves piled to the ceiling with research—I decided it was time to share.

It's taken more than a year to go through the lot—a year of perusal, sorting through, adding to and expanding upon those immense reserves of information. The result is a book of the most valuable secrets from my private files, a book that will allow you, too, to be a consumer expert and New York maven (*maven* is the Yiddish word for one who is experienced and knowledgeable).

There are hundreds of bargain stores and get-it-for-less ideas and suggestions in this book, but it's much more than a bargain book. If you can afford it, I'll send you to the best hairdressers in town; if not, I'll tell you how to have your hair done free at a posh salon. If, on your next vacation, you'd like to rent a luxurious villa in Italy for $5,000 a month, I'll tell you how to go about finding one...but I'll also steer you to luxury accommodations abroad that won't cost you a cent. I'll tell you how to throw a lavish party on a yacht...or how to arrange a very impressive affair at an eighteenth-century Georgian mansion for under $10 a person. Where to buy the most exquisite and beautifully displayed gourmet food in town...and where to skip the frills and get the same food for much less.

And I'll give you the inside scoop on New York's most fascinating ethnic neighborhoods (visiting them is like traveling without leaving town)...on areas of the city where you can still buy a building for under $40,000...on how to find a job, and how to invest the money you make...on how to keep in shape...on exploring the inner you, spiritually and psychologically...on learning everything from wok cookery to how to marry money...on losing weight and stopping smoking...on dealing with health problems...on where to get just about anything repaired, restored or otherwise serviced...on city gardening...on where to buy everything from architectural salvage to zippers (and thousands of other items)...on where to get the best blinis and burgers, not to mention dim sum, sushi, steak au poivre, soft-shell crabs, tortellini, chiles rellenos and tandoori chicken...and much more, because in New York, there's always so much more of everything.

# JOAN HAMBURG'S
# Most-for-Your-Money
## NEW YORK SHOPPING, FOOD AND SERVICES GUIDE

# I
# Shopping and Food Guide

Shopping in New York is such an adventure that even after many years as a consumerist, I'm still thrilled by it.

There are entire districts for plants and flowers, meat, beads and feathers, lamps, restaurant supplies, butcher blocks, diamonds and just about everything else. And I always find that out-of-towners' eyes pop over places (all described below) like Dean & DeLuca, Kam Man Food Products, Unique Clothing Warehouse, Caswell-Massey, the Milan Laboratory and, of course, the entire Lower East Side. The latter is best visited on a Sunday for tourism purposes, but if you're going there for serious shopping, go during the week and avoid the mob scene.

Part of the excitement is that you can purchase everything from Cuisinarts to Cacharels at prices far below retail. This is true not only in Manhattan but throughout the metropolitan area, where factory outlets, wholesalers and discount houses that buy surplus merchandise and sell it for a fraction of the original cost abound.

Also thrilling: you can get anything at all, however esoteric, rare or exotic. Looking for an out-of-print book, a little-known sculpture implement, a North African spice, an Indian sari, a set of English Edwardian officer's buttons or a sculptured marble bidet? It's here, and more often than not there's a choice of where to buy it.

Enough said. Read on, and discover the greatest shopping center in the world.

# APPLIANCES

Knowledgeable New Yorkers never pay full retail prices for appliances. If you're in the market for an expensive major appliance, decide what make and model number you want (go to the most expensive, service-oriented store and talk it over with a knowledgeable salesperson); then comparison-shop for the best price. A good place to start is:

### *The Lower East Side*

Essex and Canal Street appliance stores all carry a wide range of major-brand appliances, in perfect condition and with the usual warranties, at prices *up to 50% less than retail*. They all stock every small appliance imaginable, some major ones like refrigerators and washing machines, as well as typewriters, telephone answering machines, TVs, stereo and video equipment, cameras, movie and slide projectors, vacuum cleaners and microwave ovens. Some even carry such diverse items as luggage, fine pens and china. You can call in advance about availability, but few of these shops quote prices over the phone.

On Canal Street between Essex and Orchard Streets, check out **Benny's Import & Export**, #51, 925-7535; **Kunst Sales Corporation**, #45, 966-1909; **Bondy Export Corporation**, #40, 925-7785; and **ABC Trading Company**, #31 (this one between Essex and Ludlow Streets), 228-5080.

Along Essex between Hester and Canal Streets, **Dembitzer Bros. Export Company**, #5, 254-1310; **Lewi Supply Company**, #15, 777-6910, and **Essex Camera & Electronics**, #17, 677-6420.

On Essex between Hester and Grand Streets, **Foto-Electric Supply Company**, #31, 673-5222, and **Central Electronics**, #39, 673-3220.

All the above stores are open from Sunday to Thursday approximately from 9:00 A.M. to 5:30 P.M., with early closing on Fridays, usually at 2 P.M.

## APPLIANCES BY PHONE

**Peninsula Buying Service,** 945-4100 or 516-239-0110
This is a telephone ordering service. Just ring up Steve Cohen, give him the make and model number you want, and a brand-new appliance, fully guaranteed, will be sent out to you cash on delivery. He carries all major appliances and will quote low discount prices over the phone. Steve is an expert on every item he sells, so give him a ring even if you haven't decided what brand to buy. Tell him your budget and needs, and he'll give you the best option, possibly even recommending something less expensive than you were planning. You can ring him up Monday to Saturday between 9:00 A.M. and 6:00 P.M.

A similar operation is **Pricewatchers,** 895-1335 or 516-222-9100; call weekdays between 9:00 A.M. and 5:00 P.M.

**International Solgo,** 1745 Hempstead Turnpike, Hempstead, 895-6996 or 516-354-8816, out-of-state, 800-645-8162
Like a small department store, this catalog showroom house displays thousands of items—all quality stock sold at low, low prices. In addition to name-brand major and minor appliances—everything from refrigerator units to food processors—Solgo carries jewelry, watches and clocks, silver, glassware, luggage, cookware, some furniture, fireplace equipment, tools, infant needs (from baby bottles and potty seats to car seats and strollers), toys, typewriters, stationery items and sporting goods. It ships all over the world (phone orders are accepted) and delivers in all five boroughs, Connecticut, Long Island and New Jersey. Open weekdays 8:30 A.M. to 7:00 P.M., Saturday 9:00 A.M. to 4:00 P.M.

## ART PRINTS AND POSTERS

**Oestreicher's Prints,** 43 West 46th Street, between Fifth and Sixth Avenues, 719-1212
The city's largest selection of lithographs, silkscreens, etchings, prints, art reproductions and posters—about 500,000 pieces in all—is found at Oestreicher's. The choices span art history from the beginning of time (reproductions of cave paintings) to the current scene and include works of every major artist in every genre. You can call to find out if the shop has a particular print you're searching for. It also

does custom framing on the premises. Open weekdays 10:00 A.M. to 5:45 P.M., Sunday to 4:30 P.M.

## ART SUPPLIES AND RELATED ITEMS

**Pearl Paint Co.,** 308 Canal Street, between Broadway and Church Street, 431-7932

Pearl Paint is the favored art supply shop (more like a supermarket really) of Soho artists. The reason: an unbelievably vast selection of paints and artist's supplies—all discounted 20% to 50%—and a very knowledgeable sales staff. The first floor is devoted to house paint. Artists' supplies begin on the mezzanine, where you'll find the world's largest selection of paints—oils, acrylics, watercolors, etc.—and brushes. The second floor houses vast stocks of paper as well as pastels, pencils, markers and other things used to draw on it. Framing and canvas of every grade and variety (plus all you need for stretching) are on the third floor. Fourth floor: graphics supplies, writing pens and inks, everything in the way of airbrush equipment and artist's furniture (easels, stools, etc.). Finally, the fifth floor has printmaking equipment, art books, sculpting supplies and tools, dyes and tapes. That's just the bare bones of it. Open Monday to Saturday 9:00 A.M. to 5:30 P.M., Sunday 11:00 A.M. to 4:45 P.M.

## BEADS, BUTTONS, NOTIONS AND TRIMMINGS

**Sheru Enterprises,** 49 West 38th Street, between Fifth and Sixth Avenues, 730-0766

If you're the artsy-craftsy type, a visit to Sheru will be more fun than a trip to Disneyland. On three vast floors are stocked a mind-boggling array of beads (imported, domestic, antique, semiprecious and handmade), macramé supplies, jewelry and jewelry accessories, ribbons, hair and hat ornaments, buttons, notions, cord, rhinestone bands, trimmings, stud machines, hobby kits, shoe clips, artificial flowers—and who knows what else a good search might turn up? The store personnel are very enthusiastic and knowledgeable; they can quickly lay their hands on the item you desire and will be happy to instruct you in any craft. Sheru sells both wholesale and retail, and its prices are low; beads bought by the pound are an especially good value. Open weekdays 9:00 A.M. to 6:00 P.M., Saturday 9:30 A.M. to 5:00 P.M.

## CERAMIC AND SCULPTURE SUPPLIES

**Ceramic Supply of New York and New Jersey,** 534 La Guardia Place, between Third and Bleecker Streets, 475-7236
Don't even bother to look elsewhere. I doubt there is any item of ceramic equipment made that you won't find here—every kind of clay, chemicals for glazing, tools (there are hundreds, some of which you've probably never seen that will inspire new creations), clay mixers, slab rollers, armatures, wheels (electric and kick), molds, kilns and a tantalizing array of glaze colors. If you'd like to learn the craft, Ceramic Supply teaches pottery, porcelain dollmaking; call for a class schedule. Open weekdays 9:00 A.M. to 6:00 P.M., Saturday 10:00 A.M. to 5:00 P.M. Another location in Lodi, N.J., 201-340-3005.

**Sculpture House,** 38 East 30th Street, between Fifth and Madison Avenues, 679-7474
All things related to sculpture, of which there are thousands, are domiciled at Sculpture House. Clay is just the beginning. There are armatures, molds and casts, kilns, modeling tools, power tools, carving tools, stone tools (and stone to carve), moldmaking equipment, vises finishing materials, studio furnishings, how-to-books and a full line c ceramic equipment and glazes. Sculpture House also produces custom-manufactured tools to the artist's specifications and does custom casting in all media. Open weekdays 8:30 A.M. to 6:00 P.M., Saturday 10:00 A.M. to 4:00 P.M.

## DYES AND THEATRICAL PAINTS

**Gothic Color Co., Inc.,** 727 Washington Street, between Bank and 11th Streets, 929-7493
Specializing in paints and dyes used in theatrical scenery (its colors provide optimum brilliancy under stage lighting), Gothic was created in 1927 especially to cope with the needs of set designers. It also sells related artist's supplies and dyes for batikwork and do-it-yourselfers who want to change the color of clothing or fabrics. The staff will help you choose the correct materials for a given job and explain thoroughly how to do it. Open weekdays only, 8:30 A.M. to 5:00 P.M.

## MINIATURES, MODELS AND HOBBY SUPPLIES

**Polk's Hobby,** 314 Fifth Avenue, at 32nd Street, 279-9034

The biggest hobby shop in the country, Polk imports equipment from all over the world and sells it both wholesale and retail. The shop has four floors of merchandise, much of it geared to the boy within the man (90% of its customers are adults) who enjoys putting together model vehicles and military miniatures. There are complete kits, tools and supplies and all kinds of marvelous little motors, two-ounce fuel tanks, tiny wheels, fittings and propellers. For railroad buffs, there's not only a wide choice of rolling stock and track but almost infinite scenic accessories, tiny people, animals, Woolworth's hamburger stands, drive-in banks, etc. The military line is almost equally intriguing, including as it does every type of fighting man from ancient Cretan archers to Vietcong guerrillas, weaponry, war games, war vehicles, medieval and space figures, battlegrounds and appropriate scenery (e.g., ruined cottages and wrecked vehicles). On a lighter note, there are many educational items for kids, like chemistry sets and accessories, and Polk has a very wide selection of dollhouse kits, furnishings (even wallpaper), construction supplies and electrical wiring equipment. Open Monday to Saturday 9:30 A.M. to 6:00 P.M., Thursday until 9:00 P.M., Sunday 11:00 A.M. to 5:00 P.M.

**B. Shackman and Company,** 85 Fifth Avenue, at 16th Street, 989-5162

Shackman is a delightful world of miniatures, dollhouses, Victorian dolls and stuffed animals. Salespeople in the retail store are friendly and low-key. Prices are reasonable, too. Open Monday to Friday 9:00 A.M. to 5:00 P.M., Saturday 10:00 A.M. to 4:00 P.M. (closed Saturday in the summer).

**Pinchpenny Miniatures,** 17 Idaho Lane, Mattawan, N.J. 07747

Dollhouse and dollhouse furniture collectors will be well advised to send away for the Pinchpenny catalog, which lists hundreds of miniatures and related items for the serious and not-so-serious collector. Everything is discounted, and the selection is vast. Just send 75 cents for your illustrated catalog.

## NEEDLEWORK SUPPLIES

**Bell Yarn,** 75 Essex Street, between Broome and Delancey Streets, 674-1030

Bell Yarn is a wholesaler/retailer (since 1917), offering discounts of 10% to 30% and especially good values on its own label. Needlepointers will be thrilled with the hundreds of imported French canvases. Bell's carries every major brand of yarn and needlework thread; crewel, macramé, quilting and rug-hooking kits and supplies; a full line of embroideries, including counted cross-stitch fabrics, tablecloths, pillowcases and samplers; unclothed dolls and doll heads, and polyester pillow stuffing. Free instructions are available with any yarn purchase to get you started on your project, and custom framing and finishing (e.g., having your work made into a pillow) are available. Bell Yarn is open Sunday to Thursday 9:00 A.M. to 5:45 P.M., Friday till 5:15 P.M. There are additional stores in Rego Park, Queens; Lake Grove, N.Y.; Woodbridge and Wayne, N.J. Check out the many outlets in the telephone book.

**School Products Company,** 1201 Broadway, between 28th and 29th Streets, third floor, 679-3516

If you are interested in knitting, weaving, bookbinding or related crafts, run, do not walk to School Products Company, one of the largest suppliers to industrial and arts departments of high schools and colleges. Because it buys in such large quantities to service its wholesale accounts, the consumer can take advantage of incredible savings. In fact, its sales (four times annually) attract people from all over the tristate area. Here you can buy yarn by the pound practically at cost.

For the craftsperson this is the place to buy your hand weaving supplies, looms and equipment. I fell in love with the knitting machines. One wave of my hand and I completed a row! Take a class—School Products provides classes in spinning, weaving and knitting for $50 to $75 for the series. Ask to have your name added to the mailing list. Open Monday to Friday 8:30 A.M. to 5:00 P.M., Saturday 10:00 A.M. to 2:00 P.M. (closed Saturday in the summer).

**The New York Yarn Center,** 61 West 37th Street, between Fifth and Sixth Avenues, 921-9293

With clothing so prohibitive this year, those who can knit or crochet are truly lucky. The New York Yarn Center offers 5,000 patterns along with glorious varieties of well-known and hard-to-find yarns from all over the world and all at discount prices. Sales people are expert instructors who will gladly work with beginners. Open Monday to Friday 10:00 A.M. to 6:00 P.M., Saturday to 5:00 P.M.

**Zamart Discount Yarns and Fabrics,** 11 West 37th Street, between Fifth and Sixth Avenues, 869-7606

Ask for Judith when you visit Zamart. The sales help cares, and you may even see people sitting around knitting at this little shop. You get free instruction if you buy your yarn here, and if you need more advanced learning, a semiprivate lesson is $7.50 an hour. Open Monday to Saturday 10:00 A.M. to 7:00 P.M.

## STAINED-GLASS SUPPLIES

**S. A. Bendheim Company, Inc.,** 122 Hudson Street, corner of North Moore Street, 226-6370

Stained-glass artists could ask for no better supplier than Bendheim. A wholesaler to the trade since the turn of the century, it has four immense loft floors chock-a-block with glass and equipment, including the largest stock of antique glass in the country. Dealing in such immense volume, Bendheim is able to offer the best retail prices in town. On the first floor you'll find equipment—soldering irons, lead, foil tools, etc.—plus kits for making Tiffany-style lamps, how-to books and glass cut to a practical size for the hobbyist. On the third and fourth floors (second floor contains offices) are hundred of immense sheets of antique glass, created by the same methods that were used in the fourteenth and fifteenth centuries. Up on the fifth floor are opalescent glass, semiantique glass and machine-drawn antique glass (simulated antique glass). Open weekdays 8:30 A.M. to 5:00 P.M., Saturday 9:00 A.M. to 1:00 P.M.

## STENCIL SUPPLIES

**Stencil Magic,** 8 West 19th Street, off Fifth Avenue, 675-8892

Stenciling is an inexpensive way to do fancy decorating on just about anything, and it's the one artsy-crafty project that requires absolutely no talent. Two of the Stencil Magic owners Jim Fobel and Jim Boleach are the authors of *The Stencil Book* (Holt, Rinehart & Winston), a complete how-to guide full of innovative projects. Once you get the bug, you'll probably want to stencil-adorn everything in sight—furniture, walls, floors, boxes and baskets, clothing, the family car...there's really no limit except that imposed by the people you live with. They have precuts aplenty, including Victorian motifs, Colonial borders, flowers, fruits, animals, Christmas designs, children's storybook figures, early Americana, basket weaves, etc. Their precut, reusable stencils are made of clear plastic, so you can see through them. Send $1.00 to Dept. J and get all their stencil, supply and paint information. Open weekdays 10:00 A.M. to 5:00 P.M.

## AUCTIONS

I have personally saved thousands of dollars over the years by shopping at auctions. Bargains exist in every area, particularly in upholstered furniture, rugs and general household goods. Check out the weekly offerings of the local auction houses and estate sales in the Sunday section of your newspaper. If possible, attend a presale exhibition and inspect any item you might be interested in buying. And finally, shop the items you want. Make sure you have some idea of what the fair market price is before you are tempted to make too high a bid. **Sotheby Parke Bernet,** 1334 York Avenue, at 72nd Street, 472-3400, sells everything from priceless paintings to attic antiques in a very impressive space. **Christie's,** 502 Park Avenue, at 59th Street, 546-1000, hails from London and also offers fairly priced furnishings and art as well as priceless antiques and collectibles. **Phillips,** 867 Madison Avenue, 570-4830, too, along with its jewelry, paintings and objets d'art, has turned up surprising buys in furniture. Incidentally, all the above offer free appraisal services.

Now here is a look at some other auction opportunities that offer very good prices.

**William Doyle Galleries, Inc.,** 175 East 87th Street, between Third and Second Avenues, 427-2730.

Particularly good buys in eighteenth-, nineteenth- and twentieth-century furnishings, rugs, sterling, china, jewelry and paintings. Call for dates of auctions.

**Lubin Galleries,** 30 West 26th Street, between Broadway and Avenue of the Americas, 924-3777

Every other Saturday the year round, beginning at 11:00 A.M., Lubin auctions a wide selection of things for the home—mostly estate contents. It's a great opportunity to pick up home furnishings and valuable antiques at good prices. Last time I went, there were armoires, desks, six Louis XV side chairs, an ornate Venetian commode, an antique Hepplewhite table, a pair of Chippendale armchairs, many pieces of silver and crystal, antique chinoiserie lacquered boxes, a Dutch marquetry inlaid table and a great deal more. Pick up a catalog on viewing days, Thursday from 10:00 A.M. to 7:00 P.M. and Friday 9:00 A.M. to 3:00 P.M., before the sale. You must buy a $25 paddle (refundable) and pay in cash or certified funds.

## UNCLAIMED MERCHANDISE

**General Post Office Auctions,** 380 West 33rd Street, between Eighth and Ninth Avenues, 971-5180

About once a month the GPO auctions off items that are lost, damaged or unclaimed in the mail, and there are so many of them that it gives one to wonder. It's all rather fascinating since the merchandise might be anything at all. A recent catalog listed six undrilled bowling balls, fireplace sets, stuffed animals, a quantity of magnetic can openers, *Star Wars* toys, a Smith-Corona electric typewriter, two sewing machines, wigs, assorted glassware and Methodist religious books from 1792 among the available miscellany. Check your local post office to find the dates of upcoming auctions. Catalogs can be picked up on viewing days (always Mondays from 8:30 A.M. to 3:30 P.M.); auctions begin at 8:30 A.M. on Tuesday. Paddles cost $20 (refundable), and you have to pay 50% (in cash) immediately upon purchase of any item.

**Police Department Public Auctions,** One Police Plaza, 406-1369

These take place about every five weeks; merchandise can be viewed at different warehouses around the city (call for details). You can get sensational buys on cars, bicycles, motorcycles and mopeds that have been stolen or confiscated during crimes. Most of what's up for auction is stolen merchandise that for one reason or another could not be returned to the rightful owners (it couldn't be identified, the owners never reported the crime, etc.). The vast amount of goods here might increase your nervousness about crime, but the prices are great. Everything must be bought as is; that means you can't test-drive vehicles. General merchandise at these auctions always include many, many pieces of jewelry and watches (the catalog might be from Tiffany's), detailing as it does hundreds of items like gold rings with star sapphires and 18-karat gold chains with amethyst pendants. Then there are stereos, TVs, furniture, musical instruments, radios, lawn mowers, clothing, cameras, appliances, tools—anything, in fact, that is not usually nailed down.

**U.S. Customs Auctions,** U.S. Customs House, 6 World Trade Center, room 114, 466-2924

While you can't bid on the confiscated marijuana and cocaine seized at customs, there is jewelry, liquor (a recent catalog listed more than twenty-five pages of white wine alone) and much else that people have abandoned rather than pay the duty for. Most of it is in large lots—e.g., eighty-eight cartons of baby blouses in assorted colors—but the variety of items can be staggering: bags of anesthesia, women's boots, 10,560 empty spools, porcelain chinaware, engine parts, foreign language records, toilet seats, clothing, wallpaper, just about anything at all. Sales are always on Thursday at 9:00 A.M. (call for dates, times and locations; you can get on a mailing list if you so desire); viewing is the Tuesday before from 8:30 A.M. to 3:30 P.M. If you wish to bid, you must buy a $25 paddle (refundable).

## BATHROOM ACCESSORIES

**Sherle Wagner International, Inc.,** 60 East 57th Street, 758-3300

Sure, every suburban mall has a bath boutique these days, but none of them is like Sherle Wagner. This is the Rolls-Royce of bathroom stores, offering unlimited possibilities for that room's aesthetic enhancement. The sinks (Sherle Wagner calls them lavatory bowls) run the gamut from hand-painted porcelains with fluted pedestals to stainless steel high-tech designs; the former come with matching wallpapers. There are sculpted marble tubs, bidets and toilets (with 24-karat gold-plated seats); faucets and spouts that are shaped like cherubs and seashells; swan-design toilet handles; eighteenth-century reproduction chaises percées (cane chairs) to disguise the toilet completely (pity the hapless guest); lapis lazuli and malachite sink counters; and, of course, an opulent range of accessories like soap dishes, mirrors, toilet paper holders, towel racks, hand-painted tiles, even crystal chandeliers. Sherle Wagner will work with your designer on custom creations. Open weekdays only from 9:30 A.M. to 5:00 P.M.

## BEER- AND WINEMAKING SUPPLIES

**Milan Laboratory,** 57 Spring Street, between Lafayette and Mulberry Streets, 226-4780

Did you know that state law allows the head of a household to make 200 gallons of wine or beer each year for consumption by family and friends? At Milan Lab, brothers Paul and Anthony Miccio have all the necessary equipment and can teach you how to do it. For novices, there's a complete winemaking kit that contains everything—even the grape concentrate—and, similarly, a complete beermaking kit. Milan Laboratory is also a good place to shop for bar accessories. Open weekdays at 9:00 A.M. to 5:00 P.M., Saturday to 3:00 P.M., Sunday (September to April only) to 1:00 P.M.; hours are slightly reduced in summer, so call first.

## BICYCLES

**Gene's Bicycle Shop,** 242 East 79th Street, off Second Avenue, 249-9218

Gene's is so big—a good half block long—that you can test his bicycles right in the store. He offers the lowest prices in town on all major brands—Fuji, Peugeot, Raleigh, Motobecane, etc.—and if you see any bike for less, he'll lower the price and undersell his competitor. He also sells used bikes (and buys them), rents bicycles, does trade-in deals and handles mopeds, tricycles and children's bikes. If you use a bike in New York, the Citadel U-lock is a must, and once again Gene sells it for less than anyone else. Excellent buys, too, on racing bikes and exercise bikes. He's also reliable and low-priced for bicycle repair work of all kinds and can clean up your old bike and make it look spiffy again. Finally, if you don't know how to ride, someone at Gene's will teach you. Open daily from 9:00 A.M. to 7:00 P.M.

*SHOPPING AND FOOD GUIDE* 15

## BOOKSTORES

**The Strand Bookstore,** 828 Broadway, corner of 12th Street, 473-1452
   More than fifty years in business, the Strand is the largest secondhand bookstore in the country and every book lover's favorite haunt. You might find anything among its 2 million or so books, from a 48-cent novel to a rare first edition of James Joyce's *Ulysses*, the latter in the fifth-floor rare books department, which many people don't even know exists. The Strand buys up private libraries, reviewers' copies, remainders and publisher's overstocks. There are numerous novels (including many hard-to-find ones) and large sections devoted to books on art, history, the social sciences, Americana, and theater. Unlike many secondhand bookshops, the Strand has things arranged so that you can fairly easily lay your hands on what you're looking for. Open Monday to Saturday 9:30 A.M. to 6:30 P.M., Sunday 11:00 A.M. to 5:00 P.M.

**Samuel Weiser, Inc.,** 740 Broadway, between Astor Place and Waverly Place, 777-6363
   If you expect a store that bills itself as specialists in occult and Oriental philosophy to be musty and mysterious, you'll be surprised at Weiser's. It's as modern and slick as Brentano's, a very pleasant—and mind-expanding—place to browse. Classical or quiet meditative music is played at all times. There's a large selection of reading matter, ranging from *The Opening of the Third Eye* to Jewish yoga and including such new age subjects as holistic medicine, mythology, astrology, prophecy, witchcraft, African voodoo, nutrition, palmistry, psychic phenomena and, of course, every aspect of Eastern philosophy and religion. Weiser's also carries inspirational books for children, colorful Tibetan poetry, records and tapes (inspirational and celestial music to meditate with), crystal balls and tarot cards. Open Monday, Tuesday, Wednesday and Friday 9:00 A.M. to 6:00 P.M., Thursday 10:00 A.M. to 7:00 P.M., Saturday 9:30 A.M. to 5:00 P.M.

**Murder, Ink,** 271 West 87th Street, between Broadway and West End Avenue, 362-8905
   Appropriately fronted by a blood-red awning, Murder, Ink is the place to locate hard-to-find Agatha Christies, classic whodunits, es-

pionage thrillers and suspense stories. In addition to an immense and carefully chosen selection of in-and out-of-print, new and used, rare and easily accessible paperback and hardcover mysteries, the shop sells related games, magazines, greeting cards, records, blood-red T-shirts and sweat shirts, biographies and autobiographies of mystery writers and solid brass key chain miniatures of the Maltese Falcon. Owner Carol Brener has read every author represented in the store, so if you love Rex Stout, for instance, but have read all his books, she can suggest other authors you'll probably like. Murder, Ink is open Monday to Saturday 1:00 P.M. to 7:00 P.M., Thursday till 10:00 P.M.

**Womanbooks,** 201 West 92nd Street, 873-4121
An outgrowth of the feminist movement, Womanbooks carries about 6,000 titles specifically geared to women. They include fiction, poetry, art and music books, by or about women, books on feminism, lesbianism, older women, pregnancy and childbearing, "herstory" and even cookbooks (let's face it, most of us still cook). It's a store where you can bring the kids (there's a special play area with toys and books for them), and you can purchase nonsexist children's books here. There's also an area for women to sit and read, chat, plot or debate. There are weekly readings by women authors, a bulletin board lists events of interest to women, new works by women are reviewed in a twelve-page bimonthly newsletter and all the music played in the store is by women artists. Open Tuesday to Saturday 10:00 A.M. to 7:00 P.M., Sunday noon to 6:00 P.M.

**Eeyore's Books for Children,** 2252 Broadway, between 80th and 81st Streets, 362-0634 and 1066 Madison Avenue, between 80th and 81st Streets
The only all-children's bookstore in the city, Eeyore's has a vast number of carefully selected books, records and tapes for all ages. Everything is child-oriented. There are nooks where the kids can plop down on large pillows and read a bit, and many special events are planned throughout the year. Most Sundays, except in summer, a storyteller is on hand (call for hours), and kids get complimentary milk or juice, cookies and balloons, while their adult companions enjoy coffee and cookies. Occasionally there are author appearances, theatrical or musical performances all free. Kids love the place, and of course, it all helps create good feelings about reading. The staff is well versed in children's literature, capable of answering queries like

"What can I get for a ten-year-old girl who's read all of Judy Blume?" Open Monday to Saturday 10:00 A.M. to 6:00 P.M., Sunday 10:30 A.M. to 5:00 P.M.

**Antiquarian Booksellers' Center,** 50 Rockefeller Plaza, 246-2564

A cooperative retail bookshop, the center provides selling space to some seventy members of the Antiquarian Booksellers' Association of America. The shop also serves as the association's national headquarters and as a referral center where collectors and dealers are matched. Among the esoterica you might find here are Confederate maps and prints, nineteenth-century U.S. postal histories, medieval and modern manuscripts, autographs, atlases, sixteenth- to nineteenth-century maps, fine out-of-print books, first-edition juvenile books and old trade catalogs. No telling what fascinating item you might happen upon. Prices range from $5 to about $5,000. Open weekdays only from 10:00 A.M. to 5:30 P.M.; closed in August.

**Charles Scribner's Sons,** 597 Fifth Avenue, between 48th and 49th Streets, 758-9797

A splendid store noted for its helpful sales staff and quality. You'll find a good assortment of books from top authors along with best sellers and a complete selection of paperbacks. A perfect shop to find gift books. Open Monday through Friday from 9:00 A.M. to 6:30 P.M.; Saturday from 9:00 A.M. to 5:00 P.M.

## BOTTLES

**Bottles Unlimited,** 245 East 78th Street, 570-6571

Prior to the invention of the Owens automatic bottlemaking machine in 1905, all bottles were hand-blown into iron molds. Pre-Owens bottles are often beautiful, and they're also collectibles. The owners of Bottles Unlimited, Bill and Tara Delafield, collected so many that eventually they had to open a shop so they had some room to live in. Their inventory includes patent medicine bottles, shaped pickle jars, poison bottles (many of cobalt blue or emerald green glass), historical whiskey flasks (with pictures of a current president, eagles, sunbursts, etc.), old ink bottles, beer bottles, bitters bottles (some of these are fish-shaped), whiskey bottles and apothecary jars. There are more than 1,500 bottles in the store, some dating back to the 1800s and ranging in value from about $5 to $28,000. Open daily, noon to 6:00 P.M.

## BUTTONS AND ZIPPERS

**Tender Buttons,** 143 East 62nd Street, between Lexington and Third Avenues, 758-7004

This charming store is simply bursting with buttons—beautiful, wonderful, enchanting buttons dating from the eighteenth century on. Its collection of antique buttons is probably the most comprehensive in the world, and most are in sets. There are exquisitely painted Satsuma buttons from Japan, English Edwardian and Victorian officer's buttons, sets of hallmarked Art Nouveau silver buttons from turn-of-the-century England, real mother-of-pearl buttons, agate ball buttons with silver or brass escutcheons from England, carved ivory dragons and irises from Japan and children's buttons from the thirties shaped like mermaids, fruits, penguins, vegetables, little shoes, giraffes, etc. There are also modern buttons (many of them custom-made for the store), buckles, antique thimbles and cuff links. The best part is that practically everything is on display. Open weekdays 11:00 A.M. to 6:00 P.M., Saturday (except during July and August) to 5:30 P.M.

**Gordon Buttons Company, Inc.,** 142 West 38th Street, 921-1684

Though not as chic as Tender Buttons (that's sort of the Dean & DeLuca of button shops), Gordon has a voluminous collection (more than half a century in the making) of some 5 million buttons. He sells both wholesale and retail at very low prices, and though prices descend with large orders, there's no minimum. You'll find functional everyday buttons at Gordon's in tremendous quantity as well as the more whimsical (apple, fish, elephant, duck and star shapes, among others), the antique and the ornamental. He also sells belt buckles of all kinds and some hats and costume jewelry. Everything is well organized, so it's easy to find what you're looking for. Open weekdays 8:30 A.M. to 5:30 P.M.; closed the first week in July.

**A. Feibusch Zippers,** 109 Hester Street, between Eldridge and Forsyth Streets, 226-3964

Whether you need an ordinary zipper for a dress or skirt, a tiny two-inch zipper for doll clothes or a fifteen-foot zipper for God knows what, A. Feibusch can provide it—in any of hundreds of colors with thread to match. If it doesn't have the zipper you need in stock, it'll make it

SHOPPING AND FOOD GUIDE 19

to order. Feibusch sells wholesale and retail, and prices are considerably lower than those of department stores. Open weekdays 9:00 A.M. to 5:00 P.M., Sunday 10:00 A.M. to 4:00 P.M.

## CANDLES AND TALISMANS

**Renaissance Art Gallery,** 185 East 80th Street, between Lexington and Third Avenues, 988-3736

Dripless, odorless, smokeless, long-burning candles, handcrafted from pure honeycomb beeswax are the specialty at Renaissance Art Gallery. They're made in America using a French process, and though they're malleable enough to fit into any candleholder, they don't bend in summer. You can get them straight or tapered, in standard or made-to-order sizes and in any of thirty colors, some with evocative names like bittersweet, golden topaz and wild honey. Though candles are the mainstay of the business, Renaissance also deals in archaeological and antique objects, including a wide range of Tibetan bronzes. Open weekdays except Wednesday from 11:00 A.M. to 5:00 P.M.; closed from mid-July to mid-August.

**House of Talisman, Inc.,** 545 West 145th Street, between Amsterdam Avenue and Broadway, 281-8070

Here we enter the realms of voodoo and mysticism—of exotic oils, incense and myrrh. House of Talisman sells seven-day candles for luck (you can slip them out of the jar and write your wishes in the wax); wax doll candles for rituals (you burn them with a person's name underneath the feet, and whatever you wish for ostensibly happens to him or her); male-female candle pairs, which you keep moving closer to each other as they burn (if you want to get together with someone) until they melt together into a pool of wax; and hundreds of other such things. You can even buy actual voodoo dolls here, along with numerous mysterious-sounding items like black cat bone, swallow's heart, nutmeg with mercury in a red bag, and dove's blood ink. There are also books on the premises to instruct you in the use of this exotica, and the staff will be glad to direct you to the correct potion or candle for your particular problem. House of Talisman is the largest firm of its kind and as a wholesaler is able to offer good retail prices. Should you covet money (who doesn't?), success, fast luck or health—or simply need a jinx removed—it's open Monday to Saturday 9:30 A.M. to 7:00 P.M.

**House of Candles & Talismans,** 99 Stanton Street, between Orchard and Ludlow Streets, 982-2780

A similar operation, more conveniently located and perhaps a bit less ominous (it also carries plain old dinner table candles and more conventional religious candles), is the House of Candles & Talismans. Open daily from 10:00 A.M. to 4:30 P.M.

## CIGARS

**J & R Tobacco,** 11 East 45th Street, between Fifth and Madison Avenues, 869-8777

With more than 2,000 brands, sizes and colors in stock, his is the world's largest selection of cigars in the world's largest humidor. The entire store is a climate-controlled environment in which cigars could stay fresh for 1,000 years. The selection of quality cigars comes from all over the world except Cuba, but it does sell the Ultima Cigar from Honduras, which is closest in taste to a Cuban cigar. Not only does J & R have everything to please the most discriminating connoisseur, but it sells all its cigars at discounts of 40% to 50%. Open weekdays 8:00 A.M. to 6:00 P.M., Saturday 9:00 A.M. to 4:00 P.M. Another location is in the Financial District at 219 Broadway, between Vesey and Barclay Streets, 233-6620; open weekdays only from 8:00 A.M. to 5:00 P.M.

## CLOTHING AND ACCESSORIES

No city in the world offers a wider range of clothing options than New York. For any look you want to achieve from Nancy Reagan Republican to kinky New Wave, from Soho arty to Brooks Brothers preppy, you'll find almost infinite sources. And you can get it all wholesale—or below wholesale—on the Lower East Side, on Seventh Avenue and at secret locations throughout the metropolitan area.

### ANTIQUE CLOTHING

**Anjou Violanti, Ltd.,** 1585 Third Avenue, at 89th Street, 860-1052

In the past, owner Rick Quintane has bought up entire wardrobes, such as that of a Russian princess whose beaded and pearl-covered satin gowns cost $4,000 to $5,000 even when she bought them back in the 1920s. He also purchased the entire contents of the wardrobe of one Madame de la Rouche that included 2,000 pairs of shoes! You might find anything here from tuxedos and sequined gowns to riding jackets, antique lingerie, coats, gloves or Victoriana. Call for appointment.

**Bogie's Antique Furs & Clothing,** 201 East Tenth Street, near Second Avenue, 260-1199

There's no place quite like Bogie's. A tiny store, it's piled practically floor to ceiling with trash and treasures that are sold at unbelievable low prices. This is where many antique clothing dealers shop; they do a few simple repairs (much of Bogie's merchandise needs mending) and then sell things for five or ten times the original price. It's great fun plowing through the piles of patchwork quilts (I've picked up beauties here for just a few dollars), lingerie, antique dresses and furs, silk robes and scarves, beaded sweaters, Hawaiian shirts, coats and whatever else. The crowd is young (it's always mobbed), and a spirit of camaraderie prevails. If you're handy with a needle and thread, you could create a stunning, very complete wardrobe from Bogie's for as little as $100. Open daily noon to 5:30 P.M., except Tuesday and Friday, when the opening hour is 3:00 P.M.

**Fonda's,** 168 Lexington Avenue, between 30th and 31st Streets, 685-4035

This friendly little shop is chock-a-block with the frilly, feminine finery of a bygone era, most of it in excellent condition. There are ecru lace high-necked Victorian blouses and wedding gowns, Japanese kimonos from the twenties, eyelet fabrics and silk scarves from the thirties, secondhand furs, twenties and thirties hand-embroidered silk shawls, antique jewelry, alligator and beaded handbags, belts, gloves and hats. Fonda's also has many garments made by its own designers in contemporary styles, using antique fabrics, such as patch skirts made of vintage silks. In addition, it features contemporary designer clothing at discount prices (Dianne B, Bern Conrad, Carol Horn, Scott Barrie, etc.), and the fashion-minded sales staff loves to help a woman create a new unique image. Sizes generally are 4 to 12, but garments can be altered for fuller figures. Open Monday to Friday 10:30 A.M. to 7:30 P.M., Saturday till 6:30 P.M. Another Fonda's is at 346 East 59th Street, between First and Second Avenues, 355-7236. Opens at 11:30 A.M.

**Gene London Productions,** 106 East 19th Street, 533-4105

The most provocative selection of antique clothing you'll ever encounter has got to be costume designer Gene London's. Ranging in date from the late nineteenth century to about 1960, they include Chanel and Schiaparelli numbers, film costumes worn by movie queens (Dietrich, Harlow, Crawford and Garbo, among others), Victorian wedding gowns, Oriental robes, jewelry and accessories. Gene's collection comprises well over 2,000 garments, ranging in price from under $100 to over $1,000. He also buys antique clothing or takes it on a consignment basis, repairs it or—if you so desire—updates it.

He also has a large and unique collection of exquisite-quality wedding dresses, bridal wear and accessories, mother-of-the-bride and bridesmaid outfits for sale or rent. The wedding gowns range from Victorian styles (undergoing a renaissance of popularity these days, thanks to Princess Diana) with puff sleeves and cinched waists to actual MGM Hollywood wedding wardrobes. Fancy yourself tying the knot in Claudette Colbert's gown from *It Happened One Night*. Gene can also update, clean and refurbish your mother's or grandmother's antique wedding gown. Open weekdays 10:00 A.M. to 5:00 P.M., by appointment only.

**Harriet Love,** 412 West Broadway, between Prince and Spring Streets, 966-2280

The selection here is eclectic, running the gamut from Hawaiian shirts to turn-of-the-century wedding dresses and including alligator and beaded bags, jewelry (Victorian pins, silver Art Deco bracelets, thirties and forties watches, early plastic bracelets and pins, etc.), forties print dresses, beaded and sequined cashmere sweaters, scarves and much more. Everything is in good, if not perfect, condition. Irresistible if you crave the very best. Open Tuesday to Saturday noon to 7:00 P.M., Sunday 1:00 to 6:00 P.M.

## *CHILDREN'S CLOTHING*

Better brands of children's clothing for infants and boys and girls up to size 14 are discounted 20% at **Rice & Breskin,** 323 Grand Street, corner of Orchard Street, 925-5515. A family business since 1937, it offers an extensive line for infants and boys and girls and friendly, helpful service. Open Sunday to Friday 9:00 A.M. to 5:30 P.M.

**Klein's of Monticello,** 105 Orchard Street, between Delancey and Broome Streets, 966-1453

One of the most exclusive selections of children's wear you'll find anywhere is assembled at Klein's and sold at discounts of 20% and up. That doesn't mean it's cheap; it's simply the very best for less. Klein's carries high-fashion French and Italian imports, many Kamali and Kamali-influenced styles, Oshkosh and Lee jeans, Pierre Cardin suits, skiwear and one-of-a-kind cottage-industry items like embroidered and appliquéd denims and socks with charms around the ankle, among much other chic playwear. Open Sunday to Friday 10:00 A.M. to 5:00 P.M.

**Second Act Childrenswear, Inc.,** 1046 Madison Avenue, between 79th and 80th Streets, 988-2440

In the days of large families all but the oldest child wore hand-me-downs aplenty. Today stores like Second Act can replace the role of older siblings in this money-saving practice. Owners Jeanne Ryan and Joan Blake accept only those garments that are in excellent condition—outgrown rather than worn-out. Generally you'll find everything from ordinary play clothes to fancy French dresses (sizes infants to 14 for girls and 20 for boys), riding wear, sweat suits, Adidas, Lacoste polo shirts and toddlers' overalls. I've even come across such fancy duds as Brooks Brothers suits and Pierre Cardin blazers. This is, after all, prime preppy territory. In addition to clothing, there are usually ice skates, children's books, some toys and occasionally items like carriages, children's furniture, strollers, highchairs and bicycles. If you're looking to buy or sell something in particular, you can list it on the store's bulletin board for $1 for six months. Bring the kids along; there's a special play area with toys and books for them. This is a shop that cares. Open Tuesday to Saturday 10:00 A.M. to 5:00 P.M.; July and August same hours Monday to Friday.

For similar merchandise, **Second Cousin,** 142 Seventh Avenue South, between Tenth and Charles Streets, 929-8048 (open Monday to Saturday noon to 6:30 P.M. October through March, 11:00 A.M. to 7:00 P.M. the rest of the year); recycled jeans are a specialty, and it has many toys.

**Frugal Frog, 1707 Second Avenue,** between 88th and 89th Streets, 876-5178

Owner Arlene Leitner specializes in practical, sturdy children's wear rather than fancy designer labels, and she sells everything at very low prices. Her stock is mostly resale merchandise, but it also includes discounted irregulars, closeouts, samples and overstock. Everything's in rather a jumble, but Arlene quickly can lay her hands on any particular item you're looking for. There are many treasures like a pair of jeans for 50 cents or brand-new pajamas for $3.00. Sizes run from infants to preteen, and like Second Act, Frugal Frog has a play area stocked with toys and books to keep kids occupied while you shop. Open Monday to Thursday and Saturday 11:00 A.M. to 5:00 P.M., Friday 1:00 P.M. to 5:00 P.M.; summer hours are irregular, so call first.

**Melnikoff's,** 1594 York Avenue, at 84th Street, 288-3644

As summertime nears, grab your camp-bound kids and take them over to Melnikoff's. You can get every single item on the required clothing and equipment list here—flashlights, socks, shirts, underwear, shorts, baseball jackets, bathing suits, canteens and mess kits, duffel bags, sleeping bags, pajamas, even the trunk to pack it all in—and everything is discounted 10% to 30%. And if you order more than $100 of merchandise, the staff will sew in all your name tapes free. Melnikoff's has been outfitting campers for more than 60 years; it's an expert. It also carries a full range of adult sizes at discount. Open Monday to Saturday 9:00 A.M. to 6:00 P.M., Thursday till 9:00 P.M.

**Joey's Infants and Children's Wear,** 134 West Nyack Road, Nanuet, N.Y., 914-623-0777

One-stop shopping for infants, boys and girls—at discounts of 25% to 70%—makes Joey's very popular with budget-conscious moms. It carries more than 500 brands of clothing, including all the well-known national labels (Mighty Mac, Lee, Levi's, Oshkosh, Gunne Sax, Dijon, Jordache, Weathertamer, Pacific Trail, etc.) in everything from layette to size 20. Joey's is great for all the basics—underwear, play clothes, jeans, hats, pajamas, snowsuits, coats, sweaters, etc.—as well as those special-occasion items like Yves Saint Laurent boys' suits and the kinds of darling dresses you see at Bloomie's for $60—$35 here. Hours are Monday to Saturday 10:00 A.M. to 6:00 P.M., Thursday till 9:00 P.M. There are additional stores in Teaneck and West Orange, N.J., and Scarsdale, N.Y.

**Natan Borlam,** 157 Havemeyer Street, corner South Second Street, Brooklyn, 387-2983

Whopping discounts of up to 50% on a huge selection of national brand, imported and designer children's clothes bring mothers to Brooklyn in droves. Leave the little kids at home if possible; it's a mob scene. Besides, you'll want to be free to check out the great bargains in top label and designer clothes for women, too. The store has underwear, outerwear, tights, jeans, bathing suits, dresses, shirts, skirts and every other possible item for children, teens, juniors and women. Open Sunday to Thursday 10:00 A.M. to 5:00 P.M., Friday till 2:00 P.M.

## CLOTHING FOR WOMEN BY LOCATION

### The Lower East Side

Mecca for bargain hunters, the Lower East Side abounds with shops selling designer clothing for women at hefty discounts. The following merit exploration:

**Jay Kay**, 141 Orchard Street, between Delancey and Rivington Streets, 477-3090, specializes in designer sportswear with many French and Italian imports—all at 50% to 70% below department store prices. Among the labels here, in sizes 4 to 14, are Calvin Klein, Valentino, Pierre Cardin, Yves Saint Laurent, Ralph Lauren, Anne Klein, Cacharel—well, you get the picture. Open daily from 9:30 A.M. to 5:30 P.M.

**A. Altman**, 182 Orchard Street, between Houston and Stanton Streets, 982-7722, is one of the most famous of these Lower East Side shops—with good reason. Here top designer sportswear, dresses and evening wear (sizes 4 to 14) are discounted 30% to 50%. It's open daily 9:00 A.M. to 5:00 P.M.. If you'd like to bypass the Lower East Side scene, check out the uptown store, **Azriel Altman,** 204 Fifth Avenue, between 25th and 26th Streets, 889-0782, open daily 10:00 A.M. to 6:00 P.M. Same kind of merchandise as downtown—three floors of it.

At **Fishkin,** 314 Grand Street, corner of Allen Street, 226-6538, a family business since 1902, you'll find discounts ( a minimum of 20%) on European and American designer and name-label beachwear, sportswear, coats, accessories and even shoes (Andrew Geller, Mr. Seymour, etc.). Fishkin carries Perry Ellis coats, the Carole Little silk collection, Jack Berek hand-knit sweaters, Jack Mulqueen creations and many leather and suede garments in bright colors. Open Monday to Thursday 10:00 A.M. to 5:00 P.M., Friday to 4:00 P.M., Sunday 9:00 A.M. to 4:30 P.M..

Under the same ownership and offering similar discounted merchandise are two other stores. **The Jeans Shop,** 318 Grand Street, between Allen and Orchard Streets (same phone number and hours as above), specializes in sportswear, cruisewear, jeans, jump suits and prairie skirts in sizes 1 to 14. They feature the Norma Kamali, Bis and Jag collections, Calvin Kleins and Sassons, along with mostly California labels and designers.

**Fishkin Knitwear,** 63 Orchard Street, between Hester and Grand Streets (also same phone number and hours as above), offers classic looks in sportswear and separates for the more mature woman in sizes 4 to 16—names like Liz Claiborne, Breckenridge, Cathy Hardwick and Evan-Picone.

**JBZ,** 121 Orchard Street, between Delancey and Rivington Streets, 473-8550, is another discount store (20% to 50% off) for women's designer clothing. The main floor features outerwear; the second and third floors feature sportswear. You'll find names like Thierry Mugler, Perry Ellis, Dorothee Bis, Krizia, Armani and Leon Max. Above and beyond regular discounts, JBZ has special sales after Christmas through February and in July and August. Open Sunday to Friday 9:00 A.M. to 6:00 P.M.

**Hendel's,** 325 Grand Street, between Orchard and Ludlow Streets, 226-0440, has been at this address for fifty years. It's a good bet for outerwear—London Fog and Misty Harbor all-weather coats with zip-out linings, Bill Blass down coats, etc.—in petite and regular sizes. Hendel's also handles sportswear in sizes 4 to 18, and discounts on all merchandise average 25%. Open Sunday to Thursday 9:00 A.M. to 4:30 P.M., Friday to 3:00 P.M.

## Seventh Avenue and Around Manhattan

**Better Made Coat and Suit Company,** 270 West 38th Street, between Seventh and Eighth Avenues, 12th floor, 944-0748

Top designer coats and suits—names like Harvé Benard—that always fit properly (if they don't Better Made will alter them for you) are sold at 30% off here, along with its own high-quality creations. It has coats for all seasons, including Misty Harbor raincoats, blouses, slack and skirt suits, blazers, pants and skirts in petite sizes to 16. I'm not allowed to mention all the big designer names you'll find here, but go

up and check it out. Open weekdays 10:00 A.M. to 4:00 P.M., Saturday till 3:00 P.M.
In the same building, 17th floor, check out the ladies' wear at **Paris Fashion,** 279-6019. It's all first-quality, mostly designer merchandise—suits, dresses, blouses, skirts, pants and every kind of outerwear—at 30% to 50% off, more during special sales in May and June, sizes 2 to 16. Open weekdays 10:00 A.M. to 5:00 P.M., Saturday till 3:00 P.M.

**The Loft,** 491 Seventh Avenue, between 36th and 37th Streets, 19th floor, 736-3359
Most of the top *haute couture* designer labels (can't mention names) are represented at The Loft. It has coats, suits, dresses, slacks, tops, all kinds of sportswear in fact, in sizes 2 to 14 at discounts of 30% to 60%. All the merchandise is new, not closeout items. Open weekdays 9:30 A.M. to 5:30 P.M., Saturday 9:45 A.M. to 4:30 P.M.
While you're in the building, check out similar wares and discounts at **Abe Geller,** fifth floor, 736-8077 (weekdays 10:00 A.M. to 5:00 P.M., Saturday to 3:00 P.M., except during July and August), and **Jay's Advance Garments,** ninth floor, 239-1166, by appointment only.

**Ms., Miss or Mrs., A Division of Ben Farber, Inc.,** 462 Seventh Avenue (just opposite Macy's), 736-0557
Top-name designer clothes for women—dresses, suits, many coats, pantsuits, sweaters, shirts, etc.—are discounted 30% to 50% by this large wholesale exporter. I can't name the designers, but they're all well known and tend to create classic styles. The store carries sizes 2 to 22 (no junior sizes), and there are fifteen dressing rooms. Especially good bargains can be had during January and June, both clearance sale months. Saturdays and lunch hours the place is mobbed, so go at other times if you can. Open weekdays 9:00 A.M. to 6:00 P.M., Thursday till 8:00 P.M., Saturday to 4:00 P.M.

**Emotional Outlet,** 91 Seventh Avenue, at 16th Street, 989-0530
Discount shopping usually means giving up attractive surroundings and attentive service. Emotional Outlet is the exception. Not only are there discounts of 18% to 50%, but the service is friendly, the ambience pleasant, and frills include free coffee, wine, cookies (bagels and cream cheese for Sunday shoppers) and a TV set for accompanying boyfriends. Emotional Outlet features a fashion-forward sophisticated contemporary, but never kinky, look in designer and name-brand dresses, suits, casual coats, swimsuits, lingerie, jeans and sportswear. It also

has a full line of shoes, boots and bags, plus Danskin tights, body suits and leotards. There are two floors of merchandise. Nowhere is shopping more simpatico. Open weekdays 11:00 A.M. to 8:00 P.M., Saturday to 7:00 P.M., Sunday noon to 6:00 P.M. There are three other Manhattan locations at 242 East 51st Street, between Second and Third Avenues, 135 West 50th Street, between Sixth and Seventh Avenues, and 435 East 86th Street, between First and York Avenues.

**Shelgo,** 641 Avenue of the Americas, at 20th Street, 675-6455
A vast factory supplying many fine sportswear houses, Shelgo also dabbles in retail. It turns out a full line of sportswear—blouses, slacks, harem pants, T-shirts, warm-up suits, knitted tops, etc.—and has its own line (Ilya by Robert Krugman) of designer knits. There's no showroom (a tiny area is set aside for retail business), no advertising and minimal sales help, all of which allows Shelgo to sell to you at below wholesale prices. You might find a wool skirt here, completely lined, for under $20. Open weekdays 9:00 A.M. to 5:00 P.M., Saturday to 1:00 P.M.

## Out of Manhattan and Out of Town

**Loehmann's,** 9 West Fordham Road, at Jerome Avenue, Bronx, 295-4100
For more than fifty years Loehmann's has been offering savvy shoppers a staggering array of *haute couture* and first-quality merchandise at bargain-basement prices. It buys overruns and odd lots from hundreds of designers and manufacturers—almost nothing is damaged or irregular—and sells it for at least a third less than other discount stores. Prices spiral downward the longer the merchandise is on the racks. Loehmann's is able to offer such low prices by running a no-frills operation—that means no credit, no exchanges or refunds, no advertising of special merchandise, no fancy displays and communal dressing rooms. Labels are removed from everything, but regulars know how to decode the tickets (e.g., AK for Anne Klein), even though the store changes the codes with some frequency. Classiest designer merchandise is kept in the Back Room, a somewhat plusher area with its own fitting room. You might discover garments by Oscar de la Renta, Perry Ellis, Albert Nipon, Gloria Vanderbilt, Kenzo, Halston, Bill Blass, etc.—but you have to search the racks with some care to find the best stuff. Many women are Loehmann's addicts, and you may

easily join their ranks when you find your first Dior blouse for under $20. Hours are Monday to Saturday 10:00 A.M. to 5:30 P.M., Wednesday night until 9:30 P.M. There are additional Loehmann's stores in Brooklyn and Queens (Rego Park); New Hyde Park, Hewlett, Huntington, Bay Shore, White Plains and Mount Kisco, N.Y.; East Brunswick, Florham Park and Paramus, N.J.; and Norwalk, Conn. Check out the addresses in the telephone book.

**The Factory Outlet,** 62-43 Woodhaven Boulevard, Rego Park, Queens, 457-9200
Easy to combine with a shopping excursion to the Queens Center Mall—Orhbach's, A&S, Macy's, etc.—The Factory Outlet, just six blocks away, offers discounts averaging 35% on a vast line of first-quality current merchandise from America's largest garment manufacturers. Here you'll see a wide selection of nationally advertised brands and labels in junior, misses and half sizes—dresses, pants, sweaters, skirts, rainwear, bathing suits, etc. Open Monday to Saturday 10:00 A.M. to 5:00 P.M., Sunday 10:30 A.M. to 4:00 P.M.

**Royal Silk Ltd.,** Royal Silk Plaza, 45 East Madison Avenue, Clifton, N.J. 07011, 201-772-1800
No other fabric is as luxurious, sensual and elegant as fine silk. Unfortunately silk garments are expensive, right? Wrong. Not if you buy them from Royal Silk, a catalog operation that does its own buying and dyeing, manufacturing (in India and China from American styles) and marketing. Thus, it manages to maintain a high level of quality control and eliminate all middleman costs. Stunning high-style blouses and kurtas in sizes 5/6 to 15/16 are in the $25 to $32 range, and they come in a wide choice of colors. There are tailored shirtwaists, strapless camisoles, cowboy shirts, T-shirts, tunics, romantic and elegant continental styles. Royal Silk also makes dresses, lingerie, ensembles and shirts for men. An added boon: Despite the fact that most silk garments are marked "dry clean only," many, says Royal Silk, are hand-washable. To order a catalog, send $1 to the above address.

**Aaron's Fifth Avenue,** 627 Fifth Avenue, between 17th and 18th Streets, Brooklyn, 768-5400
Manhattanites have been crossing the bridge for more than half a century to partake of the great bargains—25% to 50% off—on first-quality designer clothes at Aaron's. Unlike most discount shops, it has a cash-refund policy within a week of purchase. You'll find an abun-

dance of designer dresses, coats, suits and sportswear at Aaron's with labels from Liz Claiborne, Trigère, Albert Nipon, Evan Picone, Belle France and many more. Don't miss the special clearout sales in February and late June and July. Open Monday to Saturday 9:30 A.M. to 6:00 P.M., Thursday till 9:00 P.M.

## CLOTHING IN EXTRA-SMALL AND EXTRA-LARGE SIZES FOR MEN AND WOMEN

**Piaffe,** 841 Madison Avenue, at 70th Street, 744-9911

If you're a size 0 to 6 (I was at birth, I believe), you don't have to brave the children's department. Piaffe offers an exquisite line of beautifully made high-fashion duds for petite women. Nothing cutesy here. The look is *très* chic and very feminine, featuring sophisticated current styles. Prices are comparable to those of better department stores. There's a large selection of dresses, evening wear, suits, sportswear, outerwear and lingerie. Open Monday, Friday and Saturday 10:00 A.M. to 6:00 P.M., Tuesday to Thursday to 7:00 P.M., Sunday noon to 5:00 P.M.

**The Minishop Boutique,** 38 West 56th Street, between Fifth and Sixth Avenues, 873-5787

Small is chic at The Minishop Boutique, where a large selection of adult styles are translated into Lilliputian sizes. Owner Alan Corday selects contemporary fashions that will look good on a small person and has the manufacturers cut identical garments for him in sizes mini-1 to 6. Alterations are free; prices, moderate (comparable to those of department stores like Macy's). The Minishop carries a full range of clothing—blouses, dresses, pants, skirts, suits, beachwear, blazers and outerwear, as well as Bonjour's line of petite jeans. Open Monday to Friday 10:00 A.M. to 8:00 P.M., Saturday to 7:00 P.M., Sunday noon to 5:00 P.M.

**Macy's,** Herald Square (Broadway at 34th Street), seventh floor, 695-4400

The best-ever development for large women is the Big City Woman department on Macy's seventh floor. Thirteen thousand square feet of floor space have been devoted to it, and in line with the Macy's image, Big City Woman buyers try to make available the same exciting styles offered in other parts of the store like Clubhouse and Young Collector.

Designer lines include Leslie Fay, Gloria Vanderbilt, Evan Picone, The Chaus Women, Pierre Cardin, Sasson and E. F. Benson. The dull and dowdy large-size look is nowhere to be seen. Bottoms, skirts and pants come in sizes 32 to 40, blouses 36 to 44, dresses 14 to 24 and 12½ to 24½. There's a full range of clothing—coats, stockings, swimwear, sports- and joggingwear, shorts, culottes, suits, lingerie and bras, as well as belts and accessories; jeans abound. A fashion consultant is on hand to help you coordinate your wardrobe, using this and other departments in the store, and there are occasional fashion shows. Macy's hours are Monday, Thursday and Friday 9:45 A.M. to 8:30 P.M., Tuesday, Wednesday and Saturday 9:45 A.M. to 6:45 P.M., Sunday noon to 5:00 P.M. Many other Macy's stores have similar departments; check your local branch.

**Jeanne Rafal, The French Boutique,** 435 Fifth Avenue, between 38th and 39th Streets, 685-8545

Leave it to the French to offer the most chic looks in large-size clothing. Many of the garments they sell are manufactured in France especially for Jeanne Rafal, but there are also designer lines like Harvé Benard and Pierre Cardin. Alterations are free. Though I've never seen a woman who looked more than a size 10 in France (except myself in the hotel mirror), there are twenty Jeanne Rafal boutiques in that country. The first New York location is conveniently close to that old standby Lane Bryant. Prices are moderate to expensive. Open Monday to Saturday 10:00 A.M. to 6:00 P.M., Thursday till 8:00 P.M.

**Ashanti,** 872 Lexington Avenue, at 65th Street, 535-0740

Its name dating to former days when it was an ethnic boutique, Ashanti now features a unique line of clothing for the large woman (sizes 14 to 26). The look is sophisticated, very New York, somewhat arty, with most garments made from natural, hand-woven and hand-dyed imported fabrics. There are many dresses, as well as blouses, separates, pants, skirts, patchwork coats, jewelry and accessories. Prices are moderate to expensive, so try to hit the sales in January and at the end of summer. Open Monday to Saturday 10:00 A.M. to 6:00 P.M., Thursday til 8:00 P.M.

**Sizes Unlimited, A Division of Roaman's,** 250 Market Street, Saddle Brook, N.J., 201-843-8374

Roaman's, alas, is one of the stores that still offers a rather dowdy line for big women—the kinds of clothes that get you back on your diet fast or drowning your sorrows in a hot fudge sundae. There is, however, some gold among the dross—designer and brand names like Gloria Vanderbilt, Sasson and Ship 'n Shore, and at this factory outlet (the Manhattan store is at 20 West 39th Street), it's all discounted 30% to 50%. What's more, Sizes Unlimited promises that if you can find the same item elsewhere for less, it'll give it to you free! Shopping here is strictly no frills, no service, no try-ons, but there is an exchange policy. Open weekdays 10:00 A.M. to 9:00 P.M., Saturday to 6:00 P.M.

**London Majesty,** 1211 Avenue of the Americas, at 48th Street, 221-1860

A subsidiary of a European company called High and Mighty, London Majesty offers the finest-quality clothing for big (46- to 58-inch chests) and tall (many basketball players shop here) men. The clothes are designed and made in England, using many imported fabrics and the finest Swiss voiles for shirts. There's a full range of clothing at London Majesty: suits, coats, shirts, outerwear, cashmere and lamb's wool sweaters from Scotland, blazers, leather and suede garments, extra-long ties and belts, etc. Only headwear and footwear are missing. Service is first-rate. Custom tailoring is done on the premises, and though prices are high, they're commensurate with quality. Open Monday to Saturday 9:00 A.M. to 6:00 P.M., Thursday till 8:00 P.M.

## *COSTUMES*

**Rainbow Party Supply,** 280 Midland Avenue, Saddle Brook, N.J., 201-791-1850

Rainbow Party Supply is just a ten-minute trip over the George Washington Bridge. If you need a costume for any occasion, take a ride to Rainbow. Here it makes top-quality costumes and sells them to retail stores. It pays to buy at its low prices, and if you are the one having the costume ball, you will be delighted by the discounts Rainbow offers on all kinds of party supplies from paper goods to piñatas. Open Monday, Tuesday, Saturday 9:00 A.M. to 5:30 P.M., Wednesday, Thursday, Friday 9:00 A.M. to 9:00 P.M.

**Lazars Stationers,** 131 Park Avenue, Box 248, Plainfield, N.J., 201-756-5868

Lazars designs and sells or rents its own costumes and has one of the largest selections around—everything from a chicken costume to a gorilla outfit. Children's costumes are for sale only, but the price is right. Adult costumes sell for $15 to $300 and rent from $15 to $40. Well worth a trip to New Jersey. Monday through Friday from 8:00 A.M. to 5:00 P.M., Thursday to 8:00 P.M.

## CUSTOM-MADE SHIRTS

**The Custom Shop, Shirtmakers,** 716 Fifth Avenue, between 55th and 56th Streets, 582-4366

Until you've tried wearing garments made to measure just for you, you've no idea what an appearance improver they are. At The Custom Shop, shirts are hand-cut to the precise specifications indicated by thirteen different measurements, yet they begin as low as $22.50. Owner Mortimer Levitt is an expert in sartorial matters, having been a shirtmaker for more than forty years. His customers have included several presidents (JFK was one), Ed Koch, Hugh Carey, Dan Rather and Walter Cronkite. The store offers a choice of 350 shirtings, mostly imported from Europe and Japan. In addition to ready-made and custom-made shirts for men and women, the shop creates linen and cotton velvet bolero vests for women, custom-made suits, slacks and ties of Moygashel linen and silk for men. Levitt sells ready-made men's blazers, men's jewelry and umbrellas and skirts and belts for women. From order to delivery takes about six weeks, and there is a minimum order of four. Open Monday to Saturday 9:00 A.M. to 6:00 P.M. There are five additional Manhattan locations and one in Hackensack, N.J.

**Prince Fashions,** G.P.O. Box 2868, Hong Kong

Everyone knows that Hong Kong offers some of the best buys in custom-made shirts. It's just a trifle inconvenient for shopping trips. However, you can take advantage of Hong Kong prices and quality without leaving home. Just write to the above address for a free catalog and samples of its silk and cotton fabrics; then send your measurements (an instruction sheet tells you how to do it) and choices as to collar, cuffs, pocket style and plain or pleated front. Prince's will send you back a custom-tailored cotton shirt for just $11.50, a silk shirt for $22.80 plus sea or air charges. This service is for both men and women.

## FURS

**Harry Kirshner & Son,** 307 Seventh Avenue, between 27th and 28th Streets, 243-4847

The Kirshners have a factory right on the premises (you can tour it if you like) where they make up all their coats. Since they're the manufacturer, they then sell to the public at prices that can go as low as 50% below retail. There's a huge stock of ready-made coats for women in sizes 4 to 16—mink, raccoon, fox, coyote, lynx, seal, etc.—and they will also custom-create anything of fur, not just coats and jackets but stoles, hats, muffs, pillows, blankets and anything else you might desire. While you're here, check out the Kirshner's sizable collection (several hundred at all times) of used coats in perfect condition; you might find a mink for as little as $100! Service is courteous and helpful. They also remodel, repair, restore and clean fur coats. Open weekdays 9:00 A.M. to 6:00 P.M., Saturday (except the first two weeks of August) 10:00 A.M. to 5:00 P.M.

**Brothers II,** 333 Seventh Avenue, between 28th and 29th Streets, third floor, 695-8469

Brothers II is pretty much the "compleat furrier." It is a vast wholesale operation that also sells to retail customers at about 20% below department-store prices. It makes gorgeous, top-quality coats, jackets and hats for men (largest manufacturer of men's fur coats and jackets in the city) and for women in mink, nutria, coyote, Canadian lynx, Alaskan otter, American gray fox, American raccoon, Tanuki (a Japanese raccoon), Finnish raccoon, natural and long-haired beaver and Norwegian Saga fox in a wide size range (petite 4 to misses 18 for women, 34 to 52 for men). Jackets can be made reversible with the other side leather. Manufacturing and tailoring are done on the premises, alterations are free and matching accessories can be made to order. There's also cold storage at Brothers II. Open weekdays 9:00 A.M. to 6:00 P.M., weekends (except May to August) 10:00 A.M. to 4:00 P.M.

**The Ritz Thrift Shop,** 107 West 57th Street, between Sixth and Seventh Avenues, 265-4559

When the very wealthy tire of their sables and minks—often after just a few months' wear—they sell them to The Ritz Thrift Shop. The Ritz pays about a quarter of the original retail price, cleans, glazes and repairs any damages and then offers them up for about half the original retail value. There are always about 1,000 coats in stock (about 10% for men), usually including 200 or so minks beginning at about $800. The rest are a mix of sable, lynx, coyote, fox, raccoon, nutria, etc. Some are bought directly from previous owners (people like Jackie Onassis and Dina Merrill); others come from major dealers who acquired them in trade-ins. And the people who buy are not just housewives from Queens; bargain-conscious customers include the glittery likes of Goldie Hawn, Mrs. Vincent Price, Celeste Holm, Redd Foxx and Susan Strasberg. Open Monday to Saturday 9:00 A.M. to 6:00 P.M., closed Saturday in July.

## HANDBAGS, HATS AND GLOVES

**Fine & Klein,** 119 Orchard Street, between Delancey and Rivington Streets, 674-6720

Catering to the carriage trade as well as to Bronx and Brooklyn bargain hunters, Fine & Klein is one of the Lower East Side's premier shops. On Sundays it's so busy you have to take a number and wait on line just to get in, and at any time you might see limos parked outside. Among the notables who come here for bargains are Zsa Zsa Gabor, Diahann Carroll and Lynda Bird Johnson. The selection is vast, with three floors of top-quality designer bags—Meyers, Finesse, Susan Gail, Oleg Cassini, Dior, Venetto, Sharif, Halston, etc.—all discounted 30%. The same discounted prices apply to umbrellas, small leather goods, attaché cases for men and women, some luggage and even jewelry. Fine & Klein isn't for el cheapos; it's for the best prices on the best bags. Open Sunday to Friday 8:45 A.M. to 5:30 P.M.

**Ber-Sel Handbags,** 79 Orchard Street, between Broome and Grand Streets, 966-5517

"If you see any bag elsewhere that you like," says owner Joseph Mittleman, "take down the model number and I'll try to get it for you cheaper." First, however, I'd advise a close perusal of his stock at Ber-Sel, where a wide selection of designer bags (Dior, Anne Klein, Meyers, Oleg Cassini, Palizzio, etc.), wallets, gloves and umbrellas (including Knirps that comes with a lifetime guarantee but not, unfortunately, a guarantee you won't lose it) are discounted 30%. There are special sales around January-February and July-August. Open Sunday to Friday 9:00 A.M. to 6:00 P.M., with earlier Friday closings in winter.

**Young's Hats,** 139 Nassau Street, just across from City Hall, 964-5693

This tiny store is crammed with hats for men—every possible variety of headgear including ten-gallon hats, berets, Stetsons, Dobbses, casual hats, fur hats, cowboy hats, caps, boaters, homburgs, derbies, tams and opera hats—all discounted 30%. They come in sizes 6 ⅝ to 8, which should take care of everyone from pinheads to melonheads. Open weekdays 9:00 A.M. to 5:15 P.M., Saturday (except July and August) 10:00 A.M. to 2:30 P.M.

**Feltly Hats,** 97 Orchard Street, between Delancey and Broome Streets, 226-0322

Feltly has been around for eighty-two years, and like the aptly named Young's (a relative newcomer established in 1930), it offers discounts—here 25%—on every variety and size of imported and domestic hats for men. Open Sunday to Friday 9:30 A.M. to 5:30 P.M.

**Bernard Krieger & Son, Inc.,** 316 Grand Street, between Orchard and Allen Streets, 226-4927

Since 1936 Krieger has been proffering top-quality designer merchandise at discounts of at least 50%. He has women's hats—felt, knit and angora hats, ski hats, berets, tams, etc.—leather gloves for men and women from Italy and the Orient in short and long lengths, ski gloves, cashmere, angora and suede gloves. Scarves and handkerchiefs here, too. Open Sunday to Friday 9:00 A.M. to 4:45 P.M.

**Modern Hatters,** 313 Third Street, Jersey City, N.J., 201-659-1113

In-the-know shoppers from all over the metropolitan area travel to Modern Hatters for big discounts on an immense selection of men's, women's and children's headwear. In business 137 years (are they ever mavens!) Modern Hatters is a wholesaler to major department stores. It'll sell you the same styles at discounts of 40% to 60% as well as overruns and show samples. There are thousands of hats for every head. Open Monday to Saturday 10:00 A.M. to 7:00 P.M.

## HIP CHIC

The following stores defy easy categorization. They sell military surplus (often dyed in fabulous colors), recycled and antique garments and much else that looks young, hip and hot and unisex but that sells at Bloomingdale's and uptown boutiques for two or three times the price.

**Unique Clothing Warehouse,** 712–718 Broadway, 1½ blocks south of Eighth Street, 674-1767
 Perhaps the most archetypical of this eclectic genre, Unique is huge, fun, colorful and cluttery with loud rock music playing at all times. If you have any fashion flair, you can put together a very, well, let's say, unique and chic complete wardrobe here for just a few hundred dollars. Everything comes in so many delicious colors—persimmon, Chinese red, aqua, peach, mauve, deep purple—it's all as irresistible as those big boxes of Crayolas you loved as a child. Merchandise includes British officers' wool coats, French peacoats, French Connection and Fiorucci lines at substantial discounts, canvas and nylon bags, parachute pants, painters' many-pocketed pants, military surplus and undershirts in a rainbow of colors, rock 'n' roll T-shirts, motorcycle gear, sailor shirts, vintage antique clothing, variegated sweat shirts and sweat pants, hot shorts, satin harem pants, Hawaiian shirts, hand-knit sweaters, shoes, sneakers, belts, costume jewelry, socks, double-pleated white Gurkha pants and much more. Prices are low because Unique deals in such large quantities. Open Monday to Thursday 11:00 A.M. to 7:00 P.M., Friday 10:30 A.M. to 8:45 P.M., Saturday 10:00 A.M. to 7:00 P.M., Sunday 11:30 A.M. to 7:00 P.M.

**Canal Jeans Company,** 504 Broadway, between Broome and Spring Streets, 226-1130
 Very much like Unique, Canal Jeans keeps two rowboats out front filled with special discounted items. The interior is jumping—neon display signs, loud rock, striking colors everywhere—and the merchandise runs the gamut from black leather motorcycle jackets to freaky items like checkered yellow pants for men. You'll also find a wide selection of jeans—Levi's, Lees, Wranglers and designer names—army field jackets, bomber jackets, Fiorucci items, karate shirts, baseball shirts, 100% cotton jump suits in every color, underwear dyed and

designed to wear as outerwear, peacoats, hot pink antler jackets, boxing shorts, sweat pants and sweat shirts, hand-embroidered bowling skirts, cowboy hats, camouflage clothing, Danskin tights and swimwear, Hawaiian shirts and so on and on and on. There's a sizable antique clothing department for both men and women. The comfortable dressing room has big mirrors and baskets to store your extra items. Open daily 10:00 A.M. to 7:00 P.M. Also at 304 Canal Street, between Mercer Street and Broadway, 431-8439.

**Reminiscence,** 175 Macdougal Street, off Eighth Street, 477-4051

About 80% of the clothing here is manufactured by Reminiscence; the rest includes army surplus, Capri pants and other fifties-look garments enjoying a New Wave renaissance, antique clothes, Hawaiian shirts and suchlike. There are cotton collarless shirts, jump suits of every variety and color, white clothing (a current craze), cotton parachute pants, Egyptian cotton flight suits, hats, socks and a fine selection of antique jewelry and hair accessories. In short, everything to assemble outfits that will get you into the trendiest discos. Open Monday to Saturday 12:15 to 8:00 P.M., Sunday only from Thanksgiving to Christmas.

**I. Buss,** 738 Broadway, just below Eighth Street, 242-3338

A traditional uniform store dating back to 1892, I. Buss branched out in 1974 to include hip surplus-military chic. Though rock and disco are always blaring, the ambience is less slick than at the above-mentioned emporiums, and nothing is dyed; but quality is excellent, the choice of goods eclectic, and prices are very low. You can still buy or rent uniforms here—doormen, chauffeurs, nurses, firemen, etc.—which some of I. Buss's customers use for costumes. Owner Stewart Busch also sells and rents real costumes—gorillas and other animals, witches, monks, Santa Claus and so on. He carries 100% wool and cotton imported sweaters, dinner jackets and old tuxedos, ruffled shirts, striped French pirate shirts, British bobby capes and wool overcoats, French cotton army pants, French army raincoats, military shorts, shoes and boots, prairie skirts, paratroopers' pants, blazers, wide-leg French military cotton shorts and many items of costume jewelry. Open Monday to Saturday from 10:00 A.M. to 7:00 P.M., sometimes on Sundays (call first).

**Kaufman Surplus,** 319 West 42nd Street, between Eighth and Ninth Avenues, 757-5670

Dating from the late thirties and fronted by two cannons from the Spanish-American War, Kaufman features Lees and Levi's, especially the original Levi's #501 shrink-to-fit, fly-button jeans (there's a pair on display with a seventy-seven-inch waist!). There's also a vast amount of military surplus here (including an unsurpassed selection of insignia), many canvas bags and soft luggage items, jump suits, overalls, fatigue pants, leather flight jackets, peacoats and all the rest. Like I. Buss, Kaufman is more low-key than its competitors; it plays country music and oldies. Open Monday to Saturday from 9:30 A.M. to 6:00 P.M.

## LINGERIE AND HOSIERY

**Charles Weiss & Sons,** 38 Orchard Street, at Hester Street, 226-1717

Claiming the largest selection of bras, lingerie and foundation garments in the city—and the largest brand diversity in the nation—Charles Weiss has it all (in all sizes) at Orchard Street discounts of between 20% to 50%. Whatever brand you favor—Bali, Lily of France, Maidenform, Vassarette, Playtex, Formfit Rogers, Pucci, Dior, Halston, you name it—Weiss has it. And if it doesn't, it'll special order it and sell it to you at a discount. Weiss is up-to-the-minute in current styles, including, of course, jogging bras. No fitting rooms here, but you ca get a full refund for up to thirty days with no questions asked. Open Sunday to Thursday 9:00 A.M. to 5:00 P.M., Friday till 2:00 P.M.

**Goldman & Cohen,** 54 Orchard Street, between Hester and Grand Streets, 966-0737

Offering similar merchandise to the above—all major brand names and top designers of lingerie and loungewear—at discounts of 20% to 60%, Goldman & Cohen has twenty to thirty salespeople to serve you at all times. Once again, no fitting room, but a liberal exchange policy. Comparison shopping is the name of the game. Open Sunday to Thursday 9:00 A.M. to 5:30 P.M., Friday till 4:00 P.M.

**A. Rosenthal,** 92 Orchard Street, between Delancey and Broome Streets, 473-5428

More of the same—everything from Pucci nightgowns to Formfit running bras and Danskin bathing suits—at discounts of 20% to 50%. All major brands and designers are represented. No dressing rooms, and Rosenthal's not too crazy about returns, so inquire before you buy if you're not sure. Open Sunday to Thursday 9:00 A.M. to 6:00 P.M., Friday till 3:00 P.M.

While you're doing Orchard Street, also try **A. W. Kaufman,** at 73, between Grand and Broome Streets, 226-1629. Open Sunday to Thursday 10:00 A.M. to 5:00 P.M., Friday till 2:30 P.M.

**D. & A.,** 22 Orchard Street, between Hester and Canal Streets, 925-4766

Owner Eliot Kivell calls himself the Underwear King. Visit his "castle," and stock up on underwear, pajamas, robes and hose for the entire family at discounts of 25%. The King stocks every major brand of women's bras and lingerie, socks and hosiery, ditto in boys' and men's underwear and hose. This is a good source for Danskin bathing suits, leotards and tights in all sizes, too; if the King doesn't have what you want, he'll special order it. There is a fitting room, but there's no trying on on Sundays, when the place is mobbed. The King has a liberal return policy, however. Open Sunday to Thursday 9:00 A.M. to 5:00 P.M., till 3:00 P.M. on Fridays.

**Anelra Lingerie,** 48½ East Seventh Street, between First and Second Avenues, 473-2454

Owner Arlene Eriksson (Anelra is vaguely Arlene spelled backwards) has filled her delightful shop with the most beautiful of foundations for frivolity and function and with lovely, lacy lingerie. She has stunning, up-to-the-moment styles in camisoles, teddies, body suits, bras, chemise slips, garter belts and sexy stockings. It's all to die from, glamorous and feminine, but never crude. There's even a small section for men, with robes, silk French-cut boxer shorts with matching tank tops and suchlike. While you're prettying up underneath, consider what shows and take a look at Anelra's special line of fine cosmetics for men and women (men, too, can cover up poor complexions, broken capillaries and circles under the eyes). A make-up consultation is $20, which you can put toward purchases. Prices are moderate to expensive, but commensurate with quality. Open Monday to Wednesday 1:00 P.M. to 9:00 P.M., Thursday and Friday till 11:00 P.M., Saturday till 8:00 P.M., Sunday to 7:00 P.M.

**Wingdale Hosiery Co.,** 34 West 30th Street, between Fifth Avenue and Broadway, 684-4291

"There isn't anything I wouldn't do to make a woman happy," says owner Sol Habler. Mrs. Habler might take exception, but she doesn't mind Sol's making you happy with discounts of at least 50% on major brands of stockings and panty hose like Hanes, Kaiser, Supp-Hose (for men and women) and a wide selection of opaques in all colors; also dance tights, leg warmers and socks. Open weekdays only from 8:00 A.M. to 4:00 P.M.

**Ultra Smart,** 15 East 30th Street, between Fifth and Madison Avenues, fourth floor, 686-1564

The same top-designer stockings you pay top dollar for in department stores are available here, sans prestige label, for about 75% less. Ultra Smart buys them from the big mills and puts them out under its own label. You can't go wrong. Open weekdays only 8:00 A.M. to 5:00 P.M.

## *MATERNITY CLOTHES*

**Chor Bazaar,** 801 Lexington Avenue, at 62nd Street, 838-2581

Pregnancy is the bane of fashionable women. It's not just that your figure is bigger, but that designers just don't seem to care how you look during those nine important months. If your response to T-shirts with arrows pointing to the word *Baby* is "yecch," head over to Chor Bazaar, where you'll discover loose, billowy and beautiful soft cotton and silk crepe de Chine garments—not specifically made for pregnant women, but amply roomy for them. Not only will you look lovely, but you can wear the clothes after Baby has been born. Chor Bazaar is not actually a maternity shop. It's a marvelously exotic high-quality import store, featuring ethnic antique dresses from Afghanistan and India, beautiful satin baby shoes from China, embroidered Mexican dresses, Moroccan shirts, Indian silks, Rumanian peasant dresses and suchlike. It's very chic. Contemporary clothing, leather and suede, shoes and jewelry are also on hand. Prices are moderate to expensive. Open Monday to Saturday 10:00 A.M. to 7:00 P.M., call to check Sunday openings.

**Reborn Maternity,** 1449 Third Avenue, at 82nd Street, 737-8817

Reborn Maternity understands the problem of coordinating a maternity wardrobe on a limited budget that must last through two different weather seasons. Many of its styles and fabrics are thus chosen to transcend seasonal differences—e.g., denim jumpers, heavy cotton dresses and linen slacks that can be worn year round. Its selection is one of the largest in the city (bigger than most of its competitors combined). Reborn carries every possible wardrobe component and includes numerous designer fashions—Jane Schaffhausen of Belle France, Regina Kravitz, Evelyn De Jonge, Sasson, Givenchy and others. They're all discounted 10% to 60%, and there's a big sale from the third week in January till the third week in February. Open weekdays 10:00 A.M. to 7:00 P.M. (till 8:30 P.M. on Thursdays), Saturdays 10:00 A.M. to 6:00 P.M., Sundays 11:00 A.M. to 5:00 P.M. There are additional locations in Paramus and Livingston, N.J.; Manhasset, Cedarhurst and Huntington, L.I.; White Plains, N.Y.; and Westport, Conn.

**Lady Madonna Maternity Boutique,** 793 Madison Avenue, at 67th Street, 988-7173

A bit out of the ordinary in the way of maternity boutiques, Lady Madonna has its own line of clothes for pregnant women; their talented designers know how to translate current styles into maternity sizes. The collection includes every possible item of clothing—dresses, pants, suits, gowns, lingerie, swimwear, even jogging clothes—and there are many garments of 100% cotton, crepe de Chine, wool, silk and linen along with the poly blends. Prices are what you'd expect in this classy Madison Avenue district, so try to catch the sales in June and December. Open Monday to Saturday 10:30 A.M. to 6:00 P.M., till 7:30 on Thursday. There are a dozen additional Lady Madonna boutiques in the metropolitan area: two in Brooklyn, one in Queens, one in White Plains, four on Long Island and four in New Jersey. Call the above number for locations.

## MEN'S CLOTHING

**Pan Am,** 50 and 59 Orchard Street, between Grand and Hester Streets, 925-7032

Orchard Street discounts aren't just for women. The finest European and American designer styles for men—Diors, Calvin Kleins, Halstons, Pierre Cardins, etc.—are reduced 20% to 50% at Pan Am's two locations. At #50 you'll find beautiful suits and sport coats (alterations are free), slacks, overcoats, raincoats, down jackets and cashmere coats. You can complete your discount wardrobe at #59, choosing from a huge line of dress and sport shirts, casual slacks, sweaters, belts and other accessories. Both stores are open Sunday to Wednesday 9:30 A.M. to 6:00 P.M., Thursday to 8:00 P.M., Friday to 2:30 P.M.

## SHOPPING AND FOOD GUIDE 43

**G & G Projections,** 53 Orchard Street, between Grand and Hester Streets, 431-4530

Very convenient for comparison shopping, G & G, on the same Orchard Street block as its above-listed competitor, offers phenomenal bargains (25% to 40% off retail with special sales January-February and July-August) on men's designer dress clothes and sportswear. Check out its Givenchy, Geoffrey Beene, Yves Saint Laurent, Stanley Blacker, Adolfo, Nino Cerruti and Egon Von Furstenberg jackets, suits and dress shirts. Also at G & G, designer ties, blazers, outerwear, slacks, jeans and leather jackets. Alterations are free. Open Sunday to Wednesday 9:00 A.M. to 6:00 P.M., Thursday till 8:00 P.M., Friday till an hour before sundown.

On the same block and under the same ownership is **Penn Garden Grand and Liberty,** 58 Orchard Street, 226-9513, featuring stunning designer shirts and sweaters—Ted Lapidus, Oleg Cassini, Oscar de la Renta, Franco Ruffini, Hathaway and many others—at the same discounts. Hours are the same, too.

**S. Sosinsky & Son,** 143 Orchard Street, between Delancey and Rivington Streets, 254-2307

The Sosinsky family has been at this location for almost seventy years, selling quality cotton and silk shirts (e.g., Arrow) and designer bathrobes (e.g., Christian Dior) for men. Its stock consists of showroom samples and irregulars, so look carefully for defects before you buy. Sosinsky also has sweaters, pajamas and knit shirts—at 50% or more below retail. Open Sunday and Tuesday to Thursday 9:00 A.M. to 5:00 P.M., Monday 10:00 A.M. to 5:00 P.M., Friday (except during July and August) 10:00 A.M. to 3:30 P.M.

**LBC Clothing, Inc.,** 337 Grand Street, between Orchard and Allen Streets, 226-1620

Some men don tuxedos only twice in their lives—at their high- or prep-school prom and their wedding. But you glamorous guys with more frequent black-tie occasions on your social calendars might consider buying instead of renting. LBC has a limited selection of tuxes amid lots of other discounted menswear—raincoats, sport jackets, outerwear and pants (some irregulars, most perfect)—all of it at 60% to 80% below retail! Irregular tuxedos, some with very minor flaws, begin at just $80. You can get a flawless tux for just over $100, the very best for $175 (elsewhere the same sells for $375). Open Sunday

9:00 A.M. to 6:00 P.M., Monday to Thursday 10:00 A.M. to 6:00 P.M., Friday 9:00 A.M. to 3:00 P.M.

Also try **First Nighter Formals,** 7 West 22nd Street, 675-5550, a manufacturer selling its own name-brand tuxes in half a dozen styles in sizes from boys' 4 to extra-large 60. Prices are about 50% below comparable retail. Open Monday to Thursday 8:00 A.M. to 4:30 P.M., Friday till 3:00 or 4:00 P.M.

**L.S. Men's Clothing,** 23 West 45th Street, between Fifth and Sixth Avenues, second floor, 575-0933

Billing itself the "executive discount store," L.S. is the source for many men who dress for success even before they've achieved it and for many others who have achieved it but still see no reason to fling money about needlessly. They all come for top-quality menswear by name-brand American manufacturers at a whopping 45% to 65% off retail prices. L.S. carries classic designer styles in suits and jackets in all sizes; cashmere, camel's hair and wool overcoats (I've seen coats for $520 in fancy men's stores just $275 here); all-weather coats; neckwear (pure silk ties for just $10); and slacks—everything, in fact, for the executive look except shirts. There's a minimal charge for alterations. Occasionally L.S. has some women's man-tailored suits and coats as well. Open Monday 10:00 A.M. to 7:00 P.M., Tuesday to Thursday to 6:00 P.M., Friday to 4:00 P.M., Sunday by appointment only between 11:00 A.M. and 4:00 P.M.

**Hilton Manufacturing Company,** 35 East Elizabeth Avenue, Linden, N.J., 201-486-2610

Semiannual sales are your ticket to the best-dressed list at Hilton, a major supplier of many of New York's finest men's shops. Classic styles in trousers, blazers, suits and sport jackets are sold at factory prices (50% below retail) for two weeks every year, one week in early May and another early in November. Call for exact dates and to be put on a mailing list that announces the sales; it'll also send driving directions if you ask. Hilton has some women's clothing—blazers, skirts and pants—that is discounted on sale weeks, too. The look for both sexes is executive/preppy. This factory outlet is not open to the public except during semiannual sales.

**Suit Yourself,** 346 Bloomfield Avenue, Bloomfield, N.J., 201-748-8605

High-quality merchandise at greatly reduced prices—savings of

20% to 50%—are what you'll find at Suit Yourself, a large, well-organized (this is no jumble sale) retail discount operator. It carries top-quality current merchandise with labels like Bill Blass, John Peel, Dimension, Adolfo and Yves Saint Laurent. A man can get a complete wardrobe here—suits, sport coats, dress and sport shirts, sweaters, designer jeans, ties, hose, underwear and belts. Tailors are right on the premises to provide quick alteration service for a fee. Open weekdays 10:00 A.M. to 8:45 P.M., Saturday to 5:45 P.M.

## MEN, WOMEN AND CHILDREN'S CLOTHING

Unfortunately for writers of guidebooks, stores were never created with easy categorization in mind. Hence the following might be largely for men with a department for women, or vice versa, or pretty evenly mixed, or also offering children's clothes. Some sell all kinds of clothing; others, just sweaters or perhaps leather and suede garments. As each listing describes exactly what you'll find, it won't, I hope, be too confusing.

**Syms,** 45 Park Place, between Church Street and West Broadway, 791-1199
  You've probably seen Marcy Syms on TV telling you how an educated consumer is the store's best customer. There are four floors plus a basement jammed with merchandise for the whole family sold at hefty discounts. In the basement are men's suits and coats, including many designer labels. The street floor contains more men's wear—slacks, shoes, socks, sport coats and outerwear—the second floor, men's shirts, ties, sweaters and knits as well as boys' sport jackets, suits and slacks. The third floor for women features suits, coats, blouses, skirts, slacks, shirts, etc., as well as children's clothing—boys, girls and toddlers. The best buys, though, are in women's pantsuits, dresses, lingerie and ensembles on the fourth floor, where an automatic markdown system is in effect. A dress retailing elsewhere for $100 will go out on the floor at $59 here. After ten days it will be reduced to $48; after twenty days, to $38; after thirty days, to a final price of $29. The tag tells the date it was put out originally, so you might want to gamble and wait for the next markdown. Syms is open Monday to Wednesday 9:00 A.M. to 7:00 P.M., Thursday and Friday till 8:00 P.M., Saturday to 6:00 P.M. There are additional Syms stores in Roslyn Heights and Elmsford, N.Y.; Paramus and Woodbridge, N.J.

**Century 21,** 12 Cortlandt Street, between Church Street and Broadway, 227-9092

The Financial District emporium is like a discount department store, offering budget buys in clothing for the entire family as well as a wide selection of merchandise ranging from home furnishings, appliances and housewares to health and beauty aids and electronic games. There are great buys—up to 50% off regular prices—on designer jeans, baby clothes, men's shirts and robes, sports clothing, lingerie, shoes and much more. One drawback: There's no try-on room. But there is a liberal return policy. Open weekdays 7:45 A.M. to 6:15 P.M. There's another Century 21 in Bay Ridge, Brooklyn, at 472 86th Street, 748-3266

**Deals,** 81 Worth Street, between Broadway and Church Street, 966-0214

If you're preppy but not rich, eschew Brooks Brothers and head downtown to Deals. Here you'll find traditional navy wool flannel and gabardine suits, classic blazers, button-down oxford shirts, pure silk regimental ties and all the rest at about 50% below regular prices. The main floor is for men; the larger basement, for women (an immense selection of both designer and traditional blouses here). In addition to preppy-look garb, Deals has name-brand fashions as well as shoes and boots. Don't miss the end-of-season sales when prices plummet to below wholesale. Open Monday to Saturday 9:00 A.M. to 6:00 P.M., Thursday till 9:00 P.M., Sunday 10:00 A.M. to 5:00 P.M.

**Victory Shirt Company,** 345 Madison Avenue, at 44th Street, 687-6375

Since 1974 Mary Sprague has been selling high-quality traditional tailored shirts for men and women right across the street from Brooks Brothers. Since she's the manufacturer, and overhead is low, prices are 25% less than comparable department-store labels. The shirts are made of 100% cotton, with hand-turned collars, single-needle tailoring and seven-button fronts that always stay closed without gaps. Styles are classic and preppy—more for the office than casual wear. They come in a wide range of sizes, and alterations, hand monogramming and custom tapering are available. Mary also offers good buys on handmade 100% silk ties. Open weekdays 9:00 A.M. to 6:00 P.M., Saturday 9:30 A.M. to 4:30 P.M. There are two other locations: 96 Orchard Street, 677-2020, and 10 Maiden Lane, 349-7111.

**San Michel Leather & Suede,** 396 Fifth Avenue, at 37th Street, 736-2000

As manufacturers of top-quality leather, suede and sheepskin garments, San Michel is able to offer retail customers 50% to 60% off department-store prices on coats, pants, skirts, jackets, hats, even bathing suits and jogging shorts of those materials. In line with the current craze, it also has down-filled leather jackets. The retail operation is taken seriously, with 5,000 square feet devoted to showroom space, including an area where fun furs are sold at popular prices (approximately $600 to $1,200). There are several thousand pieces of merchandise to choose from at all times in all sizes for men and women; also some items for children. Many special sales take place throughout the year (call for details). Open daily 10:00 A.M. to 6:00 P.M. (till 8:00 P.M. on Monday and Thursday) September to March; Monday to Saturday 10:00 A.M. to 6:00 P.M. the rest of the year.

**Mr. Ned,** 87 Fifth Avenue, between 16th and 17th Streets, 924-5042

A suit is a major purchase that generally gets several years of wear. One way to acquire a suit that fits perfectly and that you know you'll live happily with is to have it custom-made. Mr. Ned does excellent work, can create any style you have in mind and offers reasonable prices. For men or women, his two-piece suits begin at $275, three-piece suits at $300, depending mostly on the fabric selected. Mr. Ned has thousands to choose from—wools, silks, cashmeres, cottons, whatever. Open weekdays 8:00 A.M. to 5:30 P.M., Saturday till 2:30 P.M.

**Lord & Taylor Clearance Center,** 839-16 New York Avenue, Huntington, L.I., 516-673-0009

Imagine walking into Lord & Taylor and finding every single item on sale—men's suits, women's dresses, bathing suits, shoes, children's wear, toys, home furnishings, cosmetics, etc.—all at 50% to 70% below original prices. That's what it's like at the Clearance Center. Merchandise changes constantly, so you never know what treasures you'll discover. Best to go for general shopping rather than with something particular in mind. Open Monday, Thursday, Friday from 10:00 A.M. to 9:00 P.M., Tuesday, Wednesday and Saturday to 6:00 P.M., Sunday noon to 5:00 P.M.

**The Sweater Outlet,** 37 Route 17 South, East Rutherford, N.J., 201-933-3055

This factory outlet sells cashmere, camel's hair, wool and shetland sweaters for men and women at 30% to 70% below retail, with special bargains on invisible-to-the-eye irregulars. Most of the merchandise is first-quality, though. In addition to sweaters, there are women's cashmere skirts, dresses and suits, wool skirts and polyester blouses. Open 10:00 A.M. to 5:00 P.M. Tuesday to Saturday from early April to the end of July; to 6:00 P.M. Monday to Saturday the rest of the year.

**The Factory Wearhouse,** 20-24 River Road, off Route 4, Bogota, N.J., 201-343-3001

This immense factory outlet—40,000 square feet of selling space—is filled with big savings on names like Calvin Klein, Breckenridge, Jack Mulqueen, Villager and many others. Most of the name-brand and designer current first-quality stock consists of women's sportswear and outerwear, including an enormous jeans department. Sizes are 3 to 16. For men, there's also sportswear (no suits or sport jackets), once again with a tremendous selection of jeans, also jogging wear, sweaters and cotton shirts. Adjoining is the **Children's Factory Wearhouse**, offering everything from layettes to preteen sportswear, and like its adult counterpart featuring brand names (Billy the Kid, Lee, Levi's, Oshkosh, Little World, etc.). Discounts in both sections range from 30% upward with special sales on national holidays. Open Monday to Saturday 10:00 A.M. to 6:00 P.M., Thursday till 8:00 P.M. There are three New Jersey locations in Garwood, New Milford and Totowa.

## RESALE AND THRIFT SHOPS

Did you ever stop to think about what the very wealthy do with last year's fashions? They don't always give them to their help. Many, in excellent condition, end up in resale shops, where you can purchase them for a fraction of the original cost. A booklet that lists them all, and rates them with one, two or three shopping bags, is *It's Chic to Be Thrifty*, by Charlotte Harmon (call 582-1757 for information on how to order). Below, some of my personal favorites.

**I, Michael, Resale, Inc.,** 1041 Madison Avenue, at 79th Street, second floor, 737-7273

Michael began his shop with the realization that women wouldn't throw out the $2,000 gowns they'd worn just a few times—and they wouldn't give them to charity or to a friend. He contacted New York's wealthiest women and soon convinced them to empty their closets to his store. His sources even include royalty. You'll find only the best at I, Michael—designer names like Valentino, Cardin, Blass, Saint Laurent, etc.—and there's even a $10 to $25 rack. Open Tuesday to Saturday 9:30 A.M. to 6:00 P.M.; closed Saturday July and August.

**Encore Resale Dress Shop,** 1132 Madison Avenue, at 84th Street, 879-2850

Another of the shops where society women unload their slightly worn designer outfits, Encore also features a full line of brand-new furs (Seventh Avenue overstock) at discounted prices. The rest consists of dresses, gowns, bags, scarves, hats, jewelry, etc. I recently found a beautiful sweater, in perfect condition, for $175 at Encore that I had coveted at Bendel's for $700. Open Monday to Saturday 10:30 A.M. to 6:00 P.M., Sunday 12:30 to 6:00 P.M.

**Exchange Unlimited,** 563 Second Avenue, at 31st Street, 889-3229

This is one of the few resale shops in New York that carry men's clothing as well as women's. One of the reasons most don't is that men tend not to discard practically new expensive outfits, but to wear them until they're falling apart. However, Exchange Unlimited has somehow convinced fashionable men (or, more likely, their wives who discard their own duds here) to consign unwanted Ralph Lauren suits, hats, ties, shirts, belts, pants, shoes and sweaters. Many good things for women here, too—pantsuits, blazers, dresses, bags, skirts, jewelry, blouses (many designer names) and some clothing from the thirties and forties. Things go on the rack at about one-third of their original price (depending on condition). If they're still around after thirty days, they're reduced an additional 30%, sixty days 50%, ninety days 75%. Open weekdays 11:30 A.M. to 7:30 P.M., Saturday 10:00 A.M. to 6:00 P.M.

**Limited Editions,** 411 Plandome Road, Manhasset, L.I., 516-627-0221

Sponsored by Women's American ORT, this shop features a dazzling array of designer merchandise at all times—Diane Von Furstenbergs, Diors, Liz Claibornes, Gloria Vanderbilts, Oscar de la Rentas, etc. Many of the items are brand-new since a number of women who support this shop are married to men in the garment industry. The others are gently used and look new. The winning combination of low prices and high style makes Limited Editions well worth the trip to Long

Island. It's open Tuesday to Saturday 10:00 A.M. to 5:00 P.M. There's another Limited Editions in Westbury, L.I., 516-997-3693, a third in New Hyde Park, 516-746-8892, called All S'ort of Treasure that deals in resale furniture, collectibles and objets d'art from "the finest homes in Nassau County."

## SHOES

### Athletic Shoes

**Carlsen Import Shoe Co.,** 524 Broadway, at Spring Street, 431-5940
Carlsen has more than 100,000 pairs of athletic shoes in stock—for men, women and children and for every sport that requires special footwear. As a major U.S. wholesaler, Carlsen is able to offer big discounts on name-brand athletic shoes like Adidas, Spaulding, Saucony, Pony and Osaga and also on sporting goods—footballs, basketballs, bats, gloves, etc.—and sport clothes. The store is housed in a third-floor loft. It's open Monday to Friday 9:00 A.M. to 5:00 P.M., Saturday to 12:30 P.M.

### Children's Shoes

**Richie's Shoes,** 183 Avenue B, between 11th and 12th Streets, 228-5442
Moms in the know take their kids over to Richie's for everything from size 2 prewalkers to shoes for thirteen- and fourteen-year-olds. He carries all the latest styles and major American brands—Keds, Jumping Jacks, Stride Rite, Bass, Buster Brown, Little Capezio, etc.—at 40% to 60% off regular prices. Service is excellent and caring; the staff wants to be sure your child's shoes really fit. Richie's is open daily except Wednesday from 10:00 A.M. to 5:00 P.M., Sundays to 3:00 P.M.

### Men's Shoes

**Sherman Shoes,** 121 Division Street, between Orchard and Ludlow Streets, 233-7898
For more than fifty years Sherman has been selling fine men's leather

shoes and boots at sensational savings—25% to 75% less than retail! It stocks many top domestic and import designer labels, cowboy and dress boots and even has its own Italian-made brand, Paolo Ferracini. A wholesaler, Sherman buys up-to-date styles in large quantities. Open Monday to Thursday 8:00 A.M. to 4:30 P.M., Friday to 3:00 P.M., Sunday to 4:00 P.M.

Also check out **Shoes**, 94 Orchard Street, between Delancey and Broome Streets, 982-7051, where men's designer and popular-brand shoes are discounted 50%. Open Sunday to Thursday from 9:30 A.M. to 5:30 P.M., Friday till 4:30 P.M.

## Shoes for Men and Women

**Leslie Bootery for Men and Women,** 36 Orchard Street, between Canal and Hester Streets, 431-9196

A three-story operation, Leslie devotes its main floor to popular-priced brands for women, at discounts averaging 20% to 30%. Upstairs are Leslie's designer shoes for women: These are the big names, and discounts are, again, 20% to 30%. Below stairs are men's shoes—brands like Frye, Bally, Rockport and Clark's of England, once again discounted at about 20%. Open Sunday to Thursday 9:30 A.M. to 5:30 P.M., Friday to 4:30 P.M.

Also try **Designer Shoes for Men & Women** at 317 Grand Street, between Allen and Orchard Streets, 226-3977, where designer-name footwear for men and women is discounted 20%. Hours are Sunday to Thursday 9:30 A.M. to 5:30 P.M., Friday until 4:30 P.M.

**M.M. Shoe Center,** 302 Grand Street, between Allen and Eldridge Streets, 966-2702

M.M. Shoe Center has two large floors of shoe displays, including designer names like Halston, Ferragamo and Gloria Vanderbilt for women, Bill Blass, Bally and Allen Edmonds for men. There's a huge selection in sizes ranging from AA to extra-wide, and if the store doesn't have your size in stock and it's available, it'll order it. It features only current styles in perfect condition—no irregulars or closeout merchandise—but prices are discounted 20% to 25%. Open Sunday to Thursday 9:30 A.M. to 6:00 P.M.

### Shoes for Men, Women and Children

**Jonas Department Store,** 64 West 14th Street, corner of Sixth Avenue, 675-1460

Jonas has great buys in footwear for the whole family—a vast selection of canceled orders and slightly irregular shoes for infants, children, men and women. It's a self-service operation. January and February are the biggest sale months. Open Monday to Saturday 10:00 A.M. to 6:30 P.M.

### Women's Shoes

**The Orchard Bootery,** 75 Orchard Street, between Broome and Grand Streets, 966-0688

You'll find many women's designer and brand-name shoes and boots here—Olaf Daughters, Nickels, Amalfi, Jones N.Y., Ferragamo, Jacques Cohen, etc.—in AA to C widths and at discounts of 25% to 30%. For winter, there is a good selection of wide-calf boots. Open weekdays 9:30 A.M. to 5:30 P.M. (a little earlier closing on Friday in winter), Sunday 9:15 A.M. to 6:00 P.M.

**Anbar Shoes,** 93 Reade Street, between Church Street and West Broadway, 227-0253

Anbar features manufacturer's closeout and overstock merchandise—all of it first-quality (no irregulars here)—and what merchandise it is: top-name designer women's shoes, sold at prices 30% to 50% below retail! You'll find Andrew Geller, Ferragamo, Charles Jourdan, Amalfi and other first-quality lines here.

The same company also owns **Shoe Steal**, around the corner at 116 Duane Street, 964-4017, a similar operation featuring lower-priced brands like Kork-Ease, Jacques Cohen, Red Cross and Nickels. Both stores are open weekdays 8:00 A.M. to 5:30 P.M., Saturday 10:00 A.M. to 4:00 P.M.

Similar merchandise (different owner) can be found at the **Grand St. Bootery,** 65 Orchard Street, between Hester and Grand Streets, 966-6877, at discounts of 20%. They also carry top lines of men's shoes—Bally, Rockport, Frye, etc.—at similar discounts. Open Sunday to Thursday 9:30 A.M. to 5:30 P.M., Friday to 4:30 P.M.

**Aly's Hut, Inc.,** 85 Hester Street, between Orchard and Allen Streets, 226-5555

Specializing in brands like Bass, Candies, Hipoppatamus and Capezio for women (Bass shoes only for men), Aly's offers discounts of 20% to 35%. Same discounts are given on designer handbags—Anne Klein, Oleg Cassini, Pierre Cardin, etc.—and there are special sales—don't miss them—after Christmas and July 4. Open Sunday to Thursday 9:30 A.M. to 5:00 P.M., Friday till 4:00 P.M.

## SPORTING GOODS AND CLOTHING

**Herman's,** 39 West 34th Street, between Fifth Avenue and Herald Square, 279-8900

Owned by W. R. Grace & Company, Herman's is the country's leading sporting goods chain, with ninety-two stores nationwide. There's nothing in the way of major brand sporting goods that you won't find at Herman's: shoes, gear and wear for men, women and children for every imaginable sport, exercise and weight equipment, fishing gear, a full line of camping goods (tents, sleeping bags, backpacks, etc.), down jackets, coats and parkas, swimwear, gaming tables, dartboards and sporting totes. Herman's also services the equipment it sells through experienced departments that handle everything from bowling ball drilling to tennis racket restringing to ski tune-ups. Prices are moderate; however, there are almost constant sales, especially on off-season merchandise. Herman's is open weekdays 9:30 A.M. to 7:00 P.M., Saturday to 6:30 P.M., Sunday noon to 5:00 P.M.. There are additional Manhattan locations (110 Nassau Street, 135 West 42nd Street, and 845 Third Avenue) and about twenty others in the metropolitan area.

**Hudson's,** 97 Third Avenue, between 12th and 13th Streets, 473-7320

Occupying an entire city block, this immense emporium adds a big dollop of fashion flair to the sporting goods scene with many chic sporty-looking garments for men and women that are not necessarily purchased for athletic pursuits. Its clothing line includes trendy sweat suits and shirts in a rainbow of cheerful colors; one of the city's most extensive lines and size ranges of Levi's, Lee and Calvin Klein jeans; military-surplus fashion-look bags, field jackets, etc.; cowboy boots, suede rancher's hats, fringed cowhide frontiersman jackets and other western wear; beautiful 100% wool sweaters; overalls, coveralls and jump suits; down coats, jackets and parkas and much more. Its selection of footwear—work shoes, boots, hiking footwear and athletic shoes of every variety—is vast; ditto its camping and ski gear. There's also a large cutlery department. Prices are always below retail, and there are occasional sales, including a big one on ski equipment after the season. Open Monday to Saturday 9:35 A.M. to 6:35 P.M., Sunday noon to 5:00 P.M.

**Paragon Sporting Goods,** 867 Broadway, at 18th Street, 255-8036

Something like a sporting goods department store, Paragon offers an extensive major brand selection of equipment for men, women and children at discount prices with spectacular bargains on odd-lot and closeout merchandise and during special sales. There are three floors piled high with athletic clothing and equipment for all racket sports, skiing, water-skiing, windsurfing, running, golf, roller- and ice-skating, baseball, football, ice hockey and field hockey, lacrosse, billiards, fishing, boxing and weight lifting. Shopping here is a bit frantic, but it's worth braving the crowds for the low prices and vast choice. Open weekdays 9:30 A.M. to 6:25 P.M., Thursday till 7:25 P.M., Saturday 9:00 A.M. to 6:00 P.M., Sunday 11:00 A.M. to 5:00 P.M.

**The Athlete's Foot,** 739 Third Avenue, at 46th Street, 697-7870

Though this store is especially geared to runners, it also carries athletic footwear from all major manufacturers for every sport that requires special shoes (tennis, racquetball and squash, basketball, etc.) in children's through adult sizes. Though prices are normal retail, the advantage here is that all the salespeople are athletes specially trained in sports footwear. They're also up on race information and can answer all your running-related questions. Athletic shoes constitute about 75% of the store's wares. The rest consists of clothing (warm-up suits, shorts, etc.) and accessories (sport bags, visors, books on running, etc.). Open Monday to Saturday 10:00 A.M. to 7:00 P.M. There are five other stores in Manhattan and more than a dozen others in the metropolitan area.

Under the same ownership is **The Sporting Woman,** 235 East 57th Street, between Second and Third Avenues, 688-8228, whose gala 1981 opening was attended by Suzy Chaffee and Jo Jo Starbuck. The nation's (probably the world's) first complete athletic store for women only, The Sporting Woman combines fashion with function, offering a wide selection of clothing for all sports as well as weight lifting and exercise equipment, jump ropes, exercise mats, swimwear and dance wear. Salespeople are knowledgeable in sports generally and women's sports in particular. Open Monday and Thursday 10:00 A.M. to 8:00 P.M., Tuesday, Wednesday, Friday and Saturday to 7:00 P.M., Sunday noon to 5:00 P.M.

## Billiard and Gaming Tables

**Blatt Bowling and Billiard Corp.,** 809 Broadway, between 11th and 12th Streets, 674-8855

Blatt specializes in billiard tables: its extensive stock comprises more than 500 tables, among them one-of-a-kind antiques and antique reproductions. It also sells table tennis equipment, dartboards, pinball machines, poker and other game tables, board games for adults (including all bingo paraphernalia). Open Monday to Saturday 9:00 A.M. to 6:00 P.M.

## Dancewear

**Capezio Dance-Theatre Shop,** 755 Seventh Avenue, at 50th Street, 245-2130

Boasting the world's largest selection of dance and theatrical wear, Capezio supplies every major dance company with footwear, legwear and bodywear and has been doing so since 1887. This is dance headquarters. There are frequent exhibits of costumes and memorabilia, and bulletin boards keep customers *au courant* of anything happening in the worlds of dance and theater. The store carries everything in the way of conventional and unique leotards and tights, warm-up suits, socks and leg warmers, ballet shoes, tap shoes, jazz shoes, cabaret shoes, ballroom shoes, dance jump suits, sweat clothes, wrap skirts, dance bags and much more for men, women and children. Many original items come from small, very creative manufacturers. You don't have to be a dancer to shop at Capezio; its styles make beautiful exercise outfits and can be worn for the chic dancer look. The store also has books on dance and theater. Open weekdays 9:30 A.M. to 5:45 P.M., Tuesday to 7:00 P.M., Saturday till 4:45 P.M.

## Fishing and Boating Gear

**Capitol Fishing Tackle Co.,** 218 West 23rd Street, between Seventh and Eighth Avenues, 929-6132

This family-run business (since 1897 in the United States and before that in Germany) has everything you need for fresh-water, salt-water, big-game and ocean fishing. Most of it is closeout and surplus major-brand inventory that Capitol sells at 25% to 75% below retail. The remainder is purchased in volume directly from the manufacturer, with the savings thus engendered passed on to the consumer. You'll find a complete selection of tackle, rods, reels, lures, tackle boxes, accessories, books, rod-building materials, rain gear, fishing knives, boots, waders, etc. All the salespeople are experienced fisherfolk, who can advise you about equipment and where to fish, not only locally but around the world. Open weekdays from 8:30 A.M. to 5:30 P.M., Saturday 9:00 A.M. to 4:00 P.M.

**Goldberg's Marine,** 12 West 46th Street, between Fifth and Sixth Avenues, 840-8280

Every kind of boating equipment and accessory is available from Goldberg's Marine, the number one store in discount marine supplies. The selection is vast. In apparel alone there are foul-weather suits for men, women and children, Breton sweaters, navy peacoats, yachting caps, swimwear, casual boating moccasins, rubber boots and French fishermen's striped cotton pullovers, not to mention accessories like boat shoe maintenance kits and harpoon-dart belt buckles. Then you can get marine rope, anchors, dock padding, fire extinguishers, boating bags, lifesaving gear, navigation lights and instruments, teak and mahogany furnishings, radios, depth finders, tools, flags, a full range of fishing equipment and much, much more. The staff is extremely knowledgeable and helpful. Open weekdays 10:00 A.M. to 5:30 P.M., Thursday to 6:45 P.M., Saturday 10:00 A.M. to 3:00 P.M.

## Riding and Western Wear and Gear

**H. Kauffman & Son Saddlery Co.,** 139 East 24th Street between Lexington and Third Avenues, 684-6060

Founded by Herman Kauffman a year before Custer's Last Stand

and still run by his descendants, Kauffman's is housed in a converted horse auction gallery. Over the years it has been saddlers to presidents, kings and maharajas and latter-day royalty, including the Beatles and not to mention J. R. Ewing himself. There's a huge selection of riding boots, jackets and coats, jodhpurs, western boots, cowboy hats, feed bags, holsters, saddles, polo equipment and every other kind of equestrian gear as well as western art and horse prints. Many of the people who shop here do not ride at all; they come for authentic western-look fashion boots, Levi's, denim clothing, wet-weather wear and suchlike. Open Monday to Saturday 9:30 A.M. to 5:45 P.M.

**Billy Martin's Western Wear,** 812 Madison Avenue, corner of 68th Street, 861-3100

Yes, sports fans, this store is owned by New York Yankees manager Billy Martin. It's jammed with western wear for men, women and children—even cowgirl outfits for infants. Everything in this shop is American-made from southwestern states, authentic and top-quality. There are western boots, cowboy shirts, women's leather and suede outfits, belts, silver buckles, saddlebags, handmade deerskin bags, deerskin coats lined with bear and coyote fur, Indian jewelry and, of course, cowboy hats. Martin's will also create deerskin jackets and vests to order. Open Monday to Saturday 10:00 A.M. to 6:00 P.M.

**Frankel's Discount Store,** 3924 Third Avenue, corner of 40th Street, Brooklyn, 788-9402

The *Dallas* look is all the rage, but unfortunately most of it seems to be priced with the oil-rich Ewings in mind. For discounts on western wear, you have to go to Brooklyn, where Marty Frankel offers discontinued and odd-lot merchandise (about a third of it western-style) at discounts of 20% to 80% below retail. He has Sasson, Frye and Tony Lama cowboy boots, cowboy shirts, Timberland work shoes, denim clothing, jeans and work pants. Other merchandise here might include baseball gloves and bats, down jackets, Adidas sneakers and other footwear—whatever Marty has managed to buy up cheaply. Open Wednesday to Saturday 10:00 A.M. to 7:00 P.M., Sunday (except during July and August) to 5:00 P.M.

## WEDDING DRESSES

**I Do I Do Bridal Salon,** 1963 86th Street, Brooklyn, 946-0011

It's the most important dress you'll ever buy, but that's no reason to spend a fortune for it. Not when I Do I Do offers the same stunning gowns as the fanciest department-store salons and boutiques at 50% to 70% less. It has a very wide-ranging collection, from traditional Victorian and romantic styles to high-fashion contemporary looks, including, of course, copies of Lady Diana's gown. It even features heirloom slipper satin gowns from the 1930s and 1940s, all in excellent condition. Alterations are free. You can also buy any necessary bridal accessories here—veils, netting, special underwear, etc.—and there's a special section upstairs for discounted bridesmaid and mother-of-the-bride dresses. Look upstairs, too, for very good prices on prom dresses. The saleswomen (all of them I Do I Do brides) are down-to-earth professionals who take great care that the bride-to-be gets the dress of her dreams. People come to Bensonhurst from all over the metropolitan area to take advantage of the great bargains here. Service is by appointment to assure you personalized service and attention.

**Laura Ashley,** 714 Madison Avenue, between 63rd and 64th Streets, 371-0606

If you love the English romantic *Upstairs, Downstairs* look of Laura Ashley fashions, you'll want to investigate her exquisite bridal gowns in spotted voile, cotton plissé, moiré and shot taffeta. Her Victorian and Edwardian styles (many with high lace-trimmed or ruffled collars, others with big puff sleeves) reflect a time in British history when people had money and taste. There's a ready-made collection, but the shop also creates gowns to order. If you're getting your gown at Laura Ashley, you'll probably also want to purchase bridesmaid and flower girl outfits here to keep the distinctive look. Open Monday to Saturday 10:00 A.M. to 6:00 P.M.

**Paul's Veil & Net,** 66 West 38th Street, 391-3822

Originally New York's millinery district, 38th Street became something of a bridal accessory center when people stopped considering hats a wardrobe essential. Among the largest of these bridal supply shops is Paul's, a wholesaler/retailer of ready-made and customized bridal headpieces, including new, antique and imported fashions. The store is filled with hat frames, silk flowers, veiling, garters, ring-bearer pillows, lace trim, tiaras and crowns (of rhinestones, pearls, crystals and orange blossoms) and other lacy, lovely ornamentation. The staff is friendly and helpful, and prices are 30% to 40% below retail. Open weekdays from 9:00 A.M. to 5:00 P.M., Saturday 8:30 A.M. to 3:00 P.M.

## CLOSEOUT STORES

There are several stores in New York stocked entirely with closeout, discontinued, test-market, bankruptcy, overstock and damaged merchandise. You never know what you'll find in these places (that's part of the fun), but whatever you do select will be very attractively priced—often below wholesale.

**Job Lot Trading Company,** 140 Church Street, between Warren and Chambers Streets, 962-4142

Job Lot buys name-brand closeouts and overstocks in volume and sells them at a fraction of department-store prices. The place is piled floor to ceiling with merchandise, much of it on handcrafted Amish pushcarts to create an old market look. Regular departments include cutlery, clothing (for men, women and children), housewares, fishing gear, paint, electrical and automotive equipment, hardware, plumbing supplies, binoculars and telescopes, food, toys, tools and health and beauty aids. Job Lot is open Monday to Saturday from 8:00 A.M. to 5:30 P.M., Sunday 10:00 A.M. to 4:30 P.M. In addition to the Wall Street location, there's a newer Job Lot at 412 Fifth Avenue, at 37th Street, 398-9210.

**Odd Job Trading Corp.,** 7 East 40th Street, between Fifth and Madison Avenues, 686-6825

A toothbrush for 19 cents? Designer sheets for $3? Such are the steals at Odd Job, where everything is marked down at least 50%. At holiday time it has hundreds of stocking stuffers, and year round you might find office supplies, cosmetic items, discontinued china (even big names like Royal Doulton), food, tools, hardware, small appliances, sporting goods, housewares and clothing. Odd Job always has numerous toys and brand-name perfumes at better-than-duty-free prices. There's another Odd Job at 66 West 48th Street, between Fifth Avenue and Avenue of the Americas. Both stores are open weekdays 8:00 A.M.

to 6:00 P.M., Friday to 4:30 P.M.; the 40th Street store is also open Sunday 10:00 A.M. to 5:00 P.M. Additional Odd Job locations in Staten Island and Nanuet.

**The City Dump,** 332 Canal Street, between Broadway and Church Street, 226-1636

Another of this low-priced, odd-lot genre, The City Dump always has hardware, toys, camping goods, name-brand perfumes and colognes, health and beauty supplies, name-brand lingerie, automobile accessories, tools and stereo equipment on hand. I've also seen stationery supplies, kitchenware and glassware here. Almost everything is first-quality merchandise, though there are some not-too-damaged seconds. Open daily 10:00 A.M. to 6:00 P.M.

**Gabay's Outlet,** 225 First Avenue, between 13th and 14th Streets, 254-3180

It takes a lot of sifting through immense piles of clothing to separate the wheat from the chaff at Gabay's... but what wheat! I've picked up Dior sweaters here for $4, Charles Jourdan boots for $18 and an imported French bikini for $5. The store has closeout, discontinued, overstock and damaged merchandise from the city's major department stores. Unfortunately much of it is damaged, but there's no telling what your patient probing will produce. In addition to clothing for men, women and children (great toddlers' clothes), the store has furniture, housewares, shoes and boots, bedding, occasional appliances and who knows what else. New merchandise arrives daily. There are times when you'll leave Gabay's empty-handed and discouraged, others when you'll walk out laden with packages and grinning like the Cheshire cat. Open Monday to Saturday 9:00 A.M. to 5:30 P.M., Sunday 10:00 A.M. to 4:00 P.M.

## DRUGSTORES AND PHARMACIES

**Caswell-Massey Company Ltd.,** 518 Lexington Avenue, at 48th Street, 755-2254

Caswell-Massey is not just the oldest apothecary shop in the country. Established in 1752, it's older *than* the country. The Number Six cologne that it still makes was originally created for George Washington. It makes about half the products it sells, and many others are imported. Soaps run the gamut from sulfur soap (for teenage skin) to Indian sandalwood. You might purchase Tyrolean pine bath oil, special shampoo from Sweden for the sauna, its own brands of sunscreen, vanishing cream from Singapore (it's evocatively named Hazeline Snow), a mudpack from New Zealand's thermal pools, bear grease (for "salubrious effects upon the hair") or the cucumber cream used by Sarah Bernhardt. My favorites, though, are the folk remedies—porous plasters, menthol rubs for headaches and the like. Open Monday to Saturday 10:00 A.M. to 6:00 P.M.

**Kiehl Pharmacy, Inc.,** 109 Third Avenue, between 13th and 14th Streets, 475-3698

Not exactly predating the Revolution like Caswell-Massey, Kiehl's has nevertheless been on the scene since 1852. The shelves of this quaint-looking place are lined with herb-filled apothecary jars, some 800 varieties, including oddities like nettle leaves, bloodroot, horehound and peony petals. Kiehl's makes all its own products, 103 of which are in the Smithsonian. They include herbal extracts, sunscreens and sunblocks, aging-deterrent face and body creams, shampoos and conditioners, lotions, soaps and mineral-oil-free massage oils. Many Olympic teams use Kiehl's lip balm and facial products; the store is especially well known for a fragrance called Rain (it smells like a meadow after it has rained). It also creates divine talcum powders and has its own line of eye shadows. Open Monday to Friday 10:00 A.M. to 6:00 P.M., Saturday to 2:30 P.M.

**Duane Reade Drug Stores**

This marvelous drugstore chain offers extremely good prices on prescription drugs (it claims the lowest on the East Coast) as well as hefty discounts on everything else. That includes health and beauty aids, cosmetics, vitamins (national brands and its own private label), soaps, shampoos, household items, you name it. It's a good idea to go in once in a while and stock up on all the drugstore items you need. If you buy them piecemeal locally, you'll end up paying a lot more. All locations (there are twenty in Manhattan) are open from 8:00 A.M. to 6:00 P.M.. Check your phone book for the Duane Reade nearest you.

**Kaufman Pharmacy,** 557 Lexington Avenue, corner of 50th Street, 755-2266

Kaufman Pharmacy is a name you should remember. It's the only Manhattan pharmacy where prescriptions are filled twenty-four hours a day. It'll even deliver by taxi if you pay the cab fare. Kaufman handles all kinds of foreign as well as American medicines; if you've been prescribed something abroad, it'll get it—or an equivalent—for you as long as it's FDA-approved. Kaufman also carries a complete line of surgical supplies—canes, crutches, walkers for invalids, etc. And of course, should you need an eyebrow tweezer or a bottle of perfume in the middle of the night, it's readily available.

## ELECTRONICS EQUIPMENT

**American Surplus,** 324 Canal Street, between Church Street and Broadway, 966-5650

A tinkerer's paradise, this large store is crammed with electronic odds and ends—pressure transducers, accelerometers, frequency inverters, motors, laboratory ovens, environmental chambers, gyros, blowers and many other things whose uses are a sealed book to me. A large closed-circuit TV video department on the balcony has 1,000 square feet of materials for you to browse through, and should you want to build a robot, you'll find the necessary equipment here. Some customers are not electronics buffs but sculptors who come in for optical glass and Art Deco parts and jewelry makers who view the store's small hardware aesthetically. Prices are below wholesale. Open daily from 8:30 A.M. to 6:00 P.M., Saturday from 10:00 A.M. to 6:00 P.M.

## EYEGLASSES

**Cohen's Fashion Optical,** 117 Orchard Street, at Delancey Street, 674-1986

Cohen's Optical offers fabulous discounts on eyeglasses, frames and contact lenses. The price for a complete pair begins at just $9.95, and it can be ready in one hour! However, you'll probably want to spend a bit more and choose one of the thousands of frames, including all top designer lines—Dior, Givenchy, Pierre Cardin, Yves Saint Laurent, etc. Designer frames are sold at 40% off; nondesigner frames, at 50%. You can get Bausch & Lomb soft contact lenses here, too, for $88, including examination; hard lenses for $60. Cohen's also sells the relatively new color-blind-correction lenses for $150 a pair; these retail elsewhere for $400 to $500. Even if your vision is 20/20, come to Cohen's for sunglasses at half price. Customers get two hours of free parking at the Municipal Garage on Essex Street, between Rivington and Delancey Streets. Open daily 9:00 A.M. to 6:00 P.M. There are five other locations in Manhattan, others throughout the boroughs and in Nassau; check your phone book for details.

**Lugene Opticians,** 38 East 57th Street, 486-7500
 Cohen's is one of the cheapest places in New York to purchase eyeglasses; Lugene is the classiest. Operating its own laboratory, where strict standards of quality control are enforced, Lugene emphasizes precision in grinding and polishing prescription lenses. About 85% of the frames it sells are custom-designed exclusively for the store, not mass-produced designer labels. Frames begin at about $40 and go up considerably when you get to items like diamond-studded gold lorgnettes. Not surprisingly, Lugene clientele includes numerous celebrities—Lauren Bacall, Princess Margaret, Pauline Trigère, Jackie Onassis, and Katharine Hepburn among them. Lugene shares its 57th Street premises with **Dempsey & Carroll,** one of New York's oldest (1878) and most prestigious stationery engravers. The store is open weekdays 9:00 A.M. to 5:30 P.M., Thursday to 6:30 P.M., Saturday 10:00 A.M. to 5:30 P.M. There are two additional locations in New York, at the Carlyle Hotel (987 Madison Avenue) and at 660 Madison Avenue.

## FABRICS

**Stonehenge Mill Store,** 134 Sand Park Road, Cedar Grove, N.J., 201-239-9710
 Here's a store that brings many decorators over the bridge. The reason: huge savings (up to 80%) on a vast choice of designer fabrics and wallpapers that are closeout merchandise or seconds. The latter items usually contain flaws so minute that you won't even be aware of them (perhaps the color didn't live up to the artist's specifications). There are more than 2,000 cottons, chintzes and linens (some with matching wallpapers), as well as velvets, antique satins and moirés. Wallpapers can begin as low as $3 a roll. Service is excellent, and there are free workshops in paperhanging and upholstery. You can even bring your lunch and have a picnic on the lawn. To get to Stonehenge, take Route 80 West from the George Washington Bridge and go about 18 miles to Route 23 South; go about 2½ miles on 23, and make a left on Commerce Road. Open weekdays 10:00 A.M. to 4:00 P.M., Thursday to 8:00 P.M., Saturday 9:00 A.M. to 3:00 P.M.

**Bloomcrest Fabrics,** Grand Avenue, Baldwin, N.Y., 516-223-9880

Here you have 3 million yards of dress, drapery and upholstery fabric to peruse, all of it discounted 40% to 75% (more during the annual May sales). Bloomcrest buys only first-quality closeouts and overages from top designer houses like Halston, Oscar de la Renta and Geoffrey Beene. A Halston silk brocade that was used to make a $1,500 dress will sell here for $20 a yard. There's free parking on the premises. Open weekdays 9:00 A.M. to 5:30 P.M., Saturday to 6:00 P.M.

**Ashil Fabrics,** 101 West 34th Street, entrance at 1313 Broadway, 560-9049

Ashil offers a large selection of remnants—not necessarily small pieces and certainly of ample size to make just about any garment. It has cottons, polyesters, metallics, woolens, corduroys, brocades, satins, moirés, velvets, drapery and upholstery fabrics—all at greatly discounted prices. I spotted a lovely moiré selling at $9 elsewhere for $1.98 here. Open Monday to Saturday 8:30 A.M. to 5:45 P.M.

**Fabric Warehouse,** 406 Broadway, south of Canal Street, 431-9510

Four enormous floors at Fabric Warehouse are stocked with bolts of first-quality fabric of every variety, including decorator upholstery and drapery fabric, antique satins and brocades, fine silks and crepes de Chine. Everything is sold at 20% to 50% below retail. In addition, there's a large notions department, and it carries all major pattern lines. Creative ideas for dressmaking are displayed throughout the store, and Fabric Warehouse will make up custom slipcovers, drapes, quilts and bedspreads to your specifications. Open weekdays 9:00 A.M. to 6:00 P.M., to 7:30 P.M. on Thursday, weekends 10:00 A.M. to 5:00 P.M. There's another location in Queens (162-24 Jamaica Avenue, 657-9200).

**Hired Hand,** 1324 Lexington Avenue, between 88th and 89th Streets, 722-1355

This charming shop offers one of the largest selections of calico fabrics in the city, and it also sells items made from calico, supplied by hundreds of craftspeople from all over the country. These include country-look calico bags, pillows, place mats, baby quilts, potholders, dolls, clothing for newborns, soft sculpture and toys. Hired Hand also features Amish quilts, rag rugs and custom-made items (e.g., name pillows for babies). If you've always wanted to try your hand at quilting, not only is this the source for materials, but it gives classes Tuesday at 7:00 P.M. Six weeks of two-hour sessions cost $50 plus materials. Open weekdays 10:30 A.M. to 6:30 P.M., Saturday 10:00 A.M. to 5:30 P.M.

## FEATHERS AND FLOWERS

**Gettinger Feather Corp.** (A.A. Feather Co.), 16 West 36th Street, 695-9470

Isadore Gettinger grew up in the world of feathers; he's the third generation to run New York's oldest feather company, started by his grandfather in 1915. He sells feathers by the ounce or pound, fancy feathers (peacock and ostrich plumes, pheasant tails, boas, etc.), small and large feathers and quills, feathers for stuffing and feathers for masks and hats. For down jackets and bedding, Isadore recommends a mix of 80% down and 20% feathers; he carries a range of qualities of the former. Gettinger is a wholesaler who offers good prices to retail customers. Open Monday to Thursday from 10:00 A.M. to 5:30 P.M., Friday to 3:50 P.M.

**Diane Love,** 851 Madison Avenue, between 70th and 71st Streets, 879-6997

Diane Love designs exquisite fabric flowers of cottons, silks, linens, velours and velvets and has them manufactured in France and the Orient. These fake flowers adorn the finest homes and even merit a boutique at Bloomingdale's. You can buy them by the stem or in arrangements. Diane Love also sells her own design brocade bags, pure silk kimonos from the twenties, thirties and forties, wonderful baskets (ancient Japanese, turn-of-the-century American and contemporary hand-painted), Japanese lacquerware boxes, antique and modern obis and boxes made of precious stones. Open Monday to Saturday 10:00 A.M. to 5:30 P.M.

**D & D Creative Designs,** 17 Bannard Street, Freehold, N.J., 201-431-3070

If you're willing to take the trip to Freehold, you can choose from an enormous selection of silk flowers sold at 50% below store prices. D & D has a three-story warehouse, the first floor of which is mainly devoted to silk stems and arrangements; also on this level are artificial trees and plants, Lladro figurines, Lenox china, Fenton and Pilgrim glass, decorator vases and suchlike at 15% to 30% off. The latter discount applies to the jams, jellies, New England and Amish gift craft items on the second floor; at 50% off, an entire room of real dried arrangements, pods and flowers. Up on the third floor it's Christmas year round with wreaths, poinsettias, garlands and tree trimmings at 45% to 50% off. In an adjoining building, D & D houses its wedding display—bride bouquets, headpieces, aisle runners, etc., at big discounts. The firm also prints wedding invitations at a third less than normal prices. Open weekdays 9:00 A.M. to 4:00 P.M., Saturday 10:00 A.M. to 3:00 P.M., Sunday 11:00 A.M. to 3:00 P.M.

**Cinderella Flower & Feather Co.,** 57 West 38th Street, 840-0644

Cinderella imports from the Orient in vast quantities and is therefore able to sell its thousands of trimmings at very low prices. What it sells for $2, you'll see for $15 in department stores. There are thousands of styles of cloth flowers—silk, satin, cotton and velvet—to choose from, feathers galore, from ostrich plumes to maribou pins, decorated combs, silk flower wedding bouquets and headpieces, about 10,000 boas, marabou jackets made of turkey feathers, and straw and felt hats to be adorned with your choice of trimmings. Also glitter, paste and beads. Open weekdays 9:00 A.M. to 4:45 P.M., Saturday 11:00 A.M. to 2:00 P.M.

## FIREPLACE ACCESSORIES

**William H. Jackson Company,** 3 East 47th Street, at Fifth Avenue, 753-9400

If you're lucky enough to have a fireplace, Jackson's (established in 1827) has the most and the most beautiful accessories. It has hundreds of antique pieces—early American pine mantels, exquisitely carved Georgian and Adams wood mantels, Colonial andirons, English brass fenders, etc.—and its craftsmen can faithfully reproduce antiques or architect designs to the exact detail. Jackson stocks every kind of fireplace equipment, including screens, tools and fixtures, buckets, andirons and tiles. Open weekdays from 9:00 A.M. to 4:30 P.M., Saturday (from September through February only) noon to 4:30 P.M.

**Alexander's Hardware Company,** 60 Reade Street, between Church Street and Broadway, 267-0336

A great treat for hardware browsers, Alexander's is aclutter with a seventy-year accumulation of hard-to-find items and an extensive line of discounted fireplace equipment. You'll find grates, tongs, screens and andirons among such odd items as truck corners, pieces of World War I army bayonets, old clock motors, unique "hunting equipment" for mice and who knows what else. It's a large store, and all prices are discounted. Open weekdays 8:30 A.M. to 5:45 P.M., Saturday to 4:45 P.M.

## FIREWOOD

**Clark & Wilkins,** 1871 Park Avenue, at 128th Street, 534-5110

You could, of course, go chop down a tree in Central Park, but if you'd like to obtain firewood without risking arrest, give Clark & Wilkins a call. Purveyors of firewood to the metropolitan area since 1870, it has select hardwoods, fruitwoods, fireplace coal and Irish peat. A burlap bag of fourteen to eighteen split pieces of good-quality hardwood costs $8.50 to $15, depending on how many bags you order; a full cord is $250. It delivers anywhere in Manhattan.

**Woodside Wood Cutter,** 446-8984 or 424-9810

Bundled, fully seasoned hardwood costs just $3.50 per bag of six to eight pieces (minimum order is four bags) at Woodside, with ten bundles priced at $32.50. It delivers free of charge throughout the five boroughs and includes free kindling in orders of any size.

## FLEA MARKETS

**The Canal Street Flea Market,** corner of Canal and Greene Streets, 226-7541

This is an outdoor market, with hardy vendors from throughout the tristate region (about seventy of them) selling their wares regardless of weather from March 5 to December 24. I prefer it in the warmer months; shopping and freezing have just never appealed to me. It's a great market, though—like a giant garage sale where you might find anything at all. There are stalls of books, tools, coins, food, old army clothes, bottles and jars, record albums, dishes, jewelry, kitchen equipment and housewares, antique clothes and hardware, among much else. The smell of food cooking from shish kebab and sausage stalls helps evoke a carnival atmosphere. Open weekends only 9:00 A.M. to 6:00 P.M.

**The Greenwich Village Emporium,** 252 Bleecker Street, between Avenue of the Americas and Seventh Avenue, 255-0175

Hordes of New Yorkers and tourists, including celebs like Bill Murray, Andy Warhol, Johnny Cash and June Carter and Ronnie Reagan, Jr., crowd this bazaar each week. It's great fun. Housed in a former A&P, the emporium has fifty-two dealers selling everything from Presleyana to Haitian wood carvings. There are booths of antique and New Wave clothing, Oriental rugs and art, musical instruments, Art Deco sculpture, jewelry music boxes and clocks, old toys and comic books, furniture, Indian and African art, movie memorabilia, printers' type cases, stamps and coins, collectors' records, and much more. Sometimes there are even concerts. Open 1:00 P.M. to 8:00 P.M., Thursday through Sunday year round.

**SoHo Canal Antique Market,** 369 Canal Street, at West Broadway, 226-8724

This indoor Soho market houses about forty dealers on three floors, selling carefully selected, good-quality merchandise at lower than uptown but not quite garage-sale prices. There are booths of Art Deco items, jewelry (real and costume), Oriental rugs, books, antique and new kimonos, furs, clothing, paper goods, paintings, fountain pens, watches and clocks, Fiestaware and other 1930s dishes, country furnishings, uniforms, antique kitchenware, dolls and toys and beautiful Victorian clothing. Open Thursday to Sunday 11:00 A.M. to 6:00 P.M.

**Avenue I Flea Market,** Avenue I and McDonald Avenue, Brooklyn, 338-4660

It's huge, with more than 600 booths housed on one floor of a tremendous building and a parking lot that can accommodate 1,000 cars. Everything sold here is new and in perfect condition—designer clothes, furs, diamonds, furniture, appliances, jeans, whatever you'd find in a department store but at about 25% less. Each dealer jams as much merchandise as possible into his or her tiny space. Open year round Friday from 5:00 to 10:00 P.M., Saturday 10:00 A.M. to 9:00 P.M., Sunday 10:00 A.M. to 7:00 P.M.

Under the same auspices and selling the same kind of merchandise, but even larger, with 900 booths, is the **Spring Valley Flea Market,** Route 59, Spring Valley, N.Y., 914-356-1171. Take the New York State Thruway to Exit 14, and go west for 1½ miles on Route 59. Same hours as Avenue I.

## SHOPPING AND FOOD GUIDE 69

**Roosevelt Raceway Flea Market,** Roosevelt Raceway, 516-222-1530

Roosevelt Raceway has one of the largest flea markets on the East Coast, with between 900 and 2,300 vendors on hand, depending on when you go. There's a larger selection on Sundays and in November-December, but since Sunday crowds often swell to 50,000 or more ravenous shoppers, I prefer to go on Wednesdays. Merchandise is more new than old, but it does sell for about 50% below retail. Part of it is outdoors; the rest, inside on the floor where bets are placed. It's like a giant mall of mom-and-pop booths, selling stereo equipment, bonsai plants, wicker furniture, vacuum cleaners, pottery, clothing of every variety (including antique and military garb) for the entire family, gourmet food and produce, fresh-baked goods, luggage, hardware, jewelry, coins and stamps, leaded glass lamps, you name it. There's even a windmill maker. Admission is charged: $1 per carload on Wednesday, $1.50 on Sunday, 50 cents and $1, respectively, for walk-ins. Open year round on Sundays from 9:00 A.M. to 5:00 P.M., April to December on Wednesdays 9:00 A.M. to 4:00 P.M.

**Columbus Farmers' Market,** Route 206, one mile south of Columbus, N.J., 609-267-0051

Beginning as a cattle auction sixty years ago, Columbus Farmers' Market has evolved into a multifaceted operation that includes a regular supermarket where New Yorkers can stock up on essentials at Jersey prices. Indoors, Thursday (9:00 A.M. to 9:00 P.M.), Friday and Saturday (11:00 A.M. to 9:00 P.M.) and Sunday (11:00 A.M. to 6:00 P.M.), there are seventy small stores selling mostly new wares at up to 40% below retail—clothing, brass, produce, Polish meats, Pennsylvania Dutch specialties, cheeses, jewelry, TVs, etc. In addition to the above, on Thursdays from dawn to 3:00 P.M., a flea market emerges outdoors with some 1,000 stalls. More than half sell new merchandise of the department-store variety at a minimum of 50% below retail; the remainder is often used and antique items. My favorite day at the Farmers' Market is Sunday, when the outdoor area becomes an enormous garage-yard sale with about 600 vendors. The market is about 1½ hours from the city. Take the Jersey Turnpike to Exit 7 (Bordentown), and go south on Route 206.

**Rice's Sale & Country Market,** Green Hill Road, Solebury, Pa., 215-297-5993

Plan to arrive early at this very popular market. It attracts up to 15,000 people each week. There are 1,000 vendor spaces, most of them outdoors. About half deal in new, department-store merchandise, about 250 handle antiques and collectibles and the remaining 250 are food dealers. Among the latter are many Amish people, who bring homemade noodles, breads, cakes, relishes and other foodstuffs. You can also get produce, meats, fresh fish, cheeses, etc. Behind the small barn, beginning at 11:00 A.M., Rice's has "tailgate auctions." Sellers arrive with truckloads of merchandise and auction it off from the backs of their trucks. It could be anything from tires to glassware. Rice's is one of the nation's oldest flea markets. It's been in existence since before the Civil War. Take the New Jersey Turnpike to Route 287, exit at Route 22 and go to Route 202 South; one mile past the Holiday Inn make a right on Aquetong Road, then a right on Green Hill Road. Open Tuesdays only 7:00 A.M. to 2:30 P.M.

## FLOWERS

**Southflower Market,** 181 Columbus Avenue at 68th Street, 496-7100

The great thing about Southflower Market—aside from discounted prices and a very large daily selection of close to 100 varieties of fresh flowers—is that you can buy individual blossoms to make up your own bouquets. It's fun to shop here. A spirit of camaraderie develops as people wander about in a state of creative enthusiasm. Southflower delivers in Manhattan with a minimum $15 order. Hours are 10:00 A.M. to 9:00 P.M. Monday to Saturday, noon to 8:00 P.M. on Sunday. There's another Southflower Market at 1045 Second Avenue, at 55th Street, 355-6800.

## FOOD

Easy access to every kind of exotic food is one of the reasons people love New York. Dean & DeLuca, Balducci's and Zabar's alone are enough to make New York the gourmet food capital of the world. The fact that there's more—much, much more—is mind-boggling. You can lay your hands on the ingredients for anything you've ever eaten anywhere—or wanted to eat—from a complete Indonesian rijsttafel to a Senegalese stew. I've divided the following stores into categories, but they don't really break down that easily. Veteran's, a butter and egg store, also happens to sell stuffed grape leaves; you can buy cheeses, escargots and pastrami at Caviarteria, and the gourmet emporiums sell everything.

## CAVIAR

**Caviarteria,** 29 East 60th Street, between Park and Madison Avenues, 759-7410

Caviar at a discount. What a boon! Owner enthusiast Louis Sobol is a wholesaler who also sells to the public at just above wholesale prices. He stocks about twenty-five varieties of fresh caviar, the finest being Imperial ($75 for 2½ ounces), which he's supplied to presidents and royalty. He introduced American sturgeon caviar to the U.S. market and got Craig Claiborne's blessing ("remarkably like the imported"); it's processed in the Russian manner and resembles Russian caviar in appearance and flavor. Mrs. Sobol thought up Caviarteria's biggest bargain. In 200-pound barrels of imported Beluga caviar, she noticed the eggs on the bottom always got crushed. So she invented Bottom of the Barrel; it tastes exactly the same as whole-grain caviar but costs less than half as much. Open weekdays 9:00 A.M. to 6:00 P.M., Saturday 10:00 A.M. to 5:00 P.M.

## CHEESE

**Cheese of All Nations,** 153 Chambers Street, between West Broadway and Greenwich Street, 732-0752

Cheese of All Nations stocks more than 800 domestic and imported cheeses, excellent in quality and priced at about 25% to 40% less than elsewhere. My favorite is the parfait Amaretto—Neufchâtel cheese blended with nuts, dates, raisins and Amaretto. Then there's delicate Rumanian Tatra Mountain goat cheese, African Touareg made by Berber tribes, creamy Norwegian smoked herring cheese, zesty Hungarian brindza made from sheep milk, Austrian cheese made by Trappist monks, Chinese soybean cheese, smoked Emmenthaler from Czechoslovakia, classic English Stilton and blue-veined Spanish cabralos covered in grape leaves. Tasting is encouraged. Enjoy! Cheese of All Nations caters cheese and wine parties, has a Cheese-of-the-Month Club, offers gift certificates and ships cheeses around the world. Upstairs is the Big Cheese Restaurant, serving lunch weekdays. When you sit down, a complimentary plate of two cheeses, Russian pumpernickel, French bread and fresh fruit is set in front of you. The menu features soups (terrific onion generously topped with Gruyère), quiches, fondues, cheese omelets, rarebit and other mostly cheese-related items. For dessert—cheesecake, of course. A wide choice of wines and a few beers are available. Cheese of All Nations is open 8:00 A.M. to 5:30 P.M. Monday to Saturday, closed the last week of February and the first week of March.

## CHINATOWN SHOPPING

**Kam Man Food Products, Inc.,** 200 Canal Street, between Mott and Mulberry Streets, 571-0330

When showing Chinatown to out-of-town visitors, I always take them to Kam Man. It's the Chinese answer to Azuma—and then some—a bustling market for Oriental groceries, meat, fish, exotic herbs and remedies, furnishings, teas, woks, spices, Chinese cooking utensils, beautiful wicker baskets containing teapots and cups, china, exquisite bowls and much more. Between 11:00 A.M. and 2:00 P.M. the shop sells takeout lunches of cooked Chinese food. You won't find better browsing. Open daily from 9:00 A.M. to 9:30 P.M.

An almost identical store is **Kam Kuo,** 7 Mott Street, between the Bowery and Worth Street, 349-3097, with two immense floors of merchandise. Open Sunday to Thursday 9:00 A.M. to 9:00 P.M., Friday and Saturday till 10:30 P.M.

**Chef Chow Food Company,** 49 Division Street, opposite Confucius Plaza, 925-0249

Here's something you won't get from Stouffer's. In the back of this tiny takeout store, chef Yung Fu Chow cooks up moo shu pork, wontons, dumplings, eggrolls, whole carp in spicy sauce, Peking duck, crispy fried chicken with ginger sauce, and so on. Everything is then packaged and frozen for Mrs. Chow to sell at the counter up front; she'll tell you how to prepare it. Prices are very reasonable, and it's all delicious. You will amaze your friends. Chef Chow is open daily from 10:00 A.M. to 7:00 P.M.

**Chinatown Ice Cream Factory,** 65 Bayard Street, between Mott and Elizabeth Streets, 577-9701

Two Chinese brothers with the very Americanized names of William and Philip Seid operate this exotic ice creamery. They make their fresh daily ice cream in thirty-eight flavors, using high butterfat content and natural ingredients. You can opt for chocolate chip or rocky road, but the most interesting flavors are Chinese—mango, lichee, almond cookie, papaya, coconut, red bean, green tea and ginger. This may be the only place in town that serves a sundae with lichee topping. The Seid brothers make and decorate ice cream cakes to order; call a day in advance. Open noon to midnight Sunday to Thursday, Friday and Saturday till 2:00 A.M.

## CHOCOLATES

**Kron Chocolatier,** 506 Madison Avenue, between 52nd and 53rd Streets, 486-0265

Kron is the Tiffany's of chocolate shops, with each handmade morsel displayed (and, alas, priced) like a precious jewel—but oh, are they good! Kron's chocolate truffles are nonpareil; ditto the fresh strawberries, grapes, raspberries, oranges and bananas dipped daily in pure dark chocolate. They also come in marvelous shapes (inscribed with your personalized message): a magnum of champagne, solid chocolate teddy bear, tennis racket, chocolate leg, etc. Then there are chocolate greeting cards, escargot shells to fill with ice cream or mousse and Kron's own chocolate chips and hot fudge sauce to make the ultimate cookies or sundaes. Open Monday to Saturday from 8:30 A.M. to 6:00 P.M. Another store at 764 Madison Avenue, between 65th and 66th Streets, 472-1234, is open the same days and hours.

**Schwartz Candies,** 1026 Willis Avenue, Albertson, N.Y., 516-484-4670

Schwartz may not be a household word, but these hand-dipped all-chocolate candies have been satisfying chocolate lovers for the past forty-five years. The farm is famous for its marshmallows, which come in eight flavors. Schwartz will create a three-quarter-pound chocolate bar with a personal message, the perfect gift for chocoholics.

**Gabrielle's Fine Chocolates,** 5 East Pleasant Avenue, Maywood, N.J. 07607, 201-368-1738

A true chocolate lover, I spend lots of time searching the tristate area for the finest in luscious chocolate. Belgium-born Gabrielle creates her homemade candies from secret recipes. She has studied under a former White House pastry chef and frequently goes home to Belgium to purchase special molds. Her chocolates have no preservatives and are made with less sugar than other European brands. Visit her New Jersey shop, or order a pound prepaid at $10 plus $2.50 shipping. I suggest the truffles with hazelnut to start with; once you try them, you'll be back to sample the other goodies.

**The Cheese Shed,** 8043 Jericho Turnpike, Woodbury, N.Y., 516-364-1752

I told you I really travel for chocolate. At The Cheese Shed in Woodbury you can get not only Mother Margaret's handmade chocolate but also free lessons in candymaking in the evenings. Prices are lower than at comparable establishments. Call for hours; they vary.

## COFFEE AND TEA

**McNulty's Tea & Coffee Company,** 109 Christopher Street, between Bleecker and Hudson Streets, 242-5351

Talk about heavenly aromas! McNulty's (established 1895) offers forty-six varieties of gourmet coffee beans from all over the world and does custom blending and grinding on the premises. There are coffees from Kenya and Tanzania, coffees with exotic names (Old Crop Colombian, Jamaican Mountain Supreme, etc.), delicious water-processed decafs, rich espressos, French roasts and Indonesian javas and coffees flavored with coconut, almond, chocolate and maple-walnut. In addition, McNulty's carries about 100 varieties of tea, including a hard-to-find extra-fancy grade of jasmine and vintage Darjeeling. You can also purchase coffee makers, grinders and filters, teapots and tea strainers here, and McNulty's mails everywhere in the world. Ask Mr. Lee for recommendations and descriptions of the coffees and teas on display. Open Monday to Saturday 11:00 A.M. to 11:00 P.M., Sunday 1:00 to 7:30 P.M.

## DRIED FRUITS AND NUTS

**J. Wolsk & Company,** 87 Ludlow Street, between Broome and Delancey Streets, 475-7946

First-quality dried fruits, imported and domestic candy and chocolates, and nuts roasted on the premises are sold here at about half the price you'd pay uptown. Everything is very fresh. Open Sunday to Thursday 8:00 A.M. to 5:00 P.M., Friday to 2:30 P.M.; closed Sunday July and August.

Almost identical in its wares and prices is **Mutual Dried Fruit,** a block away at 127 Ludlow Street, 673-3849, open Sunday to Thursday from 9:00 A.M. to 5:30 P.M. and Friday till 4:00 P.M. Both stores have been around for a long time, Wolsk since 1938 and Mutual since 1921.

## FARMERS' MARKETS

**Greenmarkets,** 566-0990 or 477-3220

Everyone loves farmers' markets; they're a highlight of trips to the country. From June through December, however, New Yorkers can stay put, and the farmers' markets will come to them. They're called Greenmarkets, and they operate on designated days in selected areas of Manhattan, the Bronx, Brooklyn and Queens. Small farmers—plant and vegetable growers from upstate New York, Long Island and New Jersey—bring in fresh produce and sell it at lower than supermarket prices. Depending on the season, you'll find juicy sweet corn, vine-ripened tomatoes, just-picked apples and strawberries, lettuce, spinach, herbs, squash, etc. In addition to produce, the farmers sell honey and maple syrup, breads, cider, cheeses, sausages, eggs, hanging plants, fresh and dried flowers, pumpkins and gourds around Halloween and Christmas trees in December. There's a market in the Village that specializes in organically grown produce. Call the above numbers to find out the times and locations of Greenmarkets in your area.

## GOURMET EMPORIA

**Dean & DeLuca,** 121 Prince Street, between Wooster and Greene Streets, 254-7774

When I walk into Dean & DeLuca, I have the same feeling I get walking into a cathedral. The place inspires reverence. For one thing, the dazzling display of foodstuffs is an aesthetic triumph—more inspiring than anything in the nearby Soho galleries. Then there's the matter of quality. Each and every item—even a raisin or olive—is lovingly chosen with meticulous care to meet Dean & DeLuca's stringent standards of excellence. And though the store couldn't be more chic, the service is friendly to a fault. All employees know the merchandise they're selling and, no matter how busy, politely help you select what you want. There are salads, charcuterie, pastas imported from Italy, heavenly hams and sausages, 175 cheeses, fresh-baked breads, pâtés, gourmet mustards, the highest-quality olive oils and vinegars, fresh-roasted coffees, housewares, perfect produce, cookbooks, desserts and much, much more. Dean & DeLuca also does gift and picnic baskets to order and will mail out gifts for you. Don't miss this life-enhancing experience. Open Monday to Saturday 10:00 A.M. to 7:00 P.M., Sunday to 6:00 P.M.

**Zabar's,** 2245 Broadway, at 80th Street, 787-2000
Zabar's is more than an epicurean emporium with thousands of tantalizing items on display. It's the virtual hub of New York's Upper West Side. There are hundreds of cheeses (twenty goat cheeses alone), dozens of pâtés and breads (from Swiss peasant bread to Lithuanian rye), more than forty varieties of ham and an equal number of mustards to go with them, caviars, coffees, salads, salamis, sausages, desserts, homemade pastas and takeout items like duck stuffed with rice and raisins. With a few days' advance notice Zabar's will even do a whole roast suckling pig. The new 8,000-square-foot housewares section on the mezzanine sells kitchen-related appliances, every important name in cookware, French copperware, woodenware, glassware, cutlery, utensils, etc.—all at tremendously discounted prices. In one area of the mezzanine, people demonstrate how the food processors, pasta machines, espresso machines, etc. are used. Zabar's has special picnic menus and creates marvelous gift baskets; anything not perishable can be mailed from the store. A Zabar's gift certificate, by the way, is always gratefully received; it's a super wedding gift. Open Monday to Thursday from 8:00 A.M. to 7:30 P.M., Friday to 10:00 P.M., Saturday to midnight, Sunday 9:00 A.M. to 6:00 P.M.

**Balducci's,** 424 Sixth Avenue, between Ninth and Tenth Streets, 673-2600
Founded by Louis "Pop" Balducci in 1916, this famous gourmet store is still family-run. It's a huge place—a gourmet supermarket. Beautiful produce of every kind abounds. Should you crave raspberries in January (and be willing to pay the price of a steak for them), you'll find them here. There's fresh-killed poultry, the finest cuts of meat and fresh fish, even tanks of live trout and lobster. Other areas of the store are devoted to a profusion of cheeses, hams and sausages, coffee beans and teas, homemade pastas, olives, pâtés, cakes and pastries,

candies and every imaginable fancy food from marrons glacés to dried Italian wild mushrooms. You can take out dozens of scrumptious prepared dishes like saucisson en croûte, stuffed squab with fresh raspberry sauce, chicken pesto salad, even Szechuan chicken. In summer, Balducci's packs marvelous picnic baskets. It delivers in Manhattan and will ship anything sendable, gift-wrapped with a card. Open Monday to Saturday 7:00 A.M. to 8:30 P.M., Sunday to 6:30 P.M.

**The Washington Market,** 152 Duane Street, corner of Hudson Street, 233-0250

Tribeca's answer to Dean & DeLuca, this exquisite charcuterie and food store is housed in an old building of the defunct Washington Produce Market. The long list of mouth-watering takeout items prepared daily on the premises includes the likes of smoked salmon mousse, duck terrine, seafood pasta salad, sesame chicken, seasonal fresh vegetable salads with various herb vinaigrette dressings, smoked turkey with creamy horseradish sauce, mousseline of trout with pistachios and braised pork stuffed with prunes in bourbon...and that's not even a third of what's available. There are frozen gourmet meals packaged in sizes to serve one to six people, pastas imported from Italy, French herbs, top-quality produce, jams and honeys, endless spices, coffees, teas, a full line of Italian and German sausages, cheeses, breads, etc. The Washington Market also puts together themed gift boxes—e.g., The Mad Hatter: a selection of teas, preserves, Scottish shortbread, tea biscuits, Eccles English tea cakes, rose water, marinated kippers, a tea strainer and a Mad Hatter cookie cutter. Open weekdays 7:00 A.M. to 9:00 P.M., Saturday 9:00 A.M. to 9:00 P.M., Sunday to 6:00 P.M.

**Russ and Daughters,** 179 East Houston Street, between Orchard and Allen Streets, 475-4880

Joel and Bella Russ (note his gilt-framed founder's portrait on the wall) started out in 1911 selling food from a pushcart. Today the store is run by grandson Mark Federman and his wife, Ann, and people come from all over the world to buy gourmet fare for weddings and bar mitzvahs. You might even see Ed Koch surveying the smoked fish (a superb line of salmons, herrings, etc. from many countries). Fresh caviar and pâtés (Strasbourg foie gras with truffles is flown in weekly) are a specialty. There are barrels and burlap sacks full of coffee beans, a candy counter selling hand-dipped chocolates and old-fashioned confections, and big buckets of pickles, sauerkraut, olives and peppers. Not to mention such goodies as halvah, whole roasted chestnuts and dried morels from France, poppy butter, nuts and dried fruit. Russ's does catering, and you can get gift certificates. Open every day 8:00 A.M. to 6:30 P.M.

While you're here, stop in next door at **Ben's Cheese Shop**, 254-8290, for homemade baked farmer cheese. Like Baskin-Robbins ice cream, it comes in a wide variety of flavors: vegetable, pepper, scallion, walnut and raisin, peach, pineapple, blueberry, strawberry, caraway seed, chocolate chip and apple with cinnamon. Ben's also carries that delicious and hard-to-locate Pritikin-recommended hoop cheese. Open Sunday through Thursday 8:00 A.M. to 6:00 P.M., Friday to 3:30 P.M.

Finally, next door to Ben's, **Moishe's Home Made Bakery**, 475-9624, is the place to get the fresh-baked bagels and bialies on which to pile your lox from Russ and Daughters. Open Sunday to Thursday 7:00 A.M. to 6:00 P.M., Friday to 4:00 P.M.

**Paprikas Weiss, Importers,** 1546 Second Avenue, between 80th and 81st Streets, 288-6117

Paprikas Weiss dates back more than ninety-five years to the days when current owner Ed Weiss's grandfather peddled imported Hungarian paprika door to door to Yorkville housewives. Today its imports are worldwide in scope: African couscous, Irish kidney pie, Greek phyllo pastry, Russian beluga caviar, pâté de foi gras with truffles from Strasbourg, glaced fruits from Australia, etc., along with pungent Hungarian salamis, paper-thin strudel dough sheets, poppy seed grinders, homemade Hungarian-style pasta, Hungarian language records and, of course, the finest available Hungarian paprika. The store also sells cookware and bakeware (including goose feather pastry brushes); more than 200 varieties of spices, cheeses, hams, sausages, coffee beans and teas; and international and specialty cookbooks, among them Edward Weiss and Ruth Buchan's *The Paprikas Weiss Hungarian Cookbook* (William Morrow). You can get a catalog of the store's merchandise for $1 (write to Dept. J), but better to go in and enjoy it in person. Open Monday to Saturday 9:00 A.M. to 6:00 P.M.

**Lekvar-by-the-Barrel,** 1577 First Avenue, corner of 82nd Street, 734-1110

The Hungarian Roth family began offering "a little bit of Europe in New York" more than half a century ago. These days they offer not just Europe but the world. Though paprika, poppy seed filling, Hungarian cookbooks, prune butter, etc. are still prominently displayed, you'll also find Brazilian dried codfish, Indonesian peanut sauce, Szechuan hot bean sauce, Dutch chocolate, Mexican marinated jalapeño peppers and marmalades from Great Britain. For baking, Lekvar has every possible, (part of an extensive selection of all kinds of gourmet kitchenware, including cutlery, coffee makers, copperware and food processors) as well as more than thirty-five baking essences (anisette to walnut), crystal cake and cookie decorations, more than twenty-five kinds of flour, nuts, food colorings, edible leaves for decorating, marzipan figures, meringue powder, praline paste, you name it. There are fancy items here, too, like truffles along with dried beans, peas and rice, candies and chocolates, coffee beans and teas, and hundreds of herbs and spices, all ground to your order. A free catalog is available. Open Tuesday to Saturday 9:00 A.M. to 6:30 P.M.

**Aphrodisia,** 282 Bleecker Street, between Avenue of the Americas and Seventh Avenue, 989-6440

Aphrodisia is a delightful shop specializing in herbs, vitamins, spices, teas and homeopathic remedies, some of which are even said to have aphrodisiac effects. You'll find everything you need to make your own potpourri, a huge selection of ginsengs, lovely scented oils and about 100 books ranging in subject matter from American Indian medicine to natural dyes; also many cookbooks. More fascinating than these are the items like ash tree leaves (said to cure warts and ward off serpents), styrax (used in holy oils), herbal mothballs, St.-John's-wort (a medieval remedy for melancholy was made by soaking this herb in wine or brandy; it is also supposed to keep away evil spirits and ghosts) and salep root (used to ward off spells). Aphrodisia puts out a marvelous catalog; it not only lists its exotic inventory but includes recipes for everything from Lebanese cookies to May wine. Open weekdays 11:00 A.M. to 7:00 P.M., Saturday 10:00 A.M. to 7:00 P.M., Sunday noon to 5:00 P.M.

## *MEATS*

**Schaller & Weber,** 1654 Second Avenue, at 86th Street, 879-3047

Since 1937 Schaller & Weber has been purveying the highest-quality meats and sausages (it has won international awards for the latter). It's a family business, run by four Schaller sons (these guys know meat) and Dad, who's still at the helm. The store smells heavenly of more than sixty varieties of sausages, wursts, salamis and bolognas. Then there are seven kinds of ham, four varieties of bacon (Irish, Black Forest, double smoked and slab), nine types of liverwurst, French pâtés and about a dozen salads. Also, a full line of steaks, beef, lamb, veal, poultry and game (venison, rabbit, quail, pheasant, goose, duck, etc.). The folks behind the counter can tell you how to prepare anything and what goes with it. Open Monday to Thursday 9:00 A.M. to 6:00 P.M., Friday and Saturday 8:30 A.M. to 6:30 P.M.

Two other notable meat markets, **Kurowycky's** and the **East Village Meat Market,** are described in the International New York section, Ukrainian East Village entry (pp. 190–193).

## PASTA

**Piemonte Ravioli Company,** 190 Grand Street, between Mott and Mulberry Streets, 226-0475

Piemonte supplies the pasta you eat at most Little Italy restaurants as well as the spaghetti served up on Alitalia and other airlines. They're all prepared on the premises daily from the highest-grade semolina, and the green noodles get their color from fresh spinach; no artificial color, additives or preservatives mar this perfect pasta. There's ravioli, manicotti, gnocchi, tortelloni and tortellini, lasagne, fettuccini, cannelloni, cavatelli, agnolotti, macaroni, tagliorini, tagliatelli and stuffed shells. Pick up a bottle of wine, toss a salad and you have a terrific meal with a minimum of effort. Open Tuesday to Saturday 8:00 A.M. to 6:00 P.M., Sunday to 2:00 P.M.

## POULTRY MARKET

**Antzis Live Poultry Market,** 1355 Amsterdam Avenue, at 126th Street, 662-6773

You know you're getting fresh poultry when you select your bird while it's still squawking. Antzis slaughters it, plucks it, prepares it for cooking and cuts it up to your specifications. In addition to chickens, it has guinea hens, quail, squab, pheasant, rabbits, ducks, geese and turkeys, plus newly laid chicken and duck eggs. On Saturdays Antzis will deliver free in Manhattan as far south as 60th Street, East or West. Open Monday to Thursday 8:00 A.M. to 5:30 P.M., Friday 7:30 A.M. to 6:00 P.M., Saturday 7:00 A.M. to 6:00 P.M.

## SAUSAGES

**De Santis Brothers,** 158 Mott Street, between Broome and Grand Streets, 925-4540
For more than thirty years this simple little sausage shop has been making just four varieties of sausage daily on the premises: sweet (with or without fennel seeds), hot, cheese and pepper/onion. They're made from an old family recipe, using no preservatives or artificial coloring, and they're delicious. Open Monday to Saturday from 8:00 A.M. to 6:00 P.M.

## SCANDINAVIAN SPECIALTIES

**Nyborg and Nelson,** 937 Second Avenue, between 49th and 50th Streets, 753-1495
Owner Hans Booge offers a veritable smorgasbord of Scandinavian foods at this midtown emporium. He stocks Swedish crisp breads, imported herring, more than 100 cheeses (try the västervotten, a sharp Cheddar that is creamier than American varieties), Norwegian fishballs, Swedish meatballs, lingonberry jam, Slotts mustard (I got addicted to this stuff in Stockholm), Danish sausage, Scandinavian cookbooks, housewares, gifts and much more. Upstairs is a very pleasant restaurant serving inexpensive Scandinavian fare at lunch—open-faced sandwiches, beer and entrées like marinated salmon with mustard dill sauce. Open 11:30 A.M. to 9:00 P.M., Monday to Friday, Saturday noon to 6:00 P.M., Sunday noon to 7:00 P.M. There's another Nyborg and Nelson at Citicorp Center, 223-0700.

## SPANISH FOODS

**Casa Moneo,** 210 West 14th Street, between Seventh and Eighth Avenues, 929-1644
Craig Claiborne calls Casa Moneo "by far the best Spanish-American market in the U.S." Moneo carries a wide selection of foods from Spain, Mexico, South and Central America and the Caribbean, many of them hard to find, as well as the corresponding cookware—tortilla presses from Mexico, paella pans from Spain, griddles for making

arepas (meat- and cheese-filled pies), wood chocolate beaters, corn grinders, etc. You'll find every imaginable kind of chili here—red, green, yellow, dried, roasted, powdered, pickled, chopped and sliced—as well as beans both dried and refried, chocolates, coffee beans, corn husks for making tamales, fresh corn and flour tortillas, cactus, corn flour (many kinds), plantain flour, guava shells and jellies, fresh skim-milk cheeses, blood and chorizo sausages, Spanish ham, olives and olive oils from Spain and Portugal, mole paste, sweet potato paste, beer from various countries, exotic seasonings and sauces, soups and canned seafood (dried codfish, stuffed squid in oil, octopus, pickled sardines and suchlike). There are also cookbooks to tell you how to utilize them all. While you're browsing, buy a hot, crispy churro (like a doughnut) to munch on. Open Monday to Saturday 9:00 A.M. to 7:00 P.M.

## WHOLESALE MARKETS

**Basior-Schwartz,** 421 West 14th Street, between Ninth and Tenth Avenues, 929-5368

It's more delightful to shop at Dean & DeLuca, but if you want the rock-bottom prices on a wide range of gourmet foods, skip the ambience and head for Basior-Schwartz. It's conveniently, though colorfully, located in the heart of the wholesale meat district amid the bustle of trucks and men in white coats pushing huge carts. Inside, the entire store is refrigerated to keep everything fresh; wear a sweater. Basior-Schwartz sells wholesale to many of the city's finest gourmet stores and top restaurants, and it'll sell to you at wholesale prices, too—with no minimum order. There are about 100 cheeses, a dozen or so pâtés, smoked fish, all kinds of nuts, sausages and hams, pastas imported from Italy, olive oils from France and Italy, quality vinegars and mustards, jams and marmalades, tinned biscuits, dried fruits, meat and poultry and other fancy foods, along with the more mundane likes of peanut butter and mayonnaise. You won't believe the prices; you'll think it's 1960. Open weekdays only from 4:00 A.M. to noon.

**Bronx Terminal Market,** Exterior Street, between 149th and 153rd Streets, Bronx, 292-2158

If you're feeding a large family and have some room to stock up on supplies, this public market will save you plenty. About 100 dealers here sell their goods wholesale to supermarkets, food stores and restaurants—fruits, produce, meat (no fish), potted plants and flowers, cheese (more than 1,000 varieties) and other dairy products. You can buy all kinds of tropical items here, since the market supplies 75% of the Latin stores in the city. You have to buy by the boxload, but prices are about 30% below retail. The other drawback is that the market starts assembling at about 1:00 A.M. (every day except Sunday); though it goes on until about noon, the best time to shop is between 4:00 and 5:00 A.M.

## WINE AND LIQUOR

**Astor Wines and Spirits,** 12 Astor Place, between Broadway and Lafayette Street, 674-7500

This vast store offers New Yorkers an amazingly comprehensive selection of wines, ranging from the everyday to the very finest. Because Astor sells in such great volume, it's able to offer substantial discounts, and its own label wines are very competitively priced. There are frequent sales, and most wines are available by the case at additional savings. You'll also find every kind of liquor and liqueur here at the lowest prices permitted by the New York State Liquor Authority. Should you get carried away with all these bargains, you'll be glad to know Astor delivers free in the five boroughs with a minimum purchase of $35. The staff is knowledgeable and will be happy to recommend appropriate wines. Open Monday to Saturday from 9:00 A.M. to 9:00 P.M.

Also a good bet is **Brill's Liquor Mart, Inc.,** 150 Chambers Street, between Greenwich Street and West Broadway, 227-3390, across the street from the aforementioned Cheese of all Nations. Some of the wines and champagnes here actually are sold at wholesale prices, and the liquors and liqueurs are, once again, sold at the lowest prices state law allows. Open daily 8:00 A.M. to 6:00 P.M.

Discriminating shoppers will also delight in the wine bargains found at **Surrey Liquors,** 19 East 69th Street, 744-1946, and **Garnet Wines and Liquors,** 929 Lexington Avenue, 772-3211. Comparison-shop at the above, and don't forget to ask each shop for its special.

## FURNITURE

**Cardarelli Fine Furniture,** 205 West Houston Street, between Avenue of the Americas and Seventh Avenue, 924-2040

A family business since 1900, Cardarelli has ten entire floors of better-brand name furnishings and accessories in its huge showroom—couches, living room and dining room sets, bedroom sets, armoires, cabinets, clocks, desks, wall units, vases, paintings, lamps, chairs, carpeting (four or five major lines), fabrics, antiques and reproductions. You might pick up an exquisite Henredon oak china cabinet with French antique leaded-glass windows, a Drexel eighteenth-century-style highboy, an Art Nouveau mirror or a sofa covered in Oriental motif. Cardarelli emphasizes service (it will size a sofa to the very inch for you, and it does its own careful deliveries and repair work) and offers discounts of 20% to 30% on brand-name furniture. Open Monday to Saturday 9:00 A.M. to 5:00 P.M.

## *ARCHITECTURAL SALVAGE*

**Urban Archaeology Ltd.,** 137 Spring Street, between Greene and Wooster Streets, 431-6969

This unique store works with antique dealers and wrecking companies to collect architectural trim and treasures from all periods and places. In business for more than ten years, it has collected enough to fill its 5,000-square-foot premises as well as several warehouses. You never know what you'll find here: stained-glass windows, pedestals, statuary, cast-iron work, sinks, tubs, back bars, lighting fixtures, grillwork, stone lion heads, doors, gargoyles, fireplaces and much more. Open weekdays 10:00 A.M. to 6:00 P.M., weekends noon to 6:00 P.M.

## *BRASS*

**Isabel Brass Furniture,** 120 East 32nd Street, between Park and Lexington Avenues, 689-3307

The highest-quality handmade solid brass beds and furnishings—heirloom-quality items that are guaranteed for five years—come from Isabel Brass. A permanent record of the bed you choose is kept so that if fifty years from now you need to replace a foot, it has the design. Isabel beds are not inexpensive; bargain hunters stay away. Open Monday to Saturday 10:30 A.M. to 6:00 P.M., Sunday noon to 5:00 P.M.

**The Brass Bed Factory,** 3 West 35th Street, third floor, 594-8777

This really is a factory, and since you're buying direct, prices are 20% to 50% below retail. All the beds made here are carefully constructed of top-quality brass. There are about twenty-five styles to choose from, mostly antique reproductions of French, early American and New England designs but also Art Deco and contemporary styles. Four-posters and canopy beds are among the choices, and you can also purchase mattresses and box springs here. Complete queen-size beds begin at about $650 for head, foot and frame. If none of the offered styles is to your liking, the factory can execute your custom design. Open weekdays 10:00 A.M. to 6:00 P.M., weekends noon to 5:00 P.M.

## BUTCHER BLOCKS

**Alexander Butcher Block & Supply Corp.,** 176 Bowery, at Delancey Street, 226-4021

A restaurant supplier, wholesaler and retailer, Alexander ships all over the country and charges 25% to 40% less than you'd normally pay for identical furniture. It can cut hard rock maple butcher block to your specifications right on the premises and also do custom work and deliver it in no time at all (often just one day). In the store you'll find more than 100 kinds of chairs, tables and counters, as well as a selection of table bases, serving carts, barstools and counter stools, folding chairs, picnic tables, bookcases, rocking chairs, dining room sets, knife racks, hat racks, even butcher-block clocks. You can get Formica and glass here, too. All the butcher-block items are made of solid oak or maple. Open daily weekdays 10:00 A.M. to 5:00 P.M., Saturday to 4:00 P.M., Sunday 10:00 A.M. to 4:00 P.M.

## CANVAS—THAT CASUAL LOOK

**Jensen-Lewis,** 89 Seventh Avenue, corner of 15th Street, 929-4880

Charles Jensen started out making canvas sails in 1886, Edward Lewis making awnings in 1921. They merged in 1932, and in the sixties the firm expanded to include colorful canvas furnishings and other pieces that harmonize with their casual indoor-outdoor look. The store consists of two floors of merchandise: director's chairs, hammocks, canvas-upholstered couches, butcher-block furniture, tubular metal bunk beds, modernistic storage units and lamps, garden furniture and suchlike. Jensen-Lewis also carries mattresses, Martex sheets and towels and canvas luggage and bags, and it sells awning materials and canvas (in thirty-four colors) by the yard. Prices are reasonable. Open Monday to Saturday 10:00 A.M. to 7:00 P.M., Thursday till 8:00 P.M., Sunday noon to 5:00 P.M.

## CHILDREN'S FURNITURE

**Ben's Babyland,** 87 Avenue A, between Fifth and Sixth Streets, 674-1353

You can be sure that the best buys in children's furniture are on the Lower East Side...where else? Trot over to Ben's on Avenue A for discounts of 20% to 30% on Marmet and Silver Cross prams from England, Teutonia prams from Germany, Simmons cribs (the best, says Ben's) and name-brand layettes, highchairs, playpens, swing sets and related items. Open weekdays 9:00 A.M. to 6:00 P.M., Saturday till 5:30 P.M., Sunday 10:00 A.M. to 5:00 P.M.

While you're on Avenue A, walk down the street and comparison shop at Ben's competitors: **Schacter's Babyland,** 81 Avenue A., 777-1660, and **Schneider's Juvenile Furniture,** 20 Avenue A., 228-3540. Like Ben's, they're both open seven days a week.

## FURNITURE BY PHONE

Furniture is expensive these days—one of the things most people consider a major investment. So it's wise to shop around and get the best possible prices. Go to the department stores and big furniture emporiums. Peruse at leisure. Decide what you want, and write down the price, manufacturer, color and model number. Then call the following places—most quote prices on the phone—and see what kind of deal they give you.

**Furniture Distributors of America,** 708 Broadway, between Fourth Street and Astor Place, 677-3220, offers 25% to 35% off department-store prices on all major American manufacturers. You might also take a look at the 15,000-square-foot showroom—an enormous display of full bedroom, living room and dining room sets. Parking is free at the Cube Lot on Broadway just south of Eighth Street. Open Monday to Saturday 9:30 A.M. to 4:30 P.M., Sunday 11:00 A.M. to 4:00 P.M.

**Black's Furniture,** 24-54 English Rd., High Point, N.C., 919-866-5011, has a selection of hundreds of top brand names—like Drexel, Henredon and Heritage—and also quotes greatly discounted prices over the phone.

**James Roy,** 15 East 32nd Street, between Fifth and Madison Avenues, 679-2565, has a limited showroom but can obtain top-quality pieces from more than 100 nationally known American (and some Canadian) manufacturers. Bedding, too. Prices are guaranteed to be one-third off retail. No phone quotes at James Roy; you have to come in. Showroom hours are Monday to Saturday 10:00 A.M. to 5:00 P.M.

## *PILLOW FURNITURE*

**Space Makers for Living,** 33 West 21st Street, between Fifth and Sixth Avenues, 242-6619

Pillow furniture may be the answer to the high cost of couches—especially if you buy the quality creations at Space Makers' factory showroom that cost about one-third less than elsewhere. The modularized units (that means you can always add pieces) are easily assembled and beautifully crafted. Frames are of knotty sugar pine or red oak, pillows of washable polished cotton, Haitian cotton, patterned or floral prints and cotton duck. You can actually purchase an eight-foot couch here for under $400. Ottomans, love seats and other pillow furnishings are also available, along with wall bed systems (something like the old Murphy beds—a boon in small apartments) and 42-inch round oak-frame clocks. Of course, you can buy oversize pillows here, too, without buying a couch. Open weekdays 9:00 A.M. to 5:30 P.M., Thursday to 8:00 P.M., Saturday 11:00 A.M. to 5:00 P.M.

## *PLASTICS*

**The Plastic Supermarket,** 309 Canal Street, corner of Mercer Street, 226-2010

The Plastic Supermarket, in addition to custom designing, or manifesting your designs for bookcases, shelves, tables and other see-through furnishings, has 7,000 square feet of plastics of every description. There are colored sheets, rods, cubes and tubes, picture frames, boxes, bottles, lighting panels, shower enclosures, waterproofing materials, letters (for signs), parts for lampshades and shoji screens and small items for jewelry makers. Many of the Supermarket's clients are artists, and the browsing over plastic odds and ends is fun for any creative type. Open weekdays 8:30 A.M. to 5:30 P.M., Saturday till 4:00 P.M.

**Plexi-Craft Quality Products Corp.,** 514 West 24th Street, between Tenth and Eleventh Avenues, 924-3244

Come in with a sketch of a plexiglass or Lucite table, chair, lamp or pedestal, and Plexi-Craft's skilled artisans can make it up for you. They also have numerous ready-made items, including plexiglass deco tables, stack tables, TV carts, bath and kitchen accessories, even a see-through trunk. Their designs are extremely innovative, often combining the contemporary look of Lucite with classic styles, and prices are about 50% less than retail. Open weekdays 9:30 A.M. to 5:00 P.M., Saturday 11:00 A.M. to 4:00 P.M.

**Wicker Garden,** 1318 Madison Avenue, between 93rd and 94th Streets, 348-1166

Wicker Garden is absolutely enchanting, filled with new and antique Victorian furniture, the latter dating from 1870 to 1930, and includes many signed collectibles. There are rockers, love seats, chaises, couches, teacarts and bustle benches—just about everything that can be made of wicker. The Garden also features new and antique patchwork and appliqué quilts, soft-sculpture accessories, hand-painted and decoupage baskets, quilted animals, festive handmade Christmas tree ornaments and beautiful antique linens. Upstairs is **Wicker Garden's Baby** (owner Pamela Scurry conceived the idea during her pregnancy), specializing in old-fashioned infant furniture (not only wicker but brass cribs and such), quilts and blankets, antique christening dresses, a complete line of clothing, layette services, fancy pillows, gingham diaper covers, handcrafted dolls and toys—everything for infants and toddlers. Open Monday to Saturday 10:00 A.M. to 6:00 P.M., closed Saturday in August.

## HOT TUBS

**California Hot Tubs & Spas,** 60 Third Avenue, between 10th and 11th Streets, 982-3000

You don't have to live in California to be part of the hot tub set. New Yorkers are installing hot tubs in lofts, on terraces and in brownstone gardens; even outdoors you could use them year round because you stay warm in the water. Status symbols don't come cheap. Redwood hot tubs begin at about $3,500 for a tub five feet in diameter, including installation but not site preparation (you don't want it falling through the floor to the loft below) and electrical hookup. The store also sells saunas, jetted baths and fiberglass spas. There's a working model on the premises—bring your bathing suit. Open weekdays 9:00 A.M. to 6:00 P.M., Saturday by appointment.

## HOUSEWARES

Under this heading are silver, china, cookware, glassware, giftware, storage units and gadgetry.

**Eastern Silver Company,** 54 Canal Street, between Orchard and Allen Streets, second floor, 226-5708

A vast array of gleaming merchandise awaits you at Eastern—every imaginable silver item, including candelabra, vases, trays, goblets, wine decanters, sugar and creamer sets, tea and coffee sets, baby brush and comb sets, baby cups and porringers, Jewish religious items (kiddush cups, menorahs, etc.). And they're all discounted 30%. Eastern has its own factory, so it can also create silver items to your design and repair damaged pieces. Open Monday to Thursday 9:00 A.M. to 5:00 P.M., Friday to 2:00 P.M., Sunday 10:00 A.M. to 5:00 P.M.

**Jean's Silversmiths,** 16 West 45th Street, between Fifth Avenue and Avenue of the Americas, 575-0723

If you've got a gorgeous set of American silver, but are missing some necessary pieces, come into Jean's. It's been collecting silver since 1931 and stocks thousands of antique patterns on the premises. Not only will it help you fill out your set, but it'll sell you the silver at 50% to 75% off usual retail prices. If it doesn't have what you need, it'll put your pattern on file and call you when it's in. Jean's carries new silverware, too, not just flatware but hollowware (tea sets, water pitchers, creamers, etc.), once again at substantial discounts. It also does silver replating. Open weekdays from 9:30 A.M. to 5:00 P.M.

**Fae-Mart,** 108 Avenue U, corner of West Ninth Street, Brooklyn, 373-1200

Shoppers have been flocking to Brooklyn since the turn of the century to take advantage of Fae-Mart's low prices—always at least 10% to 25% below department stores—on a vast selection of houseware items. It has cookware, glassware, flatware, bed and bath accessories, appliances, lighting fixtures, gadgetry, giftware—and more than 250 patterns of fine china on display along the "Great Wall of China." It's the kind of place where you can shop for a pasta machine, a silver-plated tea set, bath towels or a vacuum cleaner. Open Monday and Thursday 9:30 A.M. to 9:00 P.M., Tuesday, Wednesday, Friday and Saturday until 6:00 P.M.

**The Pottery Barn,** 231 Tenth Avenue, at 23rd Street, 741-9120

Everyone loves The Pottery Barn, a veritable home furnishings warehouse-supermarket with three large floors of glassware, cookware, flatware, shelving, chairs and tables, storage units, earthenware crockery, china, etc. It's a twenty-store chain importing directly (no middleman) from fifty-three countries. It passes the savings on to you and also offers terrific bargains in closeout and discontinued merchandise. You can find just about anything you're looking for at The Pottery Barn, from high-tech furnishings and accessories to Chinese farmers' porcelain rice bowls and Indian dhurrie rugs. Open Monday to Saturday from 10:00 A.M. to 6:30 P.M., Sunday noon to 5:00 P.M. There are six additional locations in Manhattan; others in New Jersey, Westchester, Long Island, Connecticut and Pennsylvania. Call the above number for details on locations.

**Rainbow China Import Company,** 253-16 Northern Boulevard, Little Neck, 225-9547

It's well worth a trip to Queens for Rainbow's huge discounts on crystal, sterling, stainless, cookware and china—all of it first-quality merchandise. The china, for instance, is Gorham, Waterford, Spode, Royal Doulton, Royal Worcester and Lenox, among other top names. Rainbow is not exactly Tiffany's in the way of sumptuous displays— the setting runs more to packing boxes—but it's not Tiffany's in the way of prices either. Everything is at least 30% to 40% below usual retail. Gift wrapping is free, and you can have your purchases shipped anywhere. Open Tuesday to Saturday 9:30 A.M. to 6:00 P.M., Friday till 9:00 P.M.

**Coleman Bartick,** Blancol China Co., Ltd., 408 Harrow Road, London W9 2HU, England

If you've been to England and poked around the stores, you know how much better you can do on fine china across the Atlantic. But if you're in the market for china, crystal and glassware—and don't need it *tout de suite*—you can pay the English prices (40% to 50% less than in this country) without leaving home. Just write to the above address, and ask for an inventory and price list. Then place your order, send the money and plan to wait a few months. It's a good bet if you're missing nonessential pieces—or want to expand—your china set or know far in advance of a wedding or other gift-requiring occasion. The selection includes Royal Albert, Aynsley, Spode, Royal Worcester, Minton, Royal Doulton and many other top names.

**The Brass Loft,** 20 Greene Street, at Canal Street, third floor, 226-5467

This Soho factory outlet is a floor-to-ceiling brass bazaar of candelabra, tables, lamps, ice buckets, planters, candlesticks, fireplace equipment, chandeliers and much more—all sold at 30% to 40% below retail. Many of the pieces are made right in the building; others are imported from all over the world. Quality ranges from "as is" (possible damage) to top of the line. The Loft also handles copper cookware. Since it has its own factory, it can take on custom design work and also do repairs on solid brass. Open daily except Monday and Friday from 10:30 A.M. to 5:30 P.M.

## INTERNATIONAL HANDICRAFTS

**Folklorica,** 89 Fifth Avenue, between 16th and 17th Streets, 255-2525

Pamela Levy and Jack Bregman travel extensively in Africa, Colombia, Ecuador and Peru to seek out traditional handicraft items for their Fifth Avenue store. There are Ethiopian bread baskets, dolls from Botswana and Peru, musical instruments, rugs and tapestries, sculpture, traditional cooking and eating utensils, bells and numerous beautiful baskets. In addition to the countries they visit personally, Pamela and Jack have suppliers from India, Indonesia, Brazil, China and elsewhere. They also sell jewelry made by American craftspeople that is consistent with the spirit of the store. Everything is chosen with an eye to fine-quality workmanship. Open weekdays 10:00 A.M. to 7:00 P.M., Saturday 11:00 A.M. to 6:00 P.M.

## JEWELRY

**Rennie Ellen,** 15 West 47th Street, between Fifth and Sixth Avenues, room 401, 869-5525

Rennie Ellen is passionate about diamonds, but even more important than her enthusiasm is her long-standing reputation for scrupulous honesty. You can get a complete and detailed bill of sale with your purchase, and you can return it within five days (plenty of time for appraisals) for a full refund (no one ever has). Best of all, Rennie sells at wholesale prices. You just can't go wrong. Open weekdays 10:00 A.M. to 4:30 P.M., by appointment only.

By the way, if a diamond is beyond your ken, Rennie also runs **Kane Enterprises** (same address, phone and appointment only policy), featuring cubic zirconia (simulated diamonds that are hard to distinguish from the real thing).

**Fortunoff,** 681 Fifth Avenue, between 53rd and 54th Streets, 758-6660

"The source," or so Lauren Bacall tells us. Actually, it's a darned good one—a vast emporium for every kind of jewelry as well as hollowware, china, gift items and flatware that promises to match or beat any price from any other stores. The variety of jewelry is immense— pearl necklaces, coral strands, lapis lazuli earrings, gold rings, watches and every other tempting, beautiful thing. Fortunoff is a reliable place to buy diamonds; like Rennie Ellen, it lets you take your purchase out for appraisal with a refund available for several days. Open Monday to Saturday 10:00 A.M. to 6:00 P.M., Thursday till 8:00 P.M., Sunday noon to 5:00 P.M. Other locations in Westbury, L.I., Paramus and Wayne, N.J.

**Luxor Costume Jewelry, Inc.,** 866 Broadway, between 17th and 18th Streets, 477-3730

Now we're talking about the very affordable—about wholesale costume jewelry that's totally unimportant and fun to wear. Luxor has barrettes, feather combs, necklaces, earrings, belts, headbands, charms, key rings and novelty items—all sold at far below department-store prices. The only catch: You have to buy them in quantities of at least a dozen. So go with a few friends, or plan on some casual trinket giving. These items make great stocking stuffers and party favors for young girls. Open Monday to Friday 8:00 A.M. to 5:00 P.M., Saturday till 2:00 P.M.

Also investigate **Sac's Costume Jewelry,** around the corner at 19 East 17th Street, 675-6440.

## KITCHENWARE AND CUTLERY

**The Bridge Kitchenware Corp.,** 214 East 52nd Street, between Second and Third Avenues, 688-4220

Offering Bowery prices at an uptown location, The Bridge is in a class by itself. It's a major restaurant supplier (The Four Seasons, the Oyster Bar, etc.) and probably the largest store of its kind in the world (more than 40,000 items of kitchenware). European items are imported directly, thus eliminating middleman costs, and American-made merchandise is bought in vast quantities, making low prices viable. There's a thirty-foot wall of knives alone, including the best German cutlery at 25% off retail. You can equip your kitchen with the professional cookware used by restaurants, caterers and cooking schools, buy French porcelainware and get anything existent in the way of bakeware. I love The Bridge's vast selection of chocolate molds, shaped like roosters, bunnies, eggs, baskets, parrots, etc.; you can also use them for butter and other molded dishes. The store claims the world's largest selection of heavyweight French copperware, also much woodware (chopping boards, salad bowls, etc.), barware, gadgetry and accessories. Even Julia Child shops at The Bridge. Open weekdays 9:00 A.M. to 5:30 P.M., Saturday 10:00 A.M. to 5:00 P.M.

**Broadway Panhandler,** 520 Broadway, between Broome and Spring Streets, 966-3434

Broadway Panhandler began in 1939 as a restaurant supplier. That it still is, but it also sells every kind of kitchen equipment on a retail basis at prices much lower than those of fancy uptown shops and department stores. All its wares (about 8,000 items in all) are of the highest quality, many of them European imports. There are hundreds of intriguing kitchen gadgets; a full line of specialty bakeware, including books on cake decorating and accessories for the most intricate of decorations; everything in the way of cookware, including ethnic cooking needs (woks, bamboo steamers, pasta and ravioli makers, tortilla presses, etc.); clay cookware, glassware, china, coffee makers and cutlery. You can even order an oven or stove. Open weekdays 10:00 A.M. to 5:30 P.M., Saturday 11:00 A.M. to 5:00 P.M. (closed Saturday in summer).

**The Spice Market,** 265 Canal Street, 966-1310
The Spice Market, my source for all kinds of spices, also features kitchenware at a substantial discount. It has gourmet pots and pans, French tin bakeware, food processors, professional cooking equipment and more. Open daily from 10:00 A.M. to 5:00 P.M.

**Delbon Cutlery,** 121 West 30th Street, between Sixth and Seventh Avenues, 244-2297
The largest array of cutlery in New York is at Delbon, in business since 1840. It has every imaginable kind of scissors and shears: dressmakers' shears, pinking shears, thread clippers, sewing and embroidery scissors, left-handed scissors, poultry shears, citrus fruit clippers, rug-cutting shears, electricians' and industrial scissors, manicure and pedicure scissors, not to mention seventy-five models of hairdressing scissors alone. In knives it carries the finest domestic and imported cooking cutlery available (it finishes and hand-hones them for you, even puts on your initials at no extra charge), hunting knives, pocketknives, Swiss army knives, boot knives, multipurpose knives, divers' knives, etc. Open weekdays 9:00 A.M. to 5:30 P.M. and some Saturdays 11:00 A.M. to 3:00 P.M.—call first.

## LAMPS AND LIGHTING

**Just Bulbs,** 938 Broadway, at 22nd Street, 228-7820
The only store of its kind anywhere, Just Bulbs carries light bulbs and light bulbs only. But it can get pretty fancy. Hundreds of bulbs are displayed on the walls and freestanding pushcarts, and each can be activated by the flick of a switch. You'll be tempted to flick every switch in the shop. Go right ahead; the owners don't mind. There are more than 2,500 kinds of bulbs to choose from: bulbs in every color and wattage, bulbs to create flattering lights, fluorescent bulbs in many

colors, incandescent and fluorescent hard-to-find bulbs for foreign lamps, track-lighting bulbs, Shimmoray bulbs that produce a pattern on your walls, oven bulbs, fishtank bulbs, photography bulbs, automotive bulbs and more... everything, in fact, to light up your life. Open Tuesday, Wednesday and Friday 8:00 A.M. to 5:00 P.M., Monday and Thursday 9:30 A.M. to 6:30 P.M.

**New York Gas Lighting Company,** 146 Bowery, corner of Broome Street, 226-2840

New York Gas Lighting Company began as a gaslighting store more than seventy years ago. It still sells some gaslights, but they're no longer the store's mainstay. The emphasis today is on traditional styles of lamps and fixtures—imported chandeliers, glass shades for lamps, wall sconces, some antique fixtures and many antique reproductions, outdoor lanterns, etc. The selection is vast and includes some classic contemporary lines as well as ceiling fans, with and without lights. Everything is sold at a substantial discount. Open weekdays 9:00 A.M. to 5:00 P.M., weekends 10:00 A.M. to 4:30 P.M.; closed Saturday in summer.

**Just Shades,** 188 Bowery, corner of Spring Street, 966-2757

Another of the "Just" stores, Just Shades carries innumerable lampshades and nothing else—the largest variety in New York. They come in silk, velvet, linen, paper, vinyl and parchment (no glass), pleated and unpleated—and are priced at 20% to 30% below retail. Bring in your lamp, and you're sure to go home with a properly fitted shade. Just Shades can also re-cover shade frames in a variety of fabrics and papers. Open weekdays except Wednesday 9:30 A.M. to 4:30 P.M., Saturday and Sunday till 3:00 P.M.

**Manhattan Sales Company,** 17 East 16th Street, between Fifth and Madison Avenues, 242-8262

Manhattan Sales represents Ledu adjustable desk lamps. Basically the company sells to wholesalers, but at its 16th Street storefront it'll sell to walk-in customers—at 35% below retail price. Ledu lamps are the adjustable kind that swivel, stretch, raise or bend to any desired angle. They look like cranes—or maybe cranes from outer space—and come in a wide variety of colors and several different styles. The store also sells Duro-Lite bulbs at list price. Open weekdays only 9:00 A.M. to 4:30 P.M.

## LINENS, BEDS AND BEDDING

**J. Schachter's,** 115 Allen Street, corner of Delancey Street, 533-1150
When it comes to bedding needs, there's simply no place to compare with Schachter's. A family business since 1919, it specializes in custom-made quilts and comforters of any size, pattern or fabric (of course, there are patterns and fabrics aplenty to choose from at the store). It also offers custom- and ready-made pillows—soft-as-a-cloud down bed pillows, throw pillows and sofa cushions. You can choose from a variety of grades (the experts here will explain the difference) of goose down and lamb's wool for stuffing pillows and comforters. And if you have a patchwork quilt that you'd like made into a comforter, this is the place. A small boutique in the rear of the store handles very fine linens (top-of-the-line Wamsutta, beautifully embroidered Portuguese sheets, etc.), French towels and select tablecloths. Bathroom rugs, pillow shams, dust ruffles and fine woolen blankets are also available. Upstairs are the best bargains: closeout and discontinued merchandise, plus custom-made quilts that involved some mistake (for example, a customer ordered camel and it was made in beige); these are sold at a minimum of 40% off. Regular items sold downstairs are also discounted between 20% and 30%. Open Sunday to Thursday 9:00 A.M. to 5:00 P.M., Friday till 2:30 P.M.

**Ezra Cohen,** 307 Grand Street, at Allen Street, 925-7800
The largest selection of dry goods on the Lower East Side—towels, draperies, bedspreads, linens, shoe curtains, bathroom carpets, comforters, sheets, quilts, slipcovers, etc.—is at Ezra Cohen. There are two floors of merchandise, including all brand names and designers, and everything is sold at a minimum of 25% below retail. You'll appreciate not only the low prices and extensive selection but also the personalized attention from knowledgeable salespeople here. Open Sunday to Thursday 9:00 A.M. to 5:00 P.M., Friday till 4:00 P.M.

**Harris Levy,** 278 Grand Street, between Eldridge and Forsyth Streets, 226-3102
Here you'll find a tremendous selection of sheets, plus a department that will turn sheets into wall hangings, lampshades and dust ruffles. I've heard it rumored that even Bo-Bo Rockefeller takes advantage of

the discounts here—between 25% and 40% below retail. Tremendous savings on brand-name Dacron pillows, Belgian dish towels and fine imported table linen. I purchased my trousseau towels here twenty years ago, and I still have them. Open Monday to Thursday 9:00 A.M. to 5:00 P.M., Friday and Sunday to 4:30 P.M.

**Kleinsleep/Clearance,** 176 Avenue of the Americas, between Spring and Vandam Streets, 226-0900

Kleinsleep is a chain of ten bedding stores in the New York area featuring mattresses, box springs, high-risers and platform beds, some bedding accessories (like mattress pads and bedboards) and brass beds. At its regular stores it sells top national brands, including Sealy Posturepedic; you buy the mattress at full price and get 50% off on the matching box springs. Delivery and assembly are free and fast—within forty-eight hours—and there's a "comfort guarantee" that allows you to exchange your new bed for up to two weeks. The above clearance store—and another at 2508 Flatbush Avenue, in Brooklyn, 252-2440—have all the usual Kleinsleep merchandise, plus terrific bargains on slightly damaged and discontinued merchandise, mismatched sets and other oddities that will likely be undetectable in your bedroom. Open weekdays 10:00 A.M. to 7:00 P.M., Thursday till 9:00 P.M., Saturday 10:00 A.M. to 6:00 P.M., Sunday noon to 6:00 P.M.

**Rennert Manufacturing Company,** 93 Greene Street, between Spring and Prince Streets, 925-1463

Cotton and satin moving pads make marvelous bedspreads. They're the perfect bedroom accouterment for a high-tech décor, and they also make fine exercise mats, bed blankets, picnic blankets, sound and temperature insulation and, if you want to get creative, moving pads. That's the main reason Rennert manufactures them, but it caters to the decorator crowd by offering them in gorgeous colors. In cotton there's a choice of fifteen to twenty hues, satin pads come in black, silver gray, plum and red. You pay wholesale factory prices at Rennert's: $10 to $23.50 for cotton, $12 to $30 for satin, depending on size. Open weekdays only 8:30 A.M. to 5:00 P.M.

**The Economy Foam Center,** 173 East Houston Street, at First Avenue, 473-4462

The Economy Foam Center offers not only foam and foam mattresses but a full line of bedding items—designer sheets, comforters, bedspreads, pillows (bed and decorative, filled with foam, polyester or down), and high-riser covers among them. It's all closeout merchandise, and it's all discounted 30% to 50% below retail. There's a large selection of fabric and vinyls for upholstery and wall covering. As for foam, Economy will cut it to any size while you wait or sell it to you shredded for filler by the pound. It also sells several polyester fibers for fillers. Open Sunday to Friday 9:30 A.M. to 6:00 P.M.

## LUGGAGE

**Bettinger's Luggage Shop,** 80 Rivington Street, between Orchard and Allen Streets, 674-9411

This tiny, cluttered shop is not made for browsing. Find what you want in the relaxed atmosphere of a department store; then come down to Bettinger's and get it for 25% to 40% less. It has all major brands—Samsonite, American Tourister, Ventura, etc.—as well as exact replicas of PAX bags and a full line of wallets and attaché cases. There are even trunks. Almost all the merchandise sold here is first-quality, but Bettinger's also offers good buys on seconds and irregulars. Open Sunday to Friday 9:30 A.M. to 6:00 P.M.

## MAGIC

**Flosso Hornmann Magic Shop,** 304 West 34th Street, between Eighth and Ninth Avenues, second floor, 279-6079

Billing itself as "the world's oldest magic shop," Flosso Hornmann dates back to 1856 and was actually owned by Houdini in the early 1900s. The shop is filled with shell games, mysteriously multiplying rabbits, mind-reading secrets, handkerchief tricks, Indian rope tricks, Oriental coin tricks and, of course, card tricks. You can purchase the means to pull a dozen eggs from a volunteer's mouth, to the "wild-eyed amazement" of your audience. Aspiring child magicians are warmly welcomed, and since many of the tricks are just $1 or $2, kids can have a super time. They'll also enjoy the store's museum of magic. Flosso Hornmann provides qualified magicians to entertain at parties. Open weekdays 10:30 A.M. to 5:00 P.M., Saturday till 3:30 P.M.; other times just walk through the walls.

## MILLINERY SUPPLIES

**Manny's Millinery,** 63 West 38th Street, between Fifth and Sixth Avenues, 840-2235

It's lots of fun poking and sifting through the bins, boxes and piles of millinery accessories here. Manny's actually a wholesaler, but he sells to the public at 25% to 50% below retail. Sorting through, you'll find feathers (both decorative and for stuffing), flowers, hat frames, wire, veiling, fabrics, threads, feather boas, braid, cloth flowers and hatpins. The store makes hats to your specific design, sells a wide variety of ready-made hats (you can choose additional trimmings) and redecorates old hats. Open weekdays 9:00 A.M. to 5:30 P.M., Saturday to 3:30 P.M.

## MUSIC BOXES

**Rita Ford Inc. Music Boxes,** 19 East 65th Street, between Madison and Fifth Avenues, 535-6717

Enter here an enchanting fairy tale world, the music box realm of Rita Ford. She has one of the world's most complete and captivating collections, both antique and contemporary, ranging in price from about $13 to more than $70,000. She presented Richard Rodgers with a handmade carousel with lights and tiny up-and-down moving horses on his seventy-fifth birthday (it plays the *Carousel* waltz, of course). Johnny Cash ordered a musical watch here for Stevie Wonder that plays "You Are the Sunshine of My Life." And Robert Redford bought a jeweled box for daughter Amy that plays...well, I'm sure you can guess. The shelves are lined with intricate birds in cages that sing and whistle when wound up, clown boxes (they play "Send in the Clowns"), jewelry boxes that play arias, revolving figurines and automatons. Rita restores and repairs music boxes in addition to selling them, and she'll custom-design them, too (usually requiring a minimum twenty-four-box order). Open Monday to Saturday 9:00 A.M. to 5:00 P.M.

## MUSICAL INSTRUMENTS

**Ardsley Musical Instruments,** 219 Sprain Road, Scarsdale, 914-693-6639

You won't exactly find a priceless Stradivarius at Ardsley, but if you want musical instruments for the kids—or your own amateur use—you'll find a wide selection of more than ample quality here discounted 35% to 50%. Ardsley specializes in violins of all sizes, but it also carries a complete range of band and orchestra instruments which you can buy or rent. It has new and used, perfect and imperfect (factory seconds or slight cosmetic defects) instruments, and it also does repairs. Visits to the store are by appointment only, so call before you go.

**La Piana Piano Sales, Ltd.,** 147 West 24th Street, between Sixth and Seventh Avenues, 243-5762

Frank La Piana designs and builds his own pianos—using bird's-eye maple German-style parts (no plastic)—and sells them for one-third less than comparable commercial models. The quality of these instruments is fine, as many professional musicians who have purchased them will attest. La Piana also sells used pianos at very reasonable prices and, as an additional service, will send an expert out with you (for a $45 fee) to look at any used piano and assess its worth. On the premises, he has a professional recording and video studio which can be rented and an auditorium for recitals. During spring and summer there are sometimes free Sunday afternoon classical and jazz concerts (these often feature well-known performers), at which coffee, cake and wine are served. The store is open Monday to Saturday 9:30 A.M. to 6:30 P.M.

**Jack Kahn Music,** 158 West 55th Street, between Sixth and Seventh Avenues, 581-9420

Kahn is the guy with the late-night Crazy Eddie-style TV commercials that chastise you for putting off buying a piano. And like Crazy Eddie, he guarantees his prices can't be "beat"; if you find a lower price in thirty days, he'll refund the difference plus 10% (of the difference). He claims to have the largest selection of pianos and organs in the metropolitan area—new and used of almost every brand: grand pianos, spinet pianos, console pianos, harpsichords, spinet organs, console organs, even player pianos. Used instruments are reconditioned and rebuilt, guaranteed to be in perfect working order. Kahn's services include piano repair, tuning, rebuilding and refinishing, and the store sponsors many free piano recitals (pick up a schedule). Open Monday to Saturday 10:00 A.M. to 6:00 P.M. Additional New York locations in Staten Island, Lake Grove, White Plains, Nanuet, Freeport, Huntington and Centereach.

**Terminal Music,** 166 West 48th Street, between Sixth and Seventh Avenues, 869-5270

Located in the thick of New York's musical instrument district, Terminal offers very competitive prices (up to 50% off) on saxophones, trumpets, woodwinds, amplifiers, electric pianos and guitars and a full range of fretted instruments, as well as accessories, sheet music and instructional books and booklets. It has the world's largest selection of recorders—3,000 to 4,000 of them—and filing cabinets of recorder music. It also carries public address systems. The staff can show you how to care for the instruments you buy, and if it doesn't have an instrument you're looking for, it'll direct you to a good source. Open Monday to Saturday 9:00 A.M. to 6:00 P.M.

## NEWSPAPERS AND MAGAZINES

**Jay Bee Magazines,** 134 West 26th Street, between Avenue of the Americas and Seventh Avenue, basement, 675-1600

Jay Bee has more than 2 million back-date periodicals on tap, and from the looks of things they appear to be stacked haphazardly in every nook and cranny. Nevertheless, when you stop in for a magazine, clutter notwithstanding, the sales people can always lay their hands on it at once. Researchers, writers and students who buy magazines here can ask Jay Bee for referrals on their pet subjects. Some magazines date back to the early 1900s. Open weekdays 9:30 A.M. to 5:00 P.M., Saturday 10:00 A.M. to 5:00 P.M.

**Hotaling's,** 1 Times Square, corner of 42nd Street and Broadway, 840-1868

If you're looking for *Der Spiegel, L'Espresso,* the *Oneonta Star* or the *San Diego Union,* Hotaling's is the place most likely to have it. It carries about 250 newspapers from all over the country and the world—magazines, too. Open 7:30 A.M. to 9:30 P.M. Monday to Saturday, Sunday noon to 8:00 P.M.

## OFFICE EQUIPMENT

**Typex Business Machines,** 119 West 23rd Street, between Sixth and Seventh Avenues, 243-8086

Typex offers hefty discounts—30% to 40%—on both old and new typewriters and has them in all languages (well, maybe not Serbo-Croat, but Russian, Arabic, Greek, Spanish, French, Chinese and English at any rate). It takes trade-ins on old machines and also sells adding machines, phone-answering machines and calculators. Low rates here, too, on typewriter repair, but there's no pickup or delivery. Open Monday to Thursday 9:30 A.M. to 5:30 P.M., Friday 9:30 A.M. to 2:00 P.M., Sunday 11:00 A.M. to 4:00 P.M.

## PAINT, WALLPAPER AND WINDOW SHADES

**Pintchik Inc.,** 478 Bergen Street, corner of Flatbush Avenue, Brooklyn, 783-3333

Pintchik is a Brooklyn landmark and, as *New York* magazine aptly called it, "the ultimate paint store." It's really a decorating supermarket. The paint department stocks every major brand and color, including three house lines (its prestige brand, Imperial, is reputed to be as good as any paint on the market, and it's guaranteed 100%)—all sold at discounts of 15% to 40%. Because Pintchik carries the largest quantity of in-stock wall coverings in New York—more than a quarter million rolls—it's able to offer discounts of up to 75%, and it will order anything it doesn't have (including papers available through dealers only) and sell it to you at a huge discount. It purchases floor covering by the tractor-trailer load and passes the savings gleaned from volume buying (also closeouts) on to you (discounts of 20% to 80%). Pintchik's factory-trained personnel can handle any kind of installation. And when it comes to blinds, Pintchik is the largest Bali and Levolor dealer in the country, offering discounts of 50%, quick delivery and expert installation. The store (established 1912) is currently run by the third generation of Pintchiks; they grew up in the business and know it inside out. Pintchik delivers free to all five boroughs. Open Monday and Thursday 8:30 A.M. to 8:00 P.M., Tuesday, Wednesday and Friday 8:30 A.M. to 7:00 P.M., Saturday 8:30 A.M. to 6:30 P.M., Sunday 10:00 A.M. to

5:00 P.M. There's a branch in Manhattan at Third Ave. and 22nd Street, 982-6600, as well as two other branches in Brooklyn and one in Queens.

**Merit-Kaplan,** 227 East 44th Street, between Second and Third Avenues, 682-3585

Merit-Kaplan has good buys on wallpaper and paint, with about 100 books of the former to choose from (discounts are 20% to 50%) and all national brands of the latter at wholesale prices. Best paint buys here are on discontinued colors and custom colors that people ordered and never picked up. Sometimes you can get an $18 gallon of paint for just $4 in this section. Merit-Kaplan also sells Levolor blinds at 40% off and delivers free in all boroughs except Staten Island on minimum orders of eight gallons or $50. Look for special sales at the beginning of spring, summer and fall. Open weekdays 7:00 A.M. to 5:30 P.M.

**Window Works,** 210 Fifth Avenue, suite 1102, New York, N.Y. 10010, 258-5679

Window Works is a mail-order operation offering discounts of 35% to 55% off list on Levolor, Bali and other well-known manufacturers' brands of blinds and shades. Send $1 to the above address (refundable upon purchase), and request the "Magic with Windows Kit." It's chock-full of color brochures on available products, contains many decorator ideas and gives details on how to take exact measurements for, install and maintain your blinds. Window Works will give you an exact price quote on the phone, and Levolor Riviera blinds are sold with a five-year warranty.

**Sheila's Wall Styles,** 273 Grand Street, between Eldridge and Forsyth Streets, 966-1663

Sheila discounts both her sample book selections and her vast stock of discontinued and closeout wall coverings anywhere from 20% to 75%. She will create wallpaper in any color you need and, if you so desire, whip up custom draperies and bedspreads to match. You can consult with decorators on the premises (they'll even come to your home). Levolor, vertical and woven-wood blinds, by the way, are half price here. Everything is first quality. Open Sunday to Thursday from 9:00 A.M. to 5:00 P.M., Friday till 2:00 P.M.

Also check out **Pearl Paints,** 308 Canal Street, between Broadway and Church Street, 431-7932, a vast five-story art supply store that devotes its main floor to house paint and accessories. It carries major brands as well as its own line, does custom blending and is expert in matching paint to fabric or wallpaper. Paints at Pearl are discounted 20% to 50%. Open Monday to Saturday 9:00 A.M. to 5:30 P.M., Sunday 11:00 A.M. to 4:45 P.M.

## PERFUMES

**The Wynnewood Pharmacy,** Wynnewood Shopping Center, 50 East Wynnewood Road, Wynnewood, Pa. 19096, 215-878-4999 or 215-642-9091

The Wynnewood Pharmacy is much more than just a neighborhood drugstore. Owners Jay and Sandy Rosner call it Paris in Wynnewood, because they offer thirty-five leading perfumes, as well as bath oils, powders and body lotions, at "better-than-the-Bahamas" discounts of 20% to 70%. We're talking about fragrances like Amazone, Pierre Cardin, Halston, Bill Blass, Dior, Coriandre and Givenchy, among many others for both men and women. Open Monday to Saturday 8:00 A.M. to 9:00 P.M., Sunday 8:30 A.M. to 3:00 P.M., and you can write for a listing and order by mail.

Another good bet for discounted name-brand perfumes and colognes are above-mentioned closeout stores, especially **Odd Job Trading Corp** (p. 59) and **The City Dump** (p. 60).

**Tuli-Latus Perfumes,** 146-36 13th Avenue, P.O. Box 422, Whitestone, N.Y. 11357, 746-9337

Tuli-Latus makes quality replicas of the world's most famous fragrances, utilizing the same methods and oils from Grasse and other flower centers that the major French perfume makers use—and sells them at a fraction of the cost. Many aficionados have been unable to smell the difference. An ounce of Joy retails for about $160; the Tuli-Latus equivalent, for $22. Same price for replicas of Opium, Bal à Versailles and Oscar de la Renta. Chloe, White Shoulders, Shalimar and Madame Rochas are just $18. Tuli-Latus also copies men's fragrances like Pour Homme by Gucci ($15 an ounce), as well as body powders and lotions. Tuli-Latus offers a full money-back guarantee if you're not satisfied. You can visit the boutique at 136-56 39th Avenue, suite 450, Flushing, weekdays 9:30 A.M. to 4:30 P.M., or buy via mail order from the Whitestone address.

Similar operations: **House of Flaubert,** 68 Hemlock Road, Short

Hills, N.J. 07078, and **Essential Products,** 90 Water Street, New York, N.Y. 10005, 344-4288; write to either for a price list.

# PETS

A few tips for pet owners and would-be pet owners on how to acquire pets, take care of them, train them, find them when they're lost and even make them famous.

**Pet Clinicare,** 419 West 54th Street, between Ninth and Tenth Avenues, 581-8784

Pet Clinicare offers some of the lowest prices in town on dog and cat spaying, neutering and cat declawing—about a third less than you'd pay elsewhere for comparable services. Whether or not you have your animal altered here, you can write for its helpful free deallergizing instruction sheet that tells you how to allergy-proof your pets (a surprising number of pet lovers are allergic sufferers). Just send a stamped, self-addressed envelope to the above address with your request. Weekdays 7:00 A.M. to 6:00 P.M., only by appointment.

**Riverside Animal Hospital,** 825 West End Avenue, at 100th Street, 866-8758

You probably have Blue Cross for your own medical emergency insurance, but if your pet requires medical care and hospitalization, the fees can be almost as devastating. Riverside has a Blue Cross equivalent for pets called Pet Sure that covers 100% of most outpatient and office services and vaccinations, 80% of hospitalization, radiology, lab tests and other services and 50% of grooming and elective surgical services. That's a lot of security for just $125 a year. The same service is also available out of the **Animal Hospital of Brooklyn,** 2270 Flatbush Avenue, 258-0500. Both hospitals also have a free adoption service (they place pets and help people find homes for pets they can't care for).

**Pet Med,** Box 3400, Grand Central Station, New York, N.Y. 10163

If your dog gets cut up in a fight or your cat goes into convulsions, of course, you want to get to a vet as soon as possible. But often in the critical moments following an injury your pet's health is in your hands. Pet Med is a first-aid emergency kit for cats and dogs that includes all the pads, compresses, bandages, special safety scissors, tweezers, eyedroppers, etc. you need, plus a 200-page informative medical manual detailing emergency treatment. The kit is packaged for convenient bookshelf storage. It's especially handy when you're traveling with an animal. To order, send $15 (that includes postage and handling) to the above address, and specify whether your pet is a cat or dog.

**New York School of Dog Grooming,** 248 East 34th Street, between First and Second Avenues, 685-3777

In the beauty section of this book, I tell you about posh salons where you can have your hair done inexpensively by students. The New York School of Dog Grooming is the equivalent for your dog or cat. Under the watchful supervision of instructors, students will clip nails, brush, bathe, clean ears, style and provide any necessary finishing touches. This is the largest dog and cat grooming school in the country, so there are plenty of students to work on your pet. The cost for these services is about half of what you'd pay elsewhere, sometimes even less. Prices vary with breed. Call for an appointment.

**New York Academy of Dog Training,** 605 Third Avenue, at 37th Street, 655-0700

This is Princeton for dogs—an elite training program in your own home that teaches the highest standards of obedience, housebreaks your pet, corrects destructive habits and solves your seemingly unsolvable pet problem. It can teach an old dog new tricks! Best of all, New York Academy trains with love, praise and reward, not with punishment and scolding. The service runs from $300 to $600, depending on what you want accomplished, and includes as many sessions as necessary to get the desired results. Clients can call at any time during or after training for advice on any dog-related problems, and New York Academy can also refer them to first-rate dog groomers, kennels, veterinarians, dog foods, etc. It services all the boroughs, Nassau, Westchester and Long Island.

**Catcare,** 838-2996

Your cat doesn't want to stay with a friend when you leave town; it prefers the comforts of home, familiar surroundings, its own bowl and water dish, so next time you go away, call Catcare, a personalized service run by cat lovers-owners who come to your home, feed your cat, play with it, change the litter box, medicate and do anything else your cat needs. They don't mind doing some apartment chores as well—picking up mail, watering plants, etc. Rate per visit is about $10, and there's no charge for up to two additional cats. Catcare services most of Manhattan as far uptown as 97th Street.

**The Kennelworth,** 410 West 22nd Street, 737-9333

Where to board Rex when you go on vacation and not have to worry? Many vets recommend The Kennelworth, where pets are kept in their own rooms (not cages), special diets are catered to, maintenance and supervision are kept up twenty-four hours a day, a veterinarian is on call, animals are played with and walked individually four times a day and even music is provided (dogs especially like it). Rates, including food, range from $13 to $21 per night, depending on animal size. Indoor/outdoor facilities and outdoor runs are available, and there's a brand new cat room. You can keep any kind of pet here—cat, dog, monkey, hamster, snake, sheep, whatever—and it will get lots of TLC. There's a complete grooming facility; dog training is available.

**Petfinders,** 609 Columbus Avenue, 877-5191, 516-222-2620 (L.I.), 914-997-1094 (Westchester), 201-623-8313 (N.J.)

It's heartbreaking to lose a pet, but don't give up hope until you've tried Petfinders. For a fee of $26, it institutes a six-month search, advertising in lost-and-found columns, sending out a weekly lost pet report to more than sixty rescue organizations and humane societies, keeping in close touch with places like the ASPCA and Bide-A-Wee, subscribing to every community paper and checking "found" columns and much more. It operates throughout the metropolitan area and finds about 35% of the pets its clients are searching for. Phone 9:00 A.M. to 2:00 P.M. weekdays.

Under the same auspices is **Pet Club of America,** which provides members with a wide range of pet services. They include: health information, traveling-with-pets advice, a Petfinders tag for your animal's collar, a subscription to its newsletter, *Animal Times,* opportunity to participate in a pet show and fair, free publications, an adoption service and membership discounts on pet food, grooming, medical treatment, etc. It costs $23 a year to join, plus a one-time initiation fee of $3.50 for all your pets.

**ASPCA,** 441 East 92nd Street, at York Avenue, 876-7700

Want to adopt an orphaned animal? Head over to the ASPCA, and your only expense will be $8.50 for a license (for dogs only), which you can purchase there, and an adoption fee of $20 to $40, depending on whether it's a cat or dog, mixed breed or purebred. Adoption fee includes spaying or neutering (which you must agree to), inoculations and follow-up examinations. There are no adoption fees for rabbits, birds, hamsters or gerbils, but a donation is requested. You must be at least eighteen, have ID and be listed in the phone book. The ASPCA has hundreds of pets to choose from. While you're there, ask about its booklets and seminars on pet training. Weekdays 11:00 A.M. to 7:00 P.M., weekends noon to 6:00 P.M.

You can also try **Bide-A-Wee Home,** 410 East 38th Street, 532-4455 (a recording), or 532-4457 (a human being), a nonprofit organization that runs a similar adoption operation.

## PHOTOGRAPHIC EQUIPMENT

**Alkit Camera Shop,** 866 Third Avenue, between 52nd and 53rd Streets, 832-2101

Many top professionals and ad agencies buy their camera equipment at Alkit. The reason: competitive prices and a quality of service that is hard to come by these days. For instance, professional photographers are assigned personal salespeople who work with them on a regular one-to-one basis. With amateurs, the staff will really explain how to operate the equipment—you'll definitely know how before you leave the store—and make every effort to sell you items realistically geared to your needs. Alkit stocks a wide range of equipment and cameras—all major brands—and will rent equipment and personally service anything it sells. Open weekdays 8:00 A.M. to 6:30 P.M., Saturday 9:00 A.M. to 5:00 P.M.

**Hirsch Photo,** 699 Third Avenue, at 44th Street, 557-1150

About fifteen clerks are on the floor at all times at Hirsch, handling the daily rush of customers who come in for photographic equipment at close to wholesale prices. It's a large store, and though it's usually crowded, you can take your time browsing and discuss your needs at length with your salesperson. Hirsch carries every major still and movie camera, a full line of darkroom supplies and all other photography-related items for both the amateur and the professional. It also does expert camera repair and offers all darkroom and developing services. Open weekdays 8:30 A.M. to 5:45 P.M., Saturday 10:00 A.M. to 4:00 P.M.

## PICTURE FRAMING

**Make A Frame,** 406 Third Avenue, at 29th Street, 684-1215

Its name notwithstanding, Make A Frame does offer low-priced custom framing; however, it is cheaper—and couldn't be easier—to do it yourself. The friendly staff will help you select an appropriate frame and mat for your art, cut all the materials, dry-mount the work, if necessary, and teach you how to join the frame and fit the art into it. You'll save 40% to 60% over custom framing, and there's no wait; when you're through, your framed artwork is wrapped up and you take it home ready to hang it. Hours are Monday to Thursday 11:00 A.M. to 8:30 P.M., Friday and Saturday 11:00 A.M. to 7:00 P.M.; it is sometimes open on Sunday and Monday, but call before you go. Another store in Brooklyn at 180 Atlantic Avenue, 875-6150. Hours are Wednesday and Thursday 11:00 A.M. to 8:00 P.M.; Friday and Saturday 11:00 A.M. to 1:00 P.M.; Sunday 1:00 P.M. to 6:00 P.M.; closed Monday and Tuesday.

**Frame It Yourself,** 220 East 23rd Street, between Second and Third Avenues, 689-2908, is almost a clone of the above operation. It also has a vast selection—should you have nothing to frame—of more than 1,000 fine art posters. Open weekdays 11:00 A.M. to 7:00 P.M., Saturday 10:00 A.M. to 6:00 P.M.

**Jerry Josef,** 113 Prince Street, between Greene and Wooster Streets, 475-3837

Major New York artists, galleries, art consultants and collectors have their work custom-framed at Jerry Josef's. His work is museum-quality, and he's as concerned about conserving the longevity of artwork as he is about aesthetic considerations. Jerry uses all natural-wood frames, some hand-painted and some gold-leafed but always creating a contemporary look. Of course, this kind of prestige custom framing is not inexpensive, but if you have an important piece of art, it's worth considering. The framing operation shares the premises with an art gallery where the works of contemporary American artists are exhibited. Open Tuesday to Friday 10:00 A.M. to 6:00 P.M., Saturday 11:00 A.M. to 6:00 P.M.

**Yale Picture Frame & Molding Corp.,** 770 Fifth Avenue, at 28th Street, Brooklyn, 788-6200

Yale is a manufacturer, importer and wholesaler of picture frames, offering a huge selection to retail customers at discounts of at least 25%. It has 20,000 ready-made frames to choose from and more than a million feet of molding, as well as matting and glass. Open Monday to Thursday 8:00 A.M. to 4:00 P.M., Friday to 2:00 P.M., Sunday 9:00 A.M. to 2:00 P.M.

## RECORDS AND TAPES

**Sam Goody's,** 51 West 51st Street, corner of Avenue of the Americas, 246-8730

A reliable source for records and tapes in all music categories, Sam Goody's has an immense selection that includes many hard-to-find albums. Some of the offerings are always discounted. It also sells video and audio equipment, portable radios, Walkman units, etc. Open weekdays 9:30 A.M. to 6:45 P.M., Saturday 9:30 A.M. to 6:00 P.M., Sunday noon to 5:00 P.M. Many additional branches throughout the metropolitan area; check your phone book.

## RUGS AND CARPETS

**ABC Carpet Company,** 881 and 888 Broadway, near 19th Street, 677-6970

ABC, in business since 1897, is probably the largest carpet dealer in the country, its remnants alone comprising more than those of all other stores in New York City combined. There are two immense showrooms, both piled high with carpets and rugs of every description. At #881, the original store, ABC has four floors of new first-quality, standard-brand broadlooms—offered at 50% below department-store prices. The new showroom at #888 (Ed Koch came to the gala Labor Day opening) houses a vast array of rugs from China, Persia, Turkey, India and Pakistan—also at 50% off. This is also where you'll find that above-mentioned abundance of remnants (from scatter to mansion sizes) and machine-made rugs that sold below manufacturer's cost. ABC offers quick delivery and installation. Open Monday to Saturday 9:00 A.M. to 6:00 P.M., Thursday till 8:00 P.M., Sunday 11:00 A.M. to 5:00 P.M.

**Central Carpet,** 426 Columbus Avenue, between 80th and 81st Streets, 362-5485

Central Carpet is a long-established retailer of Oriental rugs at the lowest prices in New York (find a similar item for less, and it'll refund the difference). The store is completely blanketed with rugs layered on the floor, hanging on the walls and displayed on massive racks. There are always thousands of handmade rugs (antique, semiantique and new) from Iran, Turkey, Pakistan, Afghanistan, Russia, India and China. Central manufactures wall-to-wall carpeting, too, and sells it (in addition to used carpeting) to the public at wholesale prices. It also features a large collection of Chinese Art Deco rugs made in the 1920s and 100% wool Oriental-design reproductions. You can take a rug home on approval to see how it looks. Open weekdays 9:00 A.M. to 6:00 P.M., Thursday 10:00 A.M. to 7:30 P.M., Saturday 9:00 A.M. to 5:00 P.M., Sunday 11:00 A.M. to 5:00 P.M.

**The Rug Warehouse,** 2222 Broadway, at 79th Street, 787-6665

Like Central Carpet, The Rug Warehouse, more than fifty years on the scene, offers a lowest-price guarantee (it'll give a complete refund if you find a better price) and lets customers take rugs home, have them appraised and return them if not satisfied. Its collection of some 3,000 Oriental carpets is incredibly low-priced. I once found a Chinese rug here selling for $1,000 less than in a major department store. The collection includes Persians and Caucasians (Kashan, Tabiz, Shirvan, Kazak, Bukhara, etc.), 1920s Art Deco Chinese, European Oriental-design rugs, dhurries and kilims and new rugs made the traditional way. The Warehouse claims it will buy back any rug it's sold you at the highest prices offered by any dealer. Open Monday to Saturday 10:00 A.M. to 6:00 P.M., Sunday 11:00 A.M. to 5:00 P.M.

## SCIENTIFIC EQUIPMENT

**Edmund Scientific,** 101 East Gloucester Pike, Barrington, N.J. 08007, 609-547-3488

If your kids are into science, they'll love a trip to Edmund Scientific. In addition to thousands of scientific items, this supermarket of science offers laser light shows, has a Japanese submarine (World War II) periscope mounted through the roof and sets up hologram exhibits. The aisles are stocked with test tubes and beakers of every kind, chemistryware and labware, microscopes, telescopes, metal detectors, solar energy paraphernalia, biofeedback devices, prisms, weather instruments, astrophotography equipment and books on all the above.

Many things here are geared to interest children—including numerous toys and games—and there's lots of fascinating gadgetry, like the rodent eliminator that blasts pests with sonic waves. Though it's a two-hour drive from Manhattan, Edmund Scientific is a great destination for family weekend outings. You can also write to the above address for a free catalog. Open Monday to Saturday 9:00 A.M. to 5:30 P.M., Sunday noon to 5:00 P.M.

## SEASHELLS

**Seashells Unlimited, Inc.,** 590 Third Avenue, between 38th and 39th Streets, 532-8690

Veronica Parker Jones has the largest collection of seashells on view in the city. They come from all over the world, many of them inadvertently collected by fishermen and retrieved by her network of local dealers. They make beautiful gifts that are sure to be appreciated; everyone likes seashells. Prices begin at just 5 cents, and most shells are under $100. Open Monday to Saturday from 11:00 A.M. to 6:00 P.M.

## STAMPS, COINS AND ANTIQUITIES

**Harmer Rooke Numismatics,** 3 East 57th Street, sixth and seventh floors, 751-1900

Harmer Rooke is a world-renowned dealer in stamps and coins at all price ranges—from about $50 to a great deal higher, of course. There is also an auction house (on the seventh floor) for stamps, coins and antiquities; the latter category runs the gamut from Tibetan bronze Buddhas to Eskimo tools to ancient Egyptian glass. On the sixth floor is a beautiful gallery display of antiquities from ancient Greek, Roman, Judaic, Middle Eastern and pre-Colombian cultures, along with rare American glass and American and European autographs. Originally an English firm (established 1903), Harmer Rooke has been in New York since 1939. Though it may sound intimidating, it's actually a very friendly place where browsing is encouraged and a knowledgeable staff is happy to answer your questions. Weekday hours are 9:30 A.M. to 5:30 P.M., Saturday (except in summer) 10:00 A.M. to 3:00 P.M.

## STONE AND TILE

**Marble Modes,** 15-25 130th Street, College Point, 539-1334

This Queens marble emporium is the largest stone center on the East Coast. If you can't find the marble you want here, say the staff, "it probably doesn't exist." It has marble from all over the world in fifty different colors, as well as granite, slate, onyx, ceramic and quarry tiles for creating elegant flooring, tiling, tabletops, fireplaces, pedestals and garden paths. It also deals in statuary, terra-cotta planters and alabaster statuettes and chess sets. Open weekdays 7:30 A.M. to 4:30 P.M.

**The Quarry,** 183 Lexington Avenue, between 31st and 32nd Streets, 679-2559

Here you'll find the largest selection of ceramic wall and floor tiles in New York. They come from all over the world—France, Germany, Holland, Portugal, Mexico, etc.—and have beautiful glazed designs of animals, fruits, flowers, vegetables, zodiac signs, whatever. The Quarry will do installation or explain how to do it and rent you the necessary tools. It also carries bathroom accessories, natural marble and slate tiles. Open weekdays 9:00 A.M. to 6:00 P.M., Saturday (except in summer) 10:00 A.M. to 4:00 P.M.

Also check out **Ceramica Mia,** 405 East 51st Street, corner of First Avenue, 759-2339, where mostly Italian tiles are featured. Open weekdays 10:00 A.M. to 5:45 P.M., Saturday (except in summer) to 5:00 P.M.

## TOYS

**F.A.O. Schwarz Warehouse,** 150 Lackawanna Avenue, Parsippany, N.J., 644-9487 or 201-334-1441

The Tiffany's of toy shops has a warehouse in New Jersey where shopworn—but still working—playthings are sold at 20% to 50% less than their original prices. It's only about half an hour by car from the city, and the bargains make the trip worthwhile. With 83,000 square feet of floor space, the warehouse has quite a selection. Some toys are floor samples, some are returns, but they're the same dolls, robots, space and cowboy gear, craft items, toy cars, etc. sold on Fifth Avenue.

It's an especially great place to shop for preschoolers—they don't know from shopworn. Open 8:00 A.M. to 4:00 P.M. weekdays.

**The Gingerbread House,** 9 Christopher Street, between Avenue of the Americas and Seventh Avenue, 741-9101

This charming toy store has no Barbie dolls, no guns and spacemen, no action figures or electronic games. In a cozy, countrified setting, the Gingerbread House contains only durable, handmade toys of superior quality. The store is especially known for matching up the books it sells with dolls: huggable Beatrix Potter Peter Rabbits, Pinocchio, Babar, the Little Prince, etc. It also stocks many imported playthings, German blocks, colorful wooden Swedish toys, English sailboats and French pull toys among them. And the handmade Vermont rocking horse is a Gingerbread House classic. No discounts here, but the toys will last a lifetime or two. Shelves start just inches above the floor, so they're all at a child's-eye level. Open Monday to Saturday 11:00 A.M. to 8:00 P.M., Sunday noon to 7:00 P.M.

**Orchard Toy and Stationery Co.,** 185 Orchard Street, between Houston and Stanton Streets, 777-5133

At this Lower East Side location you can choose from thousands of toys—the ones you see advertised on TV, including the latest dolls, video games, board games, and Fisher-Price playthings—all discounted from 20% to 50%. It has toys for infants on up. Open daily 9:00 A.M. to 5:30 P.M.

**The Robotorium,** 252 Mott Street, between Houston and Prince Streets, 966-6881

Deb Huglin has collected hundreds of prototype robots, space-related objects, windup toys and automatons from all over the world, and she loves to have you come in and play with them. Meet Mr. Monster—he walks on sand (or your bed) and can carry cigarettes. One robot moves in response to a clap, a salt and pepper set dressed as maid and butler walks across the table to you, talking robots speak English and Spanish and there are even solar-powered robots. In addition to robots and windups (both new and antique—none with batteries), Deb sells a helmet that makes you talk like a robot when you have it on, space guns, hologram pendants and suchlike. Her aim is to bring the twenty-first century into the home, and in the near future she hopes to sell multifunctional household robots, too. Deb doesn't mind children playing with the toys, as long as parents keep an eye on them. She stocks only the most durable items on the market and sells them at rock-bottom prices so everyone can share the fun. Open daily from 4:00 to 11:00 P.M.

**The Last Wound-Up,** 290 Columbus Avenue, between 73rd and 74th Streets, 787-3388

Very similar to the above-listed Robotorium, The Last Wound-Up claims to have the largest windup collection in the world. There's an area called the playpen where you can set into motion the sideways-walking crab, the singing penguin, the sparkling gorilla, the self-walking shoes, the roach catcher (the roach is supposed to get a heart attack when he sees it coming), the complete monkey orchestra and the golf ball that starts to walk when struck (why should Allen Funt have all the fun?). Open daily from 11:00 A.M. to 8:00 P.M., Sunday to 6:30 P.M.

**Go Fly a Kite, Inc.,** 1201 Lexington Avenue, between 81st and 82nd Streets, 472-2623

Here is everything you ever wanted to know about kites—from the diamond-shaped kind you flew at age ten to a huge $1,000 parafoil. They come in more than 100 varieties from all over the world. There are long-tailed sky serpents, Mylar box kites, eagles and butterflies, polyethylene dragons and parrots, nylon cats, bats and octopuses, space shuttles, Chinese silk and rice paper peacocks, even a lettuce-shaped windsock. You can rent a kite or buy one; the staff'll teach you how to fly it. Go Fly a Kite sponsors numerous kite-flying events, competitions and festivals every spring and fall; inquire as to dates. Open Monday to Saturday 10:00 A.M. to 6:00 P.M., Sunday mid-March to the end of June and around Christmas from 11:00 A.M. to 5:00 P.M. Another location at Citicorp Center, 308-1666.

**The Toy Balloon,** 204 East 38th Street, between Second and Third Avenues, 682-3803

You have no idea of the possible variety of balloons until you've visited this shop. There are balloons shaped like hearts, rabbits, pandas, pigs, cats, mice, dogs and dolls. There are balloons with designs for holidays (e.g., a shamrock design for St. Patrick's Day), round and cylindrical balloons, and balloons with custom-printed messages (like "Happy Birthday, Johnny"). You can get the makings for a balloon bouquet or centerpiece here, buy balloon showers (about 100 balloons that descend when you pull a ripcord), balloons that squawk, balloons decorated with clowns, Smurfs, stripes and polka dots. Helium tanks can be rented. Open weekdays from 9:00 A.M. to 5:00 P.M.

**Play It Again,** 171 East 92nd Street, between Lexington and Third Avenues, 876-5888

Most kids are just as thrilled with a used toy as a new one (if they're not, you can always give them a lecture about when you were a child and made toys out of spools). The toys at this consignment shop, in any case, are all in good condition, brought in by Upper East Siders whose children have outgrown them. Last time I was in, it had ice skates, enough cars and trucks to jam up the Long Island Expressway, riding toys and bicycles, tennis and football equipment, books and board games as well as car seats, carriages and playpens. If you're shopping for a large item—like a bike or crib—leave your name and you'll be called when it comes in. Prices are a fraction of the original cost. Open Tuesday to Saturday from 11:00 A.M. to 6:00 P.M.; closed the entire month of August with July hours on a reduced schedule.

## UMBRELLAS

**Gloria Umbrellas,** 39 Essex Street, between Grand and Hester Streets, 475-7388

If a smile is your umbrella, because you lose your real one every time you put it down, you should know about Gloria Umbrellas. Here, at least, replacing the previous one will cost about 30% less than elsewhere. She has thousands of styles to choose from—folding umbrellas, famous brands, cotton canvas umbrellas in all colors, prints, windproof umbrellas, doorman-size umbrellas and beach umbrellas. You can even opt for a particular umbrella but choose a different handle. And if, like Mary Poppins, you're attached to your umbrella—but it's wearing out—Gloria can repair it. Open Sunday to Thursday from 10:00 A.M. to 5:00 P.M.

## VIDEOCASSETTES AND DISCS

**Video Shack, Inc.,** 1608 Broadway, at 49th Street, 581-6260

This is the world's largest source of videocassettes and discs, an immense library of more than 5,000 titles. What would you like to watch—

*Abbott and Costello in Hollywood*, rock performances of Blondie, presidential bloopers, old Tarzan flicks or the new Bo Derek version? You may never leave your house again. There are at least 100 new listings every month, including how-tos (gardening, car care, photography, etc.), sports events, rock concerts and special shows for children. You can buy or rent. A three-day film rental is $15—less than taking the family to the movies these days. Open Monday to Saturday 10:00 A.M. to 1:00 P.M., Sunday noon to midnight. Two additional locations in Manhattan and branches in New Jersey, Long Island and Westchester.

**Video to Go,** 169 West 57th Street, between Sixth and Seventh Avenues, 757-7616

Though not quite as large as Video Shack, Video to Go does have more than 1,000 titles and more coming in every day. The helpful staff is well informed on all facets of this rapidly growing industry, and prices are competitive. Its Video Club members get reduced rates on rentals, and even nonmembers pay only $9.95 to rent a film for a weekend. In addition to all the movies, Video to Go cassettes and discs allow you to work out with Jane Fonda, enjoy a Fleetwood Mac or Beatles concert, view old Super Bowl games or learn tennis with Billie Jean King. Open Monday to Saturday 10:30 A.M. to 6:15 P.M. Four additional locations in Manhattan.

# II
## Services Guide

There are services here you probably never knew existed, like yenta rentals and disaster consultants. There are artisans in New York who can repair, restore and restyle everything.

Before you buy new shoes, camping equipment, handbags, furniture, umbrellas, lamps, irons—you name it—unclutter your closets and take a good look around the house.

There are even services to help you locate other services.

## ADULT EDUCATION— A SMORGASBORD OF COURSES

For the typical New Yorker, continuing education is a way of life. Stagnation is frowned upon; growth and development are *de rigueur.* Hence Gotham's hundreds of thousands of workshops, courses and seminars in subjects ranging from income tax preparation to dim sum cookery. Courses are also a way for New Yorkers to meet each other. There are even courses in how to meet other people and, once you do, in how to make your relationships work. What follows is a random sampling to whet your educational appetite.

Some additional courses are listed in various appropriate sections of this book.

**Center for Speech Arts,** 200 West 57th Street, corner of Seventh Avenue, 664-0188

Do you find that no matter where you travel, the minute you open your mouth people say, "You're from New York, right?" Does that make you crazy? Laura Darius, founder of the Center for Speech Arts, can help you stop sounding like a Damon Runyon character via a four-week course called "How to Lose Your New York Accent," applicable, according to the course description, "to those from the entire metropolitian area." Cost is about $35 to $50. From there you might go on to the eight-week "Standard American Speech I," where you'll learn how to talk like a real American. The center also has courses in foreign accent correction, assertive speaking, how to start a conversation and suchlike.

**The Singing Experience,** 929 Park Avenue, 472-2207

"Song is everyone's birthright," says Linda Birns, whose life-enhancing workshops encourage participants (even—and maybe especially—those who have always been told, "Just mouth the words") to sing out with pride and confidence. In five warmly supportive four-hour sessions, Linda helps you overcome your fears and negative conditioning, teaches you how to sing and puts you in touch with the primal joy of it. Then—are you ready for this?—she hires a major nightclub (like Dangerfield's or the West Bank Café), the class packs the house with friends and relatives, and each member gets up and belts out a song. Salespeople, computer programmers, housewives, social workers and psychiatrists—people from all walks of life—fulfill a fantasy and become stars for a night. It's fun, it's therapy, it's immensely liberating and it's about more than just singing. If you can get up and sing before an audience, what couldn't you do? The course concludes with a reunion in which a videotape of the show is run. It costs $225. A shorter, ten-hour workshop is $75. If you think you'd like to take it but don't have the nerve right off the bat, go to one of the performances (tickets are about $6). You'll see what a beautiful experience The Singing Experience can be.

**Mind over Math,** 29-48 Bell Boulevard, Bayside, 224-6914

Are you plagued by "math anxiety"? Drs. Stanley Kogelman and Joseph Warren say your problem has more to do with attitude than aptitude, and they'd like to help you conquer your fear of figures. They debunk math myths (e.g., it's okay to count on your fingers, say these professors) and help you develop basic mathematical and problem-solving skills in workshops that are given regularly in Manhattan, Queens and Westchester. The fee is $300 for ten sessions, after which you'll be able to answer questions that begin, "If two men can dig a ditch in one hour..." without breaking into a cold sweat. Private sessions are $40. Inquire also about "The Math Solution," a six-hour cassette program for home study.

**Knowhow Workshops,** 17 West 17th Street, between Fifth and Sixth Avenues, 741-1194

Tired of being at the mercy of repairmen every time the tiniest thing goes wrong with your car or around the house? Knowhow Workshops promises it can help you achieve self-sufficiency in everyday life "even if you've never held a hammer before." In twelve-week semesters you can learn "Auto Mechanics," "Basic Carpentry and Cabinet Making" or "Home Mechanics: Home Repair and Improvement," the latter including use of tools and how to shop for them, how to choose the right wood for the job you're doing, carpentry, walls and fastening, painting, plumbing and electricity. Other courses deal with bike repair and maintenance, solar energy, motorcycle mechanics, woodworking, upholstery and furniture restoration. At the same location you can also study calligraphy (at all levels, including Chinese and Hebrew calligraphy and illumination). The courses are given in cooperation with The New School (741-5690), 66 West 12th Street, which is where you register.

**French Fashion Academy,** 600 Madison Avenue, between 57th and 58th Streets, 421-7770

Making your own clothes is the affordable way to chic, but if your Singer creations have that homespun look, you need a course at the French Fashion Academy. The academy was conceived in Paris, and its aim is to disseminate French fashion design methods throughout the world. Studio workshops modeled after famous Paris fashion houses teach patternmaking, cutting, fitting, sewing and finishing techniques for both novice and advanced couturiers. The basic course, "Creative Dressmaking," meets two hours weekly for two months. Call for details.

**Offshore Sailing School, Ltd.,** P.O. Box 119, East Schofield Street, City Island, N.Y. 10464, 885-3200

Would you, to put it in "bumperstickerese," rather be sailing? You can learn in just twenty-six hours, says the Offshore Sailing School, and you don't even need your own boat. The five basic courses are "Learn to Sail," "Advanced Sailing," "Learn to Cruise," "Introductory Racing" and "Advanced Racing." You can take them weekdays or weekends (a fun way to spend the latter). Your classroom is a twenty-seven-foot Olympic-class Solings keelboat, maximum number of students per boat is four and you'll sail from City Island. You can also take any of the courses in conjunction with a week's vacation in Florida, the British Virgin Islands, Martha's Vineyard, Bar Harbor, Maine, Virginia or Bermuda. When you are graduated from any class, you automatically become a member of the Offshore Sailing Club, which offers numerous cruises in the United States and abroad throughout the year. For a seasonal fee, members can use the club's twenty-seven-foot Solings whenever they like. There are lectures, movies and parties, too. Similar courses, vacations and options are offered from April through October at **The New York Sailing Center,** 340 Riverside Drive, 864-4472. Call both schools for brochures and complete details.

**Janovic/Plaza,** 159 West 72nd Street, between Columbus and Amsterdam Avenues, 595-2500

Are you a painter or a schmearer? Janovic/Plaza, one of New York's major paint and wallpaper emporiums, gives twice-yearly evening classes in room painting and paperhanging. The classes take place at its various stores, and you're not obligated to buy anything. "You'll learn everything you need to know to hang wallpaper perfectly," says Neil Janovic. The painting lessons cover preparation, spackling, plastering, sanding, the correct way to apply paint and how to use spray paint. Call to find out when the next class will be held.

**Metropolitan Safety Services Institute,** 60 East 42nd Street, 986-6290

Here's a course that will save you money—and it may even save your life. It's a course in defensive driving, given in eight one-hour sessions, and according to a little-known New York State Law, insurance companies must grant you a minimum 10% reduction on your motor vehicle liability insurance for three years if you complete it. But even if it wasn't for the insurance break, with over 50,000 yearly deaths from traffic accidents and some 2 million disabling injuries, the course is well worth taking. Defensive driving course graduates had 32.8%

fewer accidents than nongraduates, according to a National Safety Council Study. The fee for the course is $28, and you can take it in any of the five boroughs, Nassau or Westchester.

## BEAUTY SERVICES

Many of the world's most glamorous men and women live in New York, and there's a vast army of beauty services to cater to them. With all that's available—at all price ranges, even gratis—looking less than great is inexcusable.

### *BEAUTY BARGAINS*

**Christine Valmy International School,** 730 Fifth Avenue, between 56th and 57th Streets, 581-1520

Students being trained to work at the elegant Christine Valmy salon practice here on volunteers—both men and women—who pay just $10 for a half hour facial. The treatment includes deep pore cleansing, stimulation of circulation, facial massage and a mask geared to skin type. For $3 extra you can have a vegetable peel—a very light skin peel that removes dead cells. Waxing is also available, with the price depending on how large an area you need waxed, but whatever you have done will cost less than half regular salon rates. These training sessions are held during weekdays and on Monday and Wednesday evenings. Call a week or two in advance for an appointment. If you're very shy, be forewarned; your skin flaws may be discussed by the whole class.

**Kree International,** 1500 Broadway, between 43rd and 44th Streets, fifth floor, 730-9700

Electrolysis is the only permanent method of hair removal, but the going rate makes hairlessness a luxury. Kree International's electrolysis school, however, charges just $10 per hour session—less than a third of the usual price. The work is done by students, under very close professional supervision, weekdays between 10:30 A.M. and noon and 3:30 and 5:00 P.M. They can remove unwanted hair from any part of your body—even under your arms. The student working on you will likely wind up in a major department-store salon; Kree supplies employees to Saks, Bloomingdale's, Macy's, B. Altman's, etc. It's perfectly safe, but if you'd feel more comfortable with a trained professional, you can pay Kree's full rate, which is still less than what most other salons charge. You can also achieve hairlessness at Kree via waxing, which costs $10 an hour and is done only on Wednesday. Call for an appointment.

## BEAUTY ON THE HOUSE

Who says you can't afford to look good? You can have your hair cut and styled at some of New York's most chic salons absolutely free. The work will be done by licensed hairdressers who are being trained in the salon's techniques. You know they're good, or they wouldn't have been selected to work in these establishments. Though the work is free, you should, of course, tip the stylists.

Jean-Louis David at **Henri Bendel,** 10 West 57th Street, off Fifth Avenue, sixth floor, 247-5797, sets aside Tuesdays and Fridays from 4:00 P.M. on as training nights. Call Tuesday afternoon to make an appointment and discuss what style options are available. The hairdressers will shampoo, cut and style your hair and occasionally do coloring or perms. Mostly women are needed, but they do sometimes take men.

At **Vidal Sassoon,** 767 Fifth Avenue, between 58th and 59th Streets, 535-9200, women can just come by for a free shampoo, cutting and blow dry any Tuesday or Wednesday at 5:30 P.M. About twenty-five of those who show up will be selected. Men can come the first Wednesday of every month (women, too). One catch: You don't get any say in the style selected, so you'll have to put your trust in the Vidal Sassoon way.

**David Daines,** 833 Madison Avenue, between 69th and 70th Streets, 535-1563, trains stylists in the method of precision haircutting Tuesdays and Fridays at 6:00 P.M. Up to eight women are chosen for shampoos, cut and style each training night; just come by and hope you're selected. If you are chosen, you and the stylist decide on an acceptable style.

**John Atchison,** 44 West 55th Street, between Fifth and Sixth Avenues, 265-6870, takes four clients (women only) for free haircuts every Tuesday and Wednesday from 5:45 P.M. Call for an appointment. You can consult with the stylist as to what you'd like done.

**Glemby International,** 116 East 16th Street, between Union Square and Irving Place, 477-8816

Glemby operates prestige hair salon concessions in major department stores throughout the country. Volunteers are sometimes needed for stylists' training at various salons. The stylists may need certain types—long or short hair, whatever—for free cuts, setting, conditioning and styling. To become a volunteer, call Betty Monaco at the above number.

**Clairol Test Center and Consumer Research Center,** 345 Park Avenue, between 51st and 52nd Streets

Hundreds of women—and some men—visit the Clairol Test Center (546-2715) each week for complimentary beauty services. The staff members don't cut hair, but they will do a wash and set or blow-dry styling on a weekly basis and color, highlight, perm or straighten your hair. The reason: They need volunteers to evaluate and test new products and new shades. Don't worry, though—you take no guinea pig risks. Every product being evaluated has passed all medical and safety tests, and you won't leave without feeling satisfied that your hair looks good. Once you've availed yourself of the test center's free hair services, you can make future appointments; it's not a one-shot deal. To make an appointment, apply in person between 10:00 A.M. and 3:00 P.M., Monday to Friday.

The Consumer Research Center (546-2707) tests hair coloring, hair care, permanent and skin care products designed for home use and occasionally appliances like blow dryers and curling irons. Once again, the staff needs hundreds of weekly volunteers—men and women—to try these products. The difference is that here you do it yourself, applying them as you would at home. Then you get the chance to voice your opinions. To thank you for participating, Clairol will give you either a complimentary set or blow-dry styling and a gift pack of Clairol products or, if the product you have been testing involved styling your hair already, a free Clairol appliance. You're also entitled to a free professional make-up consultation. Call for an appointment weekdays between 9:00 A.M. and 5:00 P.M.

## *DAYS OF BEAUTY*

Want a surefire cure for the blues? Treat your wan and weary self to a full day of luxurious pampering at one of New York's most exclusive salons. It's expensive, but if you need to rationalize the expenditure, a day of combined beauty services actually represents a considerable saving over purchasing them separately—and think what it can do for your psyche!

All the salons listed below offer gift certificates, and you can work out tipping in advance. These beauteous days are naturally popular, so book as far as four to six weeks in advance.

**Elizabeth Arden,** 691 Fifth Avenue, at 54th Street, 407-7900

Just to walk in here makes you feel special. Elizabeth Arden features the Main Chance Day ($140), a full schedule including a half hour Marjorie Craig exercise workout, steam bath, massage, hairstyling, manicure, pedicure, make-up application and lunch. Four-hour sessions—the Miracle Morning ($100) and Visible Difference Day ($105)—include fewer treatments but still offer quality pampering. I could go on and on about how glamorous Elizabeth Arden is and how many famous people go here, but it's not necessary—you already know.

**Georgette Klinger,** 501 Madison Avenue, between 52nd and 53rd Streets, 838-3200

You can indulge in similar style at Georgette Klinger, where a Full Day of Beauty ($165)—facial, body massage, scalp treatment, haircut and styling, make-up lesson and lunch—is offered. It also features a four-hour version called the Half Day of Beauty for $90.00. Georgette Klinger is so chic it actually makes the society pages as one of the places the famous are seen at—and I don't mean just famous women. Paul Newman, Robert Redford and Dustin Hoffman are all Klinger clients.

**Jean-Louis David, at Henri Bendel,** 10 West 57th Street, off Fifth Avenue, sixth floor, 247-5497

Jean-Louis David has a unique Day of Beauty. It includes a dental cleaning: Bendel's Beauty floor recently installed a dentist, Dr. Daniel Rudolph, who also does tooth bonding. In addition to having their teeth cleaned (which is always in itself a big appearance improver), Day of Beauty clients get an exercise class, facial, hair consultation, full conditioning treatment, cut and styling, manicure, pedicure, make-up application and lunch for $195. Quite a package. It's also available on a six-hour basis for $145 minus the exercise class and with a less comprehensive conditioning treatment or on a four-hour basis for $100, including facial, hair consultation, cut and styling, make-up, manicure and lunch.

## FACE-LIFTS WITHOUT SURGERY

**M. J. Saffon,** 752-4195

If the face you see in the mirror has too many chins and wrinkles, the uplift you need may not be a face-lift. "Forget about surgery," says M. J. Saffon. "You can massage and exercise away your lines, wrinkles and sags...firm your neck, chin and shoulders" in just minutes a day. He should know. He's the author of two best-selling books on the subject, and his disciples have included Helen Gurley Brown, Princess Grace, Marlene Dietrich, Cher and the Duchess of Windsor. But you don't have to be rich and famous to discover Saffon's secrets. He gives a $50, six-hour seminar about once a month (it takes place on weekends) at various New York hotels in natural skin care and face-lifting without surgery. You'll learn preventive and corrective measures, how to maximize your skin care with the minimum amount of money, how to exercise and massage your lines away and how to make your own cosmetics and moisturizers, using herbs and natural ingredients. Call for details.

## MAKE-OVER MAGIC—GETTING IT/KEEPING IT

**Adrien Arpel**

You always look great when you step out of the salons—hair stunningly styled, make-up perfectly applied, skin glowing. It just never seems the same, though, when you do it yourself. With this problem in mind, Adrien Arpel recently introduced her Crash Beauty Course Clinics. They get you looking as good as you can, then teach you how to do it yourself. The forty-five minute clinics begin with a questionnaire to help gear your beauty regimen to your life-style. You're given a twelve-page workbook when you enroll, and as each beauty function is performed, personalized step-by-step instructions are detailed in it for mistakeproof use at home. You can take the crash course at any Saks or Bloomingdale's in the metropolitan area as well as at Macy's and Lord & Taylor in Manhattan. It costs about $20, and for an extra fee you can have your hair styled and get instruction on home hair care.

**Louis-Guy D,** 41 East 57th Street, between Park and Madison Avenues, 753-6077

Many of Louis Gignac's clients are models who have to redo their hair numerous times during shootings, but he believes that every woman should be able to recapture that fresh-from-the-salon look. To promote this self-sufficiency, he introduced a do-it-yourself styling bar at his salon. After your shampoo and cut at Louis-Guy D ($36 to $39), you have the option of sitting yourself down at a table equipped with blow dryers, styling brushes, electric combs, rollers, clips, etc. and doing your own hair under the expert guidance of your stylist. Not only do you learn to do it yourself, but you even save money because the fee is $7 less. The Louis-Guy D look is simple, natural, carefree and healthy.

**Beauty Checkers, at Henri Bendel,** 10 West 57th Street, off Fifth Avenue, fourth floor, 247-2829

Sit down for a make-up consultation in any salon, and you'll probably walk out with $100 worth of additional cosmetics, three-quarters of which you'll never use. Beauty Checkers has the sensible solution to cosmetic oversupply. When you come here for a make-up make-over, empty out that surplus drawer and bring everything in. Instead of dazzling you into buying everything fresh from its product line (it does have one), it'll work with your own stash. As for the lesson, it takes about an hour and costs just $20. You participate, copying on one side of your face what the instructor has done on the other. Notes are taken, and you receive colored-penciled illustrations showing you exactly what goes where. Lessons are by appointment, weekdays and alternate Saturdays.

**Vartali Salon,** 52 East 58th Street, between Madison and Park Avenues, 935-4640

The owner of this plush salon, Vartan Geudelekian, is famous for his haircuts and the kinds of make-overs you see in magazines. He did all the *Seventeen* make-overs for years, and Ford sends him all its new models for initial beauty work. This is where they attain that coveted New York high-fashion look. Both Vartan and his talented staff also do many movie and commercial shoots and coif numerous celebs, both men and women. They're concerned with bringing out your optimum beauty, regardless of current styles. A complete make-over will take in your hairstyle, possibly hair color (they're expert colorists) and make-up, and you'll get before-and-after Polaroid shots as a memento. It's a great place to send your teenage daughter so she can start looking her best at an early age—or send yourself; it's never too late to look great. The saloon often runs specials—call and ask for Vartan.

**Tomo n Tomo,** 229 East 60th Street, between Second and Third Avenues, 753-9640

Glamorous faces you see in Andy Warhol's *Interview*, on TV commercials and soap operas or on Zoli and Ford models, even the cover of *Gentlemen's Quarterly* (yes, this one is for men, too) are among the hair credits of Alan Adler, noted color director-stylist of the Tomo n Tomo salon. Though expert coloring is his specialty, Alan is also the perfect person to see when you're bored with your current look. He sees beyond the "blah" you to your greatest beauty potential, then manifests his vision while you relax in his chair, sipping sake (owner Tomo is Japanese). In choosing your hairstyle, he makes sure to take into account your life-style, including how much time and money you can afford to spend on your hair. While he's making you gorgeous, Alan will suggest changes in make-up (a consultation is free), clothing styles and accessories. His make-over stylings begin as low as $35. When he gets through with you, there's just one regret you may have: Why did you waste so many years not looking this beautiful?

## NAIL SALONS

**Moi Cosmetology Ltd.,** 38 East 63rd Street, between Madison and Park Avenues, 752-4447

The exquisitely turned-out nails of models in *Vogue* and other fashion mags are often manicured at Moi (pronounced Moy), and the salon is also frequented by many well-known actresses (Faye Dunaway, for one). If your nails are cracked and chipped, Moi will treat them, transform them and set you on the road to proper nail care and maintenance; if they're already in good shape, she'll enhance their beauty. In addition to all manicure services, you can have pedicures, facials and waxing done here.

## TRICHOLOGISTS/HAIR CARE

**Philip Kingsley, Trichologist/Hair Care,** 16 East 53rd Street, between Fifth and Madison Avenues, 735-9600

Anyone concerned about the condition of his or her hair or scalp should run to Philip Kingsley, a famous trichologist. People come here from all over the world for treatment and pampering of hair and scalp. For about $40 Mr. Kingsley will painstakingly examine your hair, take samples, go over your diet, nutrition and family hair history, develop an entire case history. Follow-up treatments are under $30.

**Michael's Children's Haircutting Salon,** 1263 Madison Avenue, between 90th and 91st Streets, 289-9612

Where do all the preppies meet? At Michael's, the "in" salon for the privileged private school set. It's totally child-oriented, including the mess. The barber seats are shaped like little cars or horses, there are comic books instead of magazines and lollipops are given out (you'd probably rather they weren't). The hairdressers, mostly flamboyant Italians, are specially trained in cutting children's hair and have a fund of stories to tell about Superman and Incredible Hulk during the clipping. They don't shampoo, just cut and style. You can bring in any child from a year old on up, even have your own hair cut here; at $10.50 it's a bargain. Special diplomas are given for first haircuts. Michael's is open Monday to Saturday from 9:00 A.M. to 5:00 P.M.; appointments are optional.

## BRIEF VACATIONS

What are you doing this weekend? You can't seriously be thinking of hanging around the house when you could be out fossil hunting, hiking the Appalachian Trail, running the rapids, antiquing, raspberry picking or attending a clambake. This section will acquaint you with sources for hundreds of fascinating day trips and in-town activities, excursions and longer holidays both in Manhattan and farther afield.

### ART TOURS

**Gallery Passport, Ltd.,** 1170 Broadway, New York, N.Y. 10001, 686-2244

If you want to penetrate the art scene but don't really know how to go about it, Gallery Passport is...well, your passport. The organization offers deluxe motor coach art tours throughout the tristate area. Groups take in gallery openings, visit art auction houses like Christie's and

Sotheby Parke Bernet, Soho and Tribeca lofts, private collections, designer showcases, historic homes, gardens and museums. Whatever is viewed is explained by lecturers with M.A.'s or Ph.D.'s in art history, some of whom write for major art magazines. Full-day tours, always including lunch, usually take place on Saturdays and are priced from about $50 to $70 per person. Recently Gallery Passport added overseas trips to its offerings. Call or write for a listing of the current schedule. It also has an excellent appraisal service.

## *ATLANTIC CITY—THE LUXURY BUS*

**Us on a Bus,** 758-0282

Maybe you'll break the bank in Atlantic City, and maybe you won't, but the least you can do is arrive and depart in style. Helene Levey's private air-conditioned motor coaches are the way to go. They transport twenty people in a luxurious living-room-like atmosphere, complete with upholstered sofas and lounge chairs, card tables, a stereo and color TV. A hostess is on board to welcome you. The bus takes off at 10:00 A.M., and breakfast (bagels with cream cheese and coffee) is served on board. Upon arrival (about 1:00 P.M.), you'll enjoy a buffet lunch in Atlantic City before hitting the casinos. And on the way back there's an open bar—drink to your winnings or drown your sorrows. The all-inclusive fee is $35, and pickups can be arranged in New York or New Jersey; reserve two weeks in advance. You can also rent the entire bus for a party with whatever extras you want supplied.

## *BED AND BREAKFAST ACCOMMODATIONS*

**The Bed & Breakfast League,** 2855 29th Street, NW, Washington, D.C. 20008, 202-232-8718

You've probably enjoyed bed and breakfast accommodations while traveling in Europe—a stay in a private home where guests meet for breakfast and conversation each morning in the dining room. This style of lodging is growing in the United States, and The Bed and Breakfast League has located numerous hosts offering such accommodations throughout the country and in Europe. As a member, you pay $15 a year for single, $25 a year for two. When you want to travel, call the league, and it'll tell you of available B & B options in the area you'll be visiting. All recommended accommodations have been carefully selected, and all are moderately priced—around $25 to $38 single, $30 to $42 double. Host members pay $50 a year and must meet the standards set by the league. Contact it if you'd like to join or become a B & B host.

## THE BEST BUS TOURS

**Biss Tours,** 426-4000

If you don't know what to do with your free time, give Biss Tours a ring and ask for the current catalog, listing hundreds of one-day, weekend and longer escorted motor coach tours departing from New York City. They're reasonably priced and extremely wide-ranging and innovative. One-day tours (via air-conditioned or heated luxury coach with a knowledgeable guide on board) include factory outlet shopping, a day of antiquing combined with a Sunday brunch buffet, square dancing at a ranch, a tour of a Pennsylvania coal mine with an all-you-can-eat Pennsylvania Dutch lunch and a ride on a narrow-gauge steam train, foliage and raspberry-picking tours, visits to farmers' markets, craft fairs and country auctions, a trip to Lost River Caverns in Pennsylvania with a clambake, winery tours, historic tours, festivals, even a mystery tour with destination unknown. Longer tours might take you to Canada, Virginia's Blue Ridge Mountains and Colonial Williamsburg, jashington, D.C., at cherry blossom time, Disney World or New Orleans. There's a lifetime of recreational activities in these catalogs.

## BRASS RUBBINGS AND ENGLISH TEA

**Church of the Resurrection Episcopal,** 115–119 East 74th Street, between Park and Lexington Avenues, 879-4320

Next time you're wondering what to do on a gloomy weekend, head over to the Church of the Resurrection Episcopal. Here every Saturday and Sunday from 2:00 to 5:00 P.M. (except in summer) people gather to learn the techniques of brass rubbing. The church houses about fifty facsimiles of English brass memorials—knights, ladies, merchants and heraldry—from the thirteenth to fifteenth century. It supplies you with all materials and provides instruction, and you'll take home a beautiful wall hanging of your own creation. The cost ranges from about $3.50 to $35, depending on the size of the memorial you rub. During the same hours a traditional English afternoon tea is served in the cozy lobby of the Parish House. Classical music is played in the background, and there's a choice of fine teas, along with buttery homemade scones with fresh cream and strawberry jam, Dundee cake, lemon curd tarts, Somerset seed cake, Chelsea buns, cucumber and watercress sandwiches, etc. A complete tea costs from $3.75 to $6. If you'd like to attend church services they're at 10:00 A.M. on Saturday and 11:00 A.M. on Sunday.

## CUT YOUR OWN CHRISTMAS TREE

Part of a traditional Christmas is cutting your own trees. In New York City you can get arrested for that, but if you write to F. E. Johnston, Jr., P.O. Box 4060, Princeton, N.J. 08540, enclosing a self-addressed, stamped envelope, he'll send a free list of New Jersey tree growers, complete with driving directions. You can wander through their lush, aromatic evergreen forests with your family on a crisp December day, choose and cut down your very own Christmas tree. Many of the farms also offer live trees with the roots embedded in balls of dirt and wrapped in burlap. When Christmas is over, you can plant them in your yard.

## FOLK DANCING

**Country Dance & Song Society of America,** 594-8833

This national society, devoted to the enjoyment, study and preservation of English and American traditional dance, song and music, has a group that meets regularly every Tuesday evening at the Metropolitan Duane Hall, 215 West 13th Street, year round except summer and holidays. Attend one of the sessions, and you might learn country dancing, English clogging, English Morris dancing or rapier sword dancing. It costs $3 for a 2½-hour session beginning at 8:00 P.M., $2.25 for full-time students; a series of nine sessions is $21, $17.50 for students. It's the cheapest date in town and lots of fun, too. The society also runs a summer camp called Pinewoods near Plymouth, Massachusetts, where adults can spend a week studying music and dance and enjoying outdoor activities. And call the society's Folk-Fone number, 594-6876, for a recorded listing of folk music events in New York City.

## FOSSIL TOURS

**Sidney Horenstein,** P.O. Box 11, Inwood Station, New York, N.Y. 10034, 569-5351

Did you know that there are 450-million-year-old snails embedded in the walls of some Manhattan buildings? Geologist Sidney Horenstein (he's on the staff of the American Museum of Natural history) will acquaint you with these and other fossils both in Manhattan and upstate New York. His tours visit old mines in the Bear Mountain region, city parks, the Palisades, even 42nd Street. Botany and other elements of natural history are also explored on these delightful and fascinating field trips. There are half-day and full-day excursions on various weekends throughout the year, the former priced at $4 per person, the latter at $7. Call or write for a schedule.

## HOME EXCHANGE VACATIONS

**Vacation Exchange Club,** 12006 111th Avenue, Unit 12, Youngtown, AZ 85363, 602-972-2186

You can eliminate one of the most expensive aspects of vacationing—the cost of accommodations—by joining the Vacation Exchange Club. Members have details about their homes published in *The Exchange Book*, which comes out twice a year, and can contact one another to arrange home exchanges. The book contains some 6,000 listings in countries all over the world—Greece, Australia, Hong Kong, all over the United States and Europe, Mexico, Kenya, Israel, the Bahamas, Canada, the Virgin Islands, in fact, almost anywhere you might think of going. Perhaps you'd like to exchange your New York apartment for an oceanfront condo in Honolulu, an Irish cottage or a villa in Spain. Many such are listed. The economic advantages go beyond the fortune you save on accommodations. You also avoid constant hotel tipping and save money on food by preparing as many meals as you like at home. Members often add to savings and benefits by exchanging cars, country club privileges, boats, etc. It's a great boon not only for vacations but for visiting out-of-town relatives and checking out an area you're thinking of moving to. You can get this year's directory for $15, be listed in next year's for $22.70. Write to the address above.

## LEARNING VACATIONS

For some the ideal vacation is lazing on the beach. Others want culture, mind expansion and intellectual enrichment. The latter should pick up a book called *Learning Vacations* by Gerson G. Eisenberg. It contains about 500 educational vacation options, running the gamut from a weekend studying wild flowers and medicinal plants in Kentucky to a one-week summer session at Johns Hopkins University in Maryland on "Geology: Chasms in Earth, Time and Perspective." There are natural history discovery tours of New Zealand, London theater and music programs, wildlife and ornithology safaris in Kenya, pottery and painting workshops, Spanish-language courses in Mexico, archaeological excavations and much, much more. If nothing else, the book makes stimulating reading on the beach. Order by sending $9.20 postpaid to Peterson's Guides, P.O. Box 2123, Princeton, N.J. 08540, 609-924-5338.

## LINCOLN CENTER TOURS

**Lincoln Center,** 877-1800, extension 512

It's fascinating to tour this renowned performing arts center and the stages on which the world's most distinguished performers appear. Lincoln Center Tours provides a behind-the-scenes visit to the Metropolitan Opera House, Avery Fisher Hall (home of the New York Philharmonic) and the New York State Theater, where the New York City Ballet and New York City Opera companies perform. Knowledgeable guides will acquaint you with the center's history and lore and take you through the auditoriums and lobby areas. You may even get to watch a rehearsal if one is going on during your visit. The hour-long tours take place several times daily except Christmas and New Year's between 10:00 A.M. and 5:00 P.M. Call the above number for the exact schedule on the day you're planning to visit. Adults pay $4.75; senior citizens and students, $4.25; children under twelve, $2.75. Prices subject to change.

You can also take a more comprehensive 1¾-hour tour called "Backstage at the Met." Visitors get to see the shops where more than 300 artisans and craftspeople design and produce the sets, costumes and wigs seen onstage, as well as the Met's rehearsal facilities, dressing rooms and the main stage set for the next scheduled performance. This tour is given weekdays at 3:30 P.M. and Saturday at 10:30 A.M. year round except August and September. It costs $5 for the general public, $3 for Opera Guild members and $2 for full-time students. To make reservations, call 582-3512, extension 219.

## LIVING LUXURIOUSLY ABROAD

**At Home Abroad,** 405 East 56th Street, apartment 6H, 421-9165

If you'd like to stay at a plush private home, sun-drenched villa or stately castle during your travels, let At Home Abroad locate the accommodation of your dreams. It'll provide you with a full detailed description and photographs of any of its personally inspected 2,000 or so properties around the world. These run the gamut from a fully equipped villa on the picturesque southern coast of Portugal to a small Tunisian marble-floored palace with an acre of gardens opening onto a white sand beach. Rates range from about $2,000 to $25,000 a month, depending on how luxurious the digs, often including services of a staff—maid, cook, housekeepers, baby-sitters, whatever. If you travel with friends, some of these places are less expensive per person than a first-class hotel.

A similar operation is **Villas International,** 213 East 38th Street, 685-4340, with more than 20,000 properties in Europe and the Caribbean.

## PICK YOUR OWN FRUITS AND VEGETABLES

**Menzel Brothers Farm and Farm Market,** Highway 34, Holmdel, N.J., 201-946-4135

A delightful day in the country for the entire family can center on a visit to Menzel Brothers Farm and Farm Market. Bring containers because at this farm you pick your own products. It's most fun from the first weekend in October through Halloween, when you can pick your own pumpkins and winter squash or dig mums (there are twenty varities). Since these fields are at the back of the farm, you reach them via a free scenic hayride, with the hay wagon attached to a tractor driven by a costumed driver (perhaps a clown or furry rabbit). Needless to say, kids love it, and with more than fifteen acres of pumpkins to choose from, you're sure to find the perfect one. To complete your fall decorations, Indian corn, dried flowers and gourds are available. The pick-your-own season actually begins in June; throughout that month you can select strawberries from forty acres grown strictly for guest picking. June crops also include spinach, string beans, broccoli, cauliflower, cabbage, peas, beets, kale, mustard and turnip greens. You can pick strawberries seven days a week, vegetables on weekends only. Menzel Brothers' roadside stand is open daily 9:00 A.M. to 6:00 P.M. from the beginning of July through the end of October, selling fresh vegetables and fruit. August is plum-tomato-picking time for people interested in canning; you must pick a minimum of ten pounds. Bushel quantities of vegetables for freezing and canning are also sold at greatly reduced prices from August through September. The farm is just forty-five minutes from Manhattan. Prices are, of course, much lower than in the city, and everything is fresh and delicious—doubly so when you've picked it yourself. To get there, take the Garden State Parkway to Exit 11, travel Route 9 to Highway 34 and go about eight miles.

**Mr. Apples,** High Falls, N.Y., 914-687-9498

Stroll through fragrant orchards and pick your own apples (there are fifteen varieties) and pears at Mr. Apples. The season begins the second week in August and runs through mid-November. There's also a farm produce stand on the premises where you can buy already-picked apples, pears, peaches and plums as well as fresh eggs, vegetables, apple and pear cider, cider vinegar, raw honey, stone-ground cereals and such. You can bring a picnic lunch to enjoy on the grass, though there are also two very nice restaurants close by—the Canal House and Top of the Falls. After lunch you can view the falls, visit the Delaware and Hudson Canal Historical Society Museum and, if it's a Sunday, peruse the merchandise at a large outdoor flea market. To get to Mr. Apples, take Exit 18 off the New York State Thruway (New Paltz), Route 32 to Rosendale, then go three miles west on Route 213.

## UNUSUAL OUTINGS

**Adventure on a Shoestring,** 300 West 53rd Street, 265-2663

Here's a way to meet new people, widen your horizons, enjoy many fascinating outings and spend very little money doing it. Adventure on a Shoestring organizes about five innovative outings a week for its members. These might include attendance at a taping of a TV talk show; a reading at a professional playwrights' workshop, preceded by coffee and cake; lessons in juggling, flamenco dancing, Japanese sword fighting, handwriting analysis, etc.; a three-hour harbor cruise on a seventy-foot sailing yacht; a chat with a vampire researcher, a hypnotist, a lie detector expert or a psychiatrist who specializes in body language; a tour of a yogurt factory; a walking tour of the historic Astor Place area; a visit to an artist's studio and hundreds of other equally interesting activities. The organization has more than 2,000 members. If you'd like to become a Shoestringer, it costs $35 a year to join plus a $3 attendance fee at most events. There are occasional additional fees for theater performances, helicopter rides and other frills, but these are usually at a group-discounted rate. Members receive a schedule of upcoming events every three months.

## WALKING TOURS

**Municipal Art Society,** 457 Madison Avenue, 935-3969

Even if you've lived here all your life, you'll "discover" New York on walking tours sponsored by the Municipal Art Society. These delightful and informative walks visit the Financial District, the Upper West Side, Brooklyn Heights, the Village (East or West), upper Fifth Avenue, South Street Seaport and other districts. The society's guides are well versed in the architecture, lore, cultural life and history of the neighborhoods you're exploring. Most of the walks are three hours in duration and take place on Sundays between May and October. It's a pleasant way to spend an afternoon, meet other people and learn something about the city we live in. Tours cost $8, $6 for members of the Municipal Art Society. In addition to the above-mentioned, there's a free one-hour tour of Grand Central Terminal every Wednesday year round at 12:30 P.M. that unveils the details of that Beaux Arts masterpiece. You can call the above number for information twenty-four hours a day.

## CITY GARDENING

Almost all New Yorkers garden, at least to the extent of tending an asparagus fern or spider plant on the windowsill. There are also countless roof gardens, window boxes, unseen-from-the-street brownstone backyards, terrace gardens and greenhouses throughout the city, and here and there you'll find frustrated farmers growing tomatoes on fire escapes or a few stalks of corn in the small patch of earth around a street tree. Herewith a few suggestions for green-thumbing in Gotham.

**Bonsai Dynasty Co., Inc.,** 851 Avenue of the Americas, at 30th Street, 695-2973

A wholesale-retail operation, Bonsai Dynasty specializes in bonsai dwarf trees from China and Japan and everything related to them—all the necessary materials, tools, special soil and pots, seeds to grow them from scratch, how-to books, even a bonsai kit with everything you need to grow your own. The selection, the largest in the Northeast, includes cypresses, elms, junipers, pines, gingkos, maples that change color with the season, flowering and fruit-bearing varieties—in fact, almost as many kinds as there are trees. Though generally bonsais are for outdoors, Bonsai Dynasty has a great many that were cultivated for indoor apartment living. They range in price from about $15 to $500, with the majority under $100. Open weekdays 8:30 A.M. to 6:00 P.M., Saturday 9:30 A.M. to 5:00 P.M., Sunday (except summer) 11:00 A.M. to 5:00 P.M.

**Farm and Garden Nursery,** 2 Avenue of the Americas, between White and Walker Streets, 431-3577

Three blocks below Canal Street, Farm and Garden is a one-stop garden shop for every kind of outdoor planting. It sells thousands of plants, small trees and bushes—begonias, zinnias, petunias, marigolds, daisies, snapdragons, eight varieties of scented geraniums and more than eighty kinds of potted herbs, berry bushes, rose bushes, evergreens, Japanese boxwoods, even bamboos. And of course, there's a full range of insecticides, fertilizers, garden hoses, planters, window boxes, seeds, plant lights, gravel, gardening tools, flower pots, you name it. Open daily from 9:00 A.M. to 6:00 P.M., Sunday 11:00 A.M. to 5:00 P.M. Closed winter Mondays.

**Maggy Geiger,** 686-5382

Maggy Geiger is the window box lady. If you already have window boxes, you can call her in for consultation on ailing plants and other troubles (she makes house calls). Or you can have her design a window box to your specifications. She uses redwood, chrome or terra-cotta containers, does all the planting, makes sure the lighting is right, foresees seasonal changes, handles installation and remedies any problems that come along. All you have to do is the watering. The service ranges from about $100, including installation.

Maggy also does exquisite flower arrangements (she's at the flower market each morning at four-thirty, selecting fresh flowers for the day) for parties or general enhancement of your home. A mixed bouquet is about $35 plus delivery (that's for one major stunning bouquet and three or four smaller arrangements). Clients are billed on a monthly basis.

Finally, she works as a landscaper for small terraces and gardens.

**Manhattan Gardener,** 316 East 92nd Street, between First and Second Avenues, 410-0900

"You'll feel better if you treat yourself to a garden," says Ron-Dean Taffel, the Manhattan Gardener. He's been making green things grow amid steel and concrete for almost thirty years and can plan or plant a roof or terrace garden for you, do indoor gardens with tropical plants and waterfalls, backyards and front yards, Japanese gardens, American gardens, English gardens and lovely window boxes. He also does cut flowers and flowering plants for parties (arrangements of the latter can be used beautifully for decoration, and you get to keep the plants afterward) and sells garden supplies, handmade terra-cotta Italian flower pots and planters as well as hard-to-find fertilizers. Ron travels to the suburbs too, and especially to the Hamptons. Call for an appointment.

**Green Guerillas,** 417 Lafayette Street, between Fourth Street and Astor Place, 674-8124

Green Guerillas is a group of more than 100 volunteers who help create and support community gardens in any area of the city. Their activities include planting street trees and caring for them; providing information to groups who are planning rooftop gardens; helping communities design and develop play lots, gardens, street plantings, recycling centers, dog runs and other open-space projects; and giving practical advice about all kinds of community gardening. Their aim is the greening of New York, and with that in mind, they give away $25,000 worth of plants each year to community groups. They also give free workshops in various aspects of gardening and can tell you how to get permission to plant a neighborhood lot. If you and your neighbors would like to see more green spaces, formulate a greening project and contact the Green Guerillas for help. Its assistance is free.

**The Grow Truck,** Council on the Environment, 51 Chambers Street, New York, N.Y. 10007, 566-0990

The Grow Truck is a way of aiding and encouraging community

groups that are involved in gardening projects in the five boroughs—especially people who are converting small vacant lots into gardens and parks in low-income neighborhoods. It delivers garden tools (on loan), supplies information and other assistance and, under the Plant-a-Lot program, provides free soil, plants, trees and shrubs to eligible groups. If you have an eyesore lot that is filled with rubble in your area and can organize a community group to turn it into a garden, write to the Council on the Environment for a Plant-a-Lot application and full details. Also inquire about the council's other services to encourage the greening of New York.

**The Plant Watcher,** 286-9423
I always feel it's a bit of an imposition asking friends or neighbors to water plants when I go away, especially over a long period of time. Fortunately it's no longer necessary to seek such favors. The Plant Watcher, an environmentally controlled umbrella terrarium, can keep your plants moist and healthy for up to ten weeks without watering. It also provides the perfect conditions for nurturing seedlings and cuttings. Easy to use and store, it comes in three sizes: 24 by 24 inches ($16); 30 by 30 inches ($20); and 36 by 36 inches ($24). Call for details on ordering.

## DRY CLEANERS, LAUNDRIES, TAILORS AND DYERS

There's a dry cleaner and Chinese laundry every third block in New York, and tailors abound. With the exception of clothes dyers, the following are not in the hard-to-find category. They're the elite, offering special services and special care. Note: For cleaning down garments and camping wear, don't forget Greenman's Down East (see Repairers, Restylers and Restorers, pp. 224–236).

### *DRY CLEANING*

**Gusenburger Pick-up and Delivery,** RH 4-2624
For more than thirty years the Gusenburger family has been taking care of the dry-cleaning needs of New York's spottiest citizens. Actually their spotter is famous in the industry. If you have a silk, sequined or beaded dress, you'll be in good hands. Everything is done by hand, and prices are fair for such reliable expert service. Call for pickup.

**Jeeves of Belgravia,** 770 Madison Avenue, at 66th Street, 674-7704

Named for Wodehouse's more than perfect valet, Jeeves, this deluxe clothes care center (to call it a dry cleaner would be much too plebeian) is the New York branch of a London-based establishment in posh Belgravia. So prestigious is the London Jeeves that clients have included both Margaret Thatcher and Princess Margaret, Prince Charles and Princess Diana, not to mention rock luminaries like Rod Stewart. If you can afford the luxury, you can join New York's glitterati who also have their Guccis, Halstons and Armanis perfectly valeted by Jeeves. It offers free pickup and delivery throughout Manhattan and pampers you and your wardrobe with the highest-quality personalized care. Jeeves offers hand laundering, alterations and expert tailoring, does repairs on leather, suede, furs and rugs and takes on the toughest stains. Send Jeeves your clothes in a suitcase, and they'll be returned cleaned and packed in tissue; when you arrive at your destination, nothing will be wrinkled. If you're moving, have Jeeves take your entire wardrobe, clean it and deliver it to your new address. It can even take fire-damaged clothes that are permeated with smoke odor and restore them to perfect condition. Is it expensive? You bet, but if you've spilled champagne on your new Perry Ellis creation, it's cheaper than buying another one. Open weekdays 8:30 A.M. to 5:30 P.M., Saturday to 1:00 P.M.

## *DYEING*

**Perry Process Cleaners & Dyers,** 1050 Avenue of the Americas, between 39th and 40th Streets, 730-0220

Dyeing clothing is a risky business, and as a result, it's almost impossible to find anyone willing to do it. According to Perry Process's owner, Seth Needleman, all dyeing must be done at the customer's risk, but it usually comes out fine. It's easiest to dye natural fibers, and you must go to a darker color. Perry Process has to examine a garment to know if it's a reasonable candidate for the dyeing process. Any defect in manufacturing will show up in the dyeing, and though there is an immense choice of colors, color accuracy cannot be guaranteed 100%. Prices begin at about $20 for a pair of pants or a blouse, $25 to $30 for a dress, $45 for a suit. On the other hand, I had Perry Process dye two blouses for me (a white silk and a beige polyester, both too easily stained), and they came out fine; I've been wearing them for years. Open weekdays 8:00 A.M. to 6:30 P.M.

**Lido Cleaners,** 990 First Avenue, between 54th and 55th Streets, 688-6789

Like Perry Process, Lido will dye most any fabric any color, but owner Dave Epstein also stresses the caveats. In addition to doing dyework, Lido is renowned as a dry cleaner; it's a good place to send your delicate garments or suede and leather items. Open weekdays 8:00 A.M. to 6:00 P.M., Saturday 8:00 A.M. to 1:00 P.M.

**Gothic Color Company, Inc.,** 727 Washington Street, between Bank and 11th Streets, 929-7493

Irving Goldman, president of Gothic Color, claims that any fabric can be dyed successfully if it is done properly, but then he does leave the risk element to you. Gothic sells every possible color of dye for batikwork and do-it-yourselfers and explains thoroughly which dyes work on any given fabric, what materials you'll need and how to do it. Open 8:30 A.M. to 5:00 P.M. weekdays. Good luck!

## HAND LAUNDERING

**Mme. Blanchevoye,** 75 East 130th Street, 368-7272

Delicate items deserve the special handling they get at Mme. Blanchevoye. Send your fancy tablecloths, your negligees, your silk hankies and fine linens and whatever else needs careful hand laundering and finishing. Unlike most laundries, Mme. Blanchevoye leaves no visible markings on your things and offers two-day service. Of course, you're not going to traipse up to 130th Street with your laundry, so pickup and delivery are free. Open weekdays 7:30 A.M. to 6:00 P.M.

## LEATHER AND SUEDE CLEANING, REPAIRING AND RESTORING

**Leathercraft Process of America,** 62 West 37th Street, between Fifth and Sixth Avenues, 586-3737

For more than seventy years Leathercraft has been in the business of cleaning and repairing leather, suede and sheepskin coats, jackets, boots, shoes, bags and clothing. All kinds of alterations—lengthening, shortening, etc.—are within its scope. It can't dye suede or leather, but it can restore the original color to its former vibrancy. Open Monday to Friday 9:00 A.M. to 6:00 P.M., Saturday 10:00 A.M. to 1:45 P.M. (closed Saturday July and August).

## MENDING AND TAILORING

**Magic Menders,** 118 East 59th Street, 759-6453

Magic Menders can restore it to its former state. The firm specializes in reweaving and reknitting tears, damages, moth holes and such, and it can match any fabric or sweater, but that's just one of its numerous services. Others include: fine French dry cleaning done by hand with special expertise on unusual spots and stains; glove cleaning and repairing (torn seams are sewn up); alterations and repairs on men's shirts (it's cheaper to replace a frayed collar and cuffs than to buy a new shirt); necktie cleaning and restyling; excellent suede and leather cleaning; handbag repairs (stitching, locks, relining, new zippers, glazing); umbrella repairs, even re-covering of old frames; monogramming on linens, towels, wearing apparel, etc.; and dressmaking, restyling and alterations. Open Monday to Friday 9:00 A.M. to 4:45 P.M.

The same service is offered by **Alice Zotta,** 2 West 45th Street, at Fifth Avenue, room 1504, 840-7657. Her prices are more than fair. Open Monday to Friday 8:00 A.M. to 6:00 P.M., Saturday to 2:00 P.M.

# EXPERTS AND CONSULTANTS

They do it all for you or tell you how to do it. In this section you'll find researchers, interior designers, people who help you move, do your shopping, organize your desk, tell you how to dress and do almost anything else you want done or need done and don't have time or the inclination to do yourself.

## ANTIQUE APPRAISALS

There may be items in your house—things you're so used to you never think about them—that are actually worth a good deal of money. Furniture, jewelry, coins, china, crystal and such could be valuable. Look around. If you think you've got something worthwhile, contact one of New York's leading auction galleries for a free appraisal. Don't just walk in off the street, though, with a chiffonier on your back. Call first and make an appointment with the department in which you're interested. If the item is too large to carry in, a photo, plus as much detailed information as possible, will do. You can also do the entire thing by sending the photo and details in the mail. Try any of the following galleries: **Sotheby Parke Bernet,** 1334 York Avenue, at 72nd Street, New York, N.Y. 10021, 472-3400; **Christie's,** 502 Park Avenue, at 59th Street, New York, N.Y. 10022, 546-1000; **Phillips,** 406 East 79th Street, between First and York Avenues, New York, N.Y. 10021, 570-4830.

## CONTRACTORS

**Decorators Contracting Service,** 424 Amsterdam Avenue, 873-5313

Decorators Contracting Service's talented tradespeople create many of New York's most chic interiors, from Park Avenue coops to Greenwich Village townhouses to Soho lofts. Owner Leonard Gleich has chosen his people with meticulous care; they're the best. They can smooth out your bumpy walls; paint, glaze or paper them perfectly; sand, finish and stencil your floors; install or renovate kitchens and bathrooms; do carpentry, electrical wiring and decorative finishes; and install new windows. Gleich is a master at organizing the work so that each job is done exactly on schedule, in its proper sequence and to your desired specifications. Call for a free estimate.

## IMAGE CONSULTANTS

**New Image,** 757-3794 or 749-6610

Emily Cho and Neila Fisher want to bring you out of the closet—your clothes closet, that is—with a new image and a well-chosen wardrobe that reflects the real you, upgrades your appearance and creates the effect you desire. The metamorphosis begins when one of them visits your home and goes through your closets to find out what is salvageable. You discuss image and life-style, your figure hang-ups (big tush?) and your budget. Having assimilated your psyche, Emily or Neila then becomes your alter ego (you stay home) as she scours New York's shops and sets aside outfits with you in mind. The next day you accompany one of them on a shopping spree and make the final decisions. They'll also recommend "whatever you select has to be 'to die from,'" says Emily. "You'll look great in everything and feel free and comfortable." The service costs about $450 to $600 (plus at least $1,200 for a season's wardrobe).

Interested in a new image, but can't afford Emily and Neila's fees? Send $26.95 c/o Emily Cho, P.O. Box 1594, Cathedral Station, New York, N.Y., 10025 for a wide-ranging and comprehensive questionnaire, fill it out and within five weeks they'll send you a personalized written wardrobe report—complete with clothing illustrations—relevant to your personality, body and life-style.

## Interior Designers

**John Fulop Associates,** Architects, 181 Mott Street, 431-9431

A small but prestigious design-oriented firm, John Fulop Associates carefully assesses your visions and images in order to create the interior of your dreams. "Instead of imposing our concepts," says Fulop, "we listen very hard to our clients and help them visualize what they want." The firm works within a variety of budgetary requirements and is energy-conservation-conscious. Fulop has designed numerous interiors for brownstones, lofts and homes throughout the metropolitan area and as far afield as Paris.

## MOVING CONSULTANTS

**M.O.V.E. (Moves Organized Very Easily),** 243-8798

Just the thought of having to move makes me want to curl up in bed with a good escapist novel. Packing, organizing, throwing things out, having members of the family retrieve them—they're overwhelming. But if you do have to move, you can take most of the trauma out of it by hiring M.O.V.E.'s Priscilla McCullough, a moving consultant. She'll do all your packing with loving care and label it all neatly for easy unpacking. She'll help you clean out closets and cabinets, get moving boxes for half price, recommend a mover, if necessary, and unpack for you when you arrive at your new home. All your valuables and fragile collectibles will be given special attention. You can hire her to help or to do the entire job. Her fee is $15 an hour, and she'll go anywhere.

**United Van Lines' Bette Malone Consumer Services Center,** 800-325-3870

People faced with a move should know about this unique service of United Van Lines. With a toll-free information number, it is staffed by professional moving consultants who will provide relocation assistance and answer your moving-related questions. Calling United Van puts you under no obligation to use its moving service. If it can't answer your question immediately (people have called with the likes of "Can you get baby bottles in Saudi Arabia?"), it'll have the answer in the mail in a few days. It'll also send you, upon request, an informative free brochure called *Answers to Questions About Moving*. In addition, it publishes and offers, free of charge, a group of fact sheets that provide details about every major U.S. city and some smaller towns and international destinations. These deal with subjects like geography, climate, government, culture, commerce and industry, food, housing—really the works. Call weekdays 9:00 A.M. to 6:00 P.M.

**Consumer News, Inc.,** 813 National Press Building, Washington, D.C. 20045

Consumer News, Inc. is an independent, nongovernment organization dedicated to making the buyer beware. Its sixteen-page booklet *A Shopper's Guide to Choosing a Mover* tells you how the government rates professional household moving companies on the basis of customer complaints and annual Interstate Commerce Commission performance reports. It also gives many suggestions on how to choose a mover. To order, send $2 to the above address.

## *SHOPPERS, GIFT BROKERS AND PEOPLE WHO WILL DO ANYTHING AT ALL*

**Creative Resources,** 114 East 72nd Street, between Park and Lexington Avenues, 794-2161

If you constantly forget birthdays and anniversaries, turn all your annual gift-buying occasions over to Janey Klein. She specializes in devising unusual and distinctive one-of-a-kind gifts. To have her handle your Christmas shopping is a joy. You can tell her what to buy or leave it in her very capable hands. She knows where to get just about everything wholesale and has her own stable of artisans. Among her innovative gifts are themed baskets—e.g., a kitchen basket (lovely dishcloths, mitts, utensils, a cookbook and a houseplant). Janey gets them beautifully wrapped and sends them off for you. Clients usually pay a fee of about 20% above the cost of the gifts plus postage. Janey's "creative resources" extend to every kind of service. In the past she's planned surprise parties for clients, scouted apartments, arranged for shiatsu massage, Rolls limos, tarot card readings and breakfasts in bed. And once she even set up a hotel room for a romantic tryst, complete with caviar, champagne and flowers. If you can imagine it, Janey can do it, and if you can't imagine it, she can.

**Gift Brokers, Inc.,** P.O. Box 701, Gracie Station, N.Y., 10028 749-6610

Similar to the above, but specializing in gifts only, is Gift Brokers, run by Kathleen Bastis. She'll take the time to locate hard-to-find items, especially one-of-a-kind and limited editions, arts and crafts, come up with unique gift ideas and suggestions and deliver presents on the right day in stunning wrappings, and all at a discount. Most of her work is corporate, but she'll also take on individual clients.

**Bear Essentials,** 60-15 Hewlitt Street, Little Neck, N.Y. 11362, 224-3150

Gifts that make a child's eyes light up often originate at Bear Essentials, where owner Sherri Kenner has the perfect solution to all your present-purchasing problems. For birthdays, Valentine's Day, Christmas, camp gifts, hospital gifts, for no occasion or any occasion, Sherri puts together imaginative, toy-filled packages that are geared to a child's special skills and interests and are festively wrapped in colored cellophane with ribbons, bows and stickers. Every package contains four to ten items packed in baskets or other kid-usable containers— e.g., a strawberry shortcake wastebasket. Sherri's New Jersey warehouse is chock-a-block with toys, so she can easily "theme" the package to suit your child's fixations (Dukes of Hazzard, Disney or Sesame Street characters, art supplies, etc.); a catalog is available. Packages for newborns are super-popular; they contain developmental toys to help Baby discover the world and develop his or her senses, as well as gifts for Mom. Bear Essentials will ship anywhere in the world. Packages begin at about $20.

**Mouthpiece,** 511 East 20th Street, 677-1772

Donna Kennedy has made a profession out of chutzpah. If you don't care to take assertiveness training, Donna will fight the battles and deal with the hassles you're too timid—or busy—to handle yourself. She'll argue with the phone company or Con Ed for you, return unwanted gifts or damaged merchandise (even to Gucci!), straighten out your magazine subscription problems (she doesn't mind arguing with a computer), have your tennis racket restrung or wait on long lines for concert tickets. "I complain better than anyone else," says Donna, but she does other chores as well. In fact, she'll take on just about anything except settling personal disputes. She's comparison-shopped, Christmas-shopped, scouted apartments and houses, helped complete a silver service, driven people to the airport and to driving tests, planned parties and provided models, secretaries and other personnel. Fees are based on the amount of time and difficulty involved in any given job.

See also **Lend-a-Hand,** listed under Household Cleaning in this section (p. 176).

**Let Millie Do It!,** 532-8775

Millie Emory is a professional organizer, but that doesn't mean she spends her time inciting labor to riot. What she organizes is your life. If your closets are overflowing with items you haven't used in years and you haven't filed your income tax since 1975, it's time to give her a call. She'll either set you on the road to self-organization or come in on a regular basis to keep things from getting out of hand. In addition to organizing homes and offices (the latter might include setting up systems, finding and/or training employees, doing confidential work, etc.), Millie is a veritable Jill-of-all-trades who will take on any job, large or small, as long as it's legal and moral. Past assignments have included house-sitting (loving care to plants and pets); conducting garage sales; finding a rare Mexican dish for Anthony Quinn; supervising moving, house and apartment hunting; taking kids to the doctor; research of all kinds; holiday shopping; bidding in place of celebrities at auctions; meeting people at the airport; selecting contestants for a TV game show. Her rates are about $25 an hour, with a three-hour minimum, a bit higher for corporate work.

Another "life organizer," **Stephanie Winston,** 533-8860, works only with businesses. Founder of the Organizing Principle, a consulting firm, she has written a book on the subject for the general public called *Getting Organized: The Easy Way to Put Your Life in Order* (Warner Books). It deals with every aspect of getting your act together: managing time and paper work, setting up your desk area, financial planning, storage and closet space, books and records, the kitchen, bathroom, bedroom, workroom, even teaching your children to organize. She also has another book called *The Organized Executive* (Norton). If you feel your mess is beyond the pale, take heart: Stephanie claims she has never encountered a situation so complex that it could not be unraveled.

You can take a course called **"How to Get Organized"** at the New School (741-5690). Taught by a pro in the field, Ronni Eisenberg, it is designed to help you eliminate unnecessary everyday chaos and allow you more time for success in achieving personal goals. Among the topics covered are procrastination, defining priorities, setting goals, scheduling your time and the handling and filing of papers. You know if you need it.

## WRITERS AND RESEARCHERS

**Marshe InfoService, Inc.,** P.O. Box 207, Roslyn, N.Y. 11576, 516-627-3127, 516-826-4261

If you're writing a murder mystery and want to know about untraceable poisons, need to locate an out-of-print textbook, want to check out job opportunities in other countries or need help tracing your family roots, get in touch with Marshe librarians Marilyn Stern and Sherry Powell. They'll ferret out the information you need, be it obvious or obscure, and present it to you in a concise, easy-to-read format. Fees vary with the project, averaging about $35 an hour. In addition to research, Stern and Powell can organize libraries. And in 1980 they compiled a directory of hot line numbers in the five boroughs, Westchester, Nassau and Suffolk counties called *Help in a Hurry*. It's a handy (and possibly lifesaving) little publication that tells you whom to contact in a wide range of emergency situations—battered women, alcohol, drug and psychiatric problems, poison, rape, suicide, etc.—while providing useful information on financial aid to students, parenting, weight control and suchlike. To order, send $1.50 plus tax to the above address.

**American Society of Journalists and Authors, Inc.,** 1501 Broadway, suite 1907, New York, N.Y. 10036, 997-0947

If you need to hire a free-lance writer, editor, researcher or speech writer, you should know about ASJA. A nationwide organization of independent nonfiction writers, ASJA offers a referral service called Dial-a-Writer (398-1934). Listed writers can do articles, books, brochures, annual reports, speeches, TV and film scripts, advertising copy, press releases—anything written, in fact. So if you know you've got the concept for a best seller or dynamite screenplay but can't write, get yourself a writer. There's usually a search fee of $25, after which you negotiate with the writer.

**For Your Information,** 310 Madison Avenue, 661-4730

Many major publishing houses, writers and professionals use the computer and research capabilities of For Your Information. If you are a business without a library or research person, if you are involved in a job hunt and need pertinent information about an industry or company, its strengths, its problems; if you are writing a book and need expertise, you might well take advantage of this service. Talented duo Naomi Bernstein and Pat Bear will scour libraries and publications in their constant quest for hard-to-find information. Their prices are fair, and their track record is excellent.

## MISCELLANEOUS SERVICES

The rest of the uncategorized best, listed alphabetically.

### Baby-sitters

**P/T Child Care, Inc.,** 19 East 69th Street, 879-4343

P/T has been providing New York moms and dads with baby-sitters and temporary live-in nannies and governesses since the days when Mom and Dad might have had nannies themselves. The employees are very carefully checked out, and many have been accepting P/T positions for ten years or more. Though often the agency can provide someone on a same-day basis, it makes sense to call at least a week ahead, especially if you're going away for a weekend or longer (maximum is three weeks). Rates at this writing are about $4 an hour for one child, a bit more for each extra child or a child under three months. There's a four-hour minimum, a fee of 12% and a maximum carfare charge of $3 during the day, $4 in the evening. If you'd like to give Baby a three-week course in a foreign language while you're on vacation, P/T will try to provide a bilingual nanny.

**New York University Student Employment Office,** 598-2971

When you call this office, your listing gets posted on a job bulletin board which students constantly check out in hopes of employment. There's no screening done, but you, of course, meet the student applicant and can make your own decision. You just might find the sitter of your dreams, the perfect mother's helper to take along to Martha's Vineyard this summer or even someone to live in and take care of the kids. There's no fee to the agency, and you can work out any mutually acceptable financial arrangement with the student. Open Monday, Thursday and Friday 9:00 A.M. to 5:00 P.M., Tuesday and Wednesday to 6:30 P.M. all year.

## Dating Service

**People Resources, Inc.,** 30 West 57th Street, 765-7770

Tired of the bar scene? People Resources, a one-step service for singles, brings people together via video introductions. It's a class act—it advertises only in the *New York Times* and *New York* magazine, and participants are carefully screened. If selected, you make a videotape about yourself and the kind of person you'd like to meet. Then you view other tapes. If you'd like to meet someone you've seen on the screen, he or she is alerted and comes in to view your tape. When the feeling is mutual, a meeting is arranged. Members also get to attend People Resources' numerous seminars, parties, lectures and workshops and to use the Living Yellow Pages—a professional video library of members' services. You can choose to avail yourself of all, or just some (even only activities), of People Resources' offerings. Call for details.

## Diet Food Delivery

**Skinny Dip,** 1395 Second Avenue, between 72nd and 73rd Streets, 570-6926

Hot news! You *can* pig out on cookies (yes, I mean eating twenty or thirty of them) and not even go off your diet—if you buy cookies at Skinny Dip, where they have only 5½ calories each. They're scrumptious, too—especially the chewy chocolate meringues. Barbara Haroche, owner of this low-calorie food emporium, may be the best friend any dieter ever had. Not only does she make 5½-calorie cookies, but she features a complete line of gourmet diet foods prepared by a French chef. Everything she sells is fresh (including all vegetables), prepared right on the premises, labeled as to calorie count. You can go in and shop for a variety of low-cal treats (like the 110-calorie apple strudel) or have complete meals of your own or Skinny Dip's devising sent to your home. If you want to lose weight fast, opt for Barbara's five-day 700-calorie-a-day plan. You can pick up the five days of food or have it delivered (all at once). A typical day of this diet begins with a breakfast of a half grapefruit, a wedge of cheese and a breadstick; for lunch, chicken salad, green bean salad, two breadsticks and a fruit mousse; dinner: chicken parmigiana, zucchini delight and ice cream cake. There's also a daily snack such as chocolate cream cheese pie. The entire five days' food costs $60, plus a delivery fee ($1.75 to $5, depending on where you live; Manhattan only). Barbara has other planned diets at higher-calorie counts and plenty of sound dieting advice (e.g., "Buy your dishes at F.A.O. Schwarz"). Open weekdays 11:00 A.M. to 8:00 P.M., Saturday to 7:00 P.M. Gift certificates are available.

## *Divorce and Will Kits—Do It Yourself*

**Divorce Yourself,** 10 East 39th Street, room 504, 986-3300

A lawyer might charge $1,000 for an uncontested divorce, but if you and your soon-to-be-ex can agree on all the thorny issues—custody, alimony, child support, property division, visitation, etc.—you don't have to go broke to break up. In a month or less, for a little more than $200 (including court costs), you can take care of the entire business yourself, using Dale Robbins's Divorce Yourself Kit. No legal knowledge or special aptitude is required. The kit contains separate envelopes, each with complete instructions, work sheets and necessary legal forms—all designed at a grade-school level. Robbins will be happy to answer any questions you have at any step of the procedure. It's all perfectly legal. The only danger is, working closely with your mate on the kit, you just might get back together again. Robbins also offers do-it-yourself legal separations (once again for about a fifth of what a lawyer would charge) and sells a Will Kit for $7.50. Call for an appointment.

## Fireplace and Heating Stove Installation and Renovation

**Welles Fireplace Company,** 287 East Houston Street, between Clinton and Suffolk Streets, 777-5440

At Welles a staff of fully insured and licensed fireplace specialists offers a full range of services. They design and install both traditional-style and contemporary fireplaces and renovate defunct ones. The latter involves more than cosmetic work, as many people have found out to their chagrin. Close to 30% of Welles's work is redoing incorrectly done cosmetic renovations. This often involves tearing up walls, having to refinish floors and other expensive headaches. Better to employ Welles's experts in the first place. They foresee all possible complexities—safety factors, wind conditions, energy considerations, etc.—at the outset. Specific and thorough estimates are given, and all work is done in compliance with local building codes. Costs begin at about $5,000 for a new fireplace on the top floor of a loft or in a house. Other Welles services include installing dampers, glass doors and mantels, lining flues, chimney maintenance and decorative brickwork. Call for an appointment.

**The Alternative Heat Company,** 63 Fourth Avenue, near Bergen Street, Brooklyn, 596-0493

With the cost of home heating rising each year, this may be the time to consider options other than fuel oil. That's the specialty of Alternative Heat. According to owner Tom Godfrey, wood and coal stoves (legal in New York City, by the way) pay for themselves in the first year as a result of cost saving. His company sells and installs the stoves, including the beautiful French Petit Godin (designed in 1889) and the Norwegian Jotul, the Mercedes of coal stoves. It also builds, designs, maintains and renovates fireplaces and stoves, builds and cleans chimney systems, restores marble mantels and delivers coal and firewood. Stoves and fireplaces are on display in the Brooklyn showroom. Call for an appointment.

## Flagmakers

**Valley Forge Flag Company,** 1 Rockefeller Plaza, 586-1776

For three generations the "skilled American workers" at Valley Forge have been hand-sewing flags, using only the best-quality weather-resistant fabrics. In addition to American flags in all sizes, they make up state and territorial flags, Confederate flags, historic flags (including Betsy Ross replicas), religious flags, parade flags, logo flags, golf flags, foreign flags, drill team flags, yacht flags, pennants and banners, and they carry every imaginable flag accessory (poles, ornaments, rods, rain covers, you name it). They can design a flag to your specifications (allow at least four weeks). Open weekdays 9:00 A.M. to 5:00 P.M.

## Florists

**Rialto Florists, Inc.,** 707 Lexington Avenue, between 57th and 58th Streets, 688-3234

Rialto is open twenty-four hours a day, and though exactly why you should need flowers at 3:00 A.M. is open to fanciful conjecture (fight with your spouse, games in the graveyard?), if the need should arise, you now know where to go. Just because the service operates almost without competition doesn't mean the selection is limited either. Regardless of the season, Rialto features an immense selection—everything from anemones to zinnias—of good-quality flowers as well as artificial flowers and flowering and green plants. It can do any kind of arrangement for an occasion, too (it once created a full floral motorcycle for a Hell's Angel's funeral). The shop delivers from 7:00 A.M. to midnight (minimum order of $20) throughout the metropolitan area, including parts of New Jersey and Westchester; If you want flowers at odder hours, you'll have to pick them up yourself.

## Homework Help

**Homework Hotline,** 780-7766 or 914-682-9759

Children deserve services, too. The Homework Hotline, operated by Intershare, a state-funded information network in the metropolitan area, is set up to help kids with homework. Working out of the Brooklyn Public Library, a staff of moonlighting teachers and librarians fields questions Monday to Thursday from 5:00 to 8:00 P.M. (schooldays only). They never just give the answer; instead, they direct callers to sources where they can find the information themselves or work through similar problems. Sometimes kids just need clarifying an assignment (remember those thorny questions like "What were the factors that led to the

Romantic Movement in English literature?"). Math questions account for 50% of the calls, and though they won't do the specific problem, they'll work through the procedure until the caller has it down pat. Pupils at any grade level as well as puzzled parents can receive assistance.

## Knife Sharpening

**Delbon Cutlery,** 121 West 30th Street, between Sixth and Seventh Avenues, 244-2297

Delbon is one of New York's most famous cutlery stores, offering a vast array of every kind of knife and scissors, including the complete Wusthof-Trident line of high-carbon knives for fine cookery, discounted at 20%. The staff finishes, hand-hones and adjusts all cutlery bought on the premises and will put your initials on at no extra charge. Not only does Delbon sell every imaginable item of cutlery, but it also services same and can sharpen anything from your hunting knife to your cuticle clippers. Note the big grinding and polishing wheels in the back of the store. Open weekdays 9:00 A.M. to 5:30 P.M. and some Saturdays from 11:00 A.M. to 3:00 P.M. (call first).

## Marriage Counseling

**Save a Marriage, Inc.,** 799-0101

"We used to be so close, but after four years of marriage we don't seem to have anything to say to each other." "My husband's been out of work for seven months, and I feel furious and resentful." These are the kinds of problems you can take to Save a Marriage, a free telephone hot line manned by psychiatrists, psychologists and social workers (all trained in marital therapy) who offer their time and expertise to callers. With about half the marriages in the United States ending in divorce nowadays, the service is obviously needed, and for those who can't afford a therapist or don't want their spouses to know they're seeking help, it's a godsend. Calls are accepted Monday, Wednesday and Friday from noon to 2:00 P.M., and Tuesday to Friday from 6:00 to 8:00 P.M.; Fridays Spanish-speaking therapists are available. You can talk as long as you want and call back if you need to or even get a referral for more long-range counseling.

## Massage

**Armando Zetina,** 211 West 56th Street, 586-1342

A former ballet dancer himself, Zetina is the favored masseur of many top dancers, performers and theater people. Mikhail Baryshnikov, Natalia Makarova, Pam Sousa (*A Chorus Line*), Joseph Papp, Better Midler, George de la Pena and Fernando Bujones are among his faithful clientele. His method combines elements of Swedish massage with the strong finger pressure used in Japanese shiatsu. It's a soothing experience rather than a pounding, creating a heightened body awareness that Zetina claims might even help you lose weight (you'll become more aware of overeating). His specialty, however, is injuries. "I love to work on a good sprain," says Zetina enthusiastically. With such a glittery clientele, he is, of course, booked up far in advance. If you'd rather not wait, have him recommend an associate he has personally trained.

## Office and Office Personnel Rental

**World-Wide Business Centres, Inc.,** 575 Madison Avenue, between 56th and 57th Streets, 486-1333

A beautifully furnished and fully staffed executive office or suite at a prestige address (the above-listed) can materialize overnight when you contact World-Wide Business Centres. It has 140 offices that can be rented for any amount of time from a half day to forever, and though all services are available, you pay only for what you use. Your employees might include receptionists, typists, secretaries, bookkeepers, messengers, administrative assistants, salespeople and cleaning and maintenance staff. You can avail yourself of an exclusive telephone number which switchboard operators answer with your company name, a building directory listing, fully equipped conference rooms, a mailroom, facsimile equipment for transmitting documents, domestic and international telex service, word processors, dictaphones, photocopiers, etc. You'll have twenty-four-hour access to the building and employee availability from 9:00 A.M. to 5:30 P.M. weekdays. Another bonus: As a WWBC client you're freed of any need to play the role of office manager and can concentrate 100% on the business at hand.

## Postal Services

**Citipostal,** 175 Fifth Avenue, between 22nd and 23rd Streets (Flatiron Building), 460-9550, and 207 East 85th Street, between Second and Third Avenues, 772-7909

We all know what a drag the post office can be, what with the long lines, dawdling civil servants and rough handling of your delicate parcels. Citipostal takes the frustration out of mailing things. It operates like a postal supermarket, bringing together at each location all the services of the U.S. mail, UPS, Federal Express and Purolator Courier. There are never long lines at either branch, and friendly Citipostal employees will tell you the most economical way to send your packages and provide the proper labels and mailing envelopes. The service offers postal lockboxes at lower rates than the regular post office, and you can use the actual street address of Citipostal (your box is called a suite number) as a business address. You can also call to find out if there's mail and have your mail held or forwarded if you're out of town. Citipostal bills each month, unlike the post office, which requires a six-month advance payment. Other Citipostal services include package receiving (you're called when it arrives) and a telephone answering service for just $15 a month. Furthermore, it's open more hours than the post office: Hours at 373 Fifth Avenue are weekdays 8:00 A.M. to 7:00 P.M., Saturday 9:00 A.M. to 3:00 P.M.; at 85th Street, hours are 7:00 A.M. to 7:00 P.M. weekdays, 9:00 A.M. to 3:00 P.M. on Saturday.

## Realistic Environmental Portraiture

**Jill Watson,** 777-8772

The typical family portrait, in which everyone is stiffly posed and smiling, is about as evocative of the people in it as their collective embalmed corpses would be. If you'd like a portrait (of yourself, the kids, the entire family, whatever) that really captures the essence and unique personality of each person photographed, give Jill a call. She specializes in photo portraits of people in their home surroundings and workplaces, portraits that tell a story about the people in them. Her relaxed way with people (including kids—they love her) makes it easy for subjects to be natural—to be themselves—and the intimate view she captures is what portraiture is really about. Her prices are very reasonable.

## Sanding Machines—Rental

**Zelf Tool & Die Works,** 44 Greene Street, between Grand and Broome Streets, 925-8586

Zelf (that's what the owner calls himself) maintains that anyone can sand a floor properly without digging holes in it. His Soho shop rents out floor-sanding equipment and gives a lecture and demonstration to be sure you know how to use it. The machines are carefully maintained and, according to Zelf, "have a lot of power and pep." It will run you about $12 to rent a sander, an edger and sandpaper for twenty-four hours—a huge savings over having someone come in and do the job. Zelf also rents hand tools, nailing machines, electric hammers, hand sanders, airless paint sprayers and other equipment. Open Monday to Saturday from 8:30 A.M. to 3:30 P.M.

## Seltzer Delivery

**Gimme Seltzer,** 226-6079

It ain't exactly Perrier, but it's cheaper, you can have it delivered to your home and you can make an egg cream with it. What it is, actually, is triply filtered (sand, charcoal and blotting paper) carbonated New York City tap water. It comes in attractive antique bottles and will keep for weeks in the refrigerator without losing carbonation. A case of ten bottles, the minimum order, is just $6.50. With it, you'll get a long, humorous dissertation on the history of seltzer ("The origins of seltzer go way back through the mists of time to when the gods reigned on Mt. Olympus..."); gourmet egg cream recipes for aficionados, utilizing such unorthodox ingredients as Haagen-Dazs, Kahlua and red ginger tea, and a list of additional uses and curative properties of seltzer ("It cures cancer, radiation poisoning and warts, is ideal for fights and squirting anything from roaches to Hare Krishnas, makes your plants grow to breathtaking sizes, can stop a snorer or wake a heavy sleeper and cool down a nuclear reactor in danger of a meltdown"). In addition to the miracle elixir, Gimme Seltzer carries a full line of syrups—U-Bet chocolate, root beer, vanilla, cherry, raspberry, orange, etc.—and even Tab and Sprite for diet egg creams. Manhattan deliveries only.

## Singing Telegrams, etc.

**Eastern Onion Singing Telegrams,** 741-0006
If a 280-pound girl dressed in red velvet and a feather boa smothers you with kisses on your birthday, give in graciously. It only means that one of your warped friends has chosen to send you a greeting of song via Manhattan Mama. She may also appear in tutu and tennis shoes, waving a magic wand in the guise of Fairy Onion. Eastern Onion has bizarre telegrams for every occasion, from bridal showers to bar mitzvahs, to announcing to your husband (you hope) that he is going to be a father or even that you want a divorce (to the tune of "Toot, Toot, Tootsie, Goodbye"). For holidays there's a singing Thanksgiving turkey, a Halloween vampire, a St. Patrick's Day leprechaun, Santa and his elves, etc. You can send strippers, both male (e.g., Naughty Cop) and female (e.g., Saucy Secretary). And then there are gorillagrams, bellygrams, dancing cakes, big apples, Carmen "Marumba" and Mae East. Eastern Onion is the biggest singing telegram company in New York and probably in the nation, with offices in fifty states. It has ninety-five stock songs—all humorous—to cover just about every contingency, but for an additional fee you can have a song written just for you. Charges depend on location (it services all five boroughs, New Jersey and parts of Connecticut and Long Island) and the act you select. You can bill your telegram to any major credit card.

**Yenta-gram,** 475-0566
Life isn't all balloon bouquets and strip-a-grams. Sometimes you deserve a yenta-gram. So what is it? It's a comic "guilt trip" delivered by an improvisational actress effectively disguised as a yenta. She enters your life in a pillbox hat, rumpled stockings and a schmatte dress. She's wearing too much make-up, carrying too many shopping bags and talking in shrill Brooklynese. Vicki Grossfeld designed the service "to give New Yorkers a novel way to express discontent, vent frustrations and generally make other people aware of their shortcomings and idiosyncrasies." You provide your yenta with background material about the recipients, and she'll harangue them for ten minutes with hilarious pertinent quips. The cost is about $45 in Manhattan, $50 in most of Brooklyn and Queens, more for Long Island and New Jersey, but you can try *handling* for the price. So why haven't you called yet? The phone is broken?

## Stretcher Makers

**Framemasters and The Stretcher Company,** 153 Waverly Place, between Avenue of the Americas and Seventh Avenue, 989-3939

These are actually two companies sharing one location. The Stretcher Company builds, for artists and needlepointers, custom stretchers of any shape or size from a tiny oval to a large heavy-duty rectangle for wall-size paintings. It also stretches raw canvas (bring your own or buy it here), painted canvas and other fabrics. The latter service costs about $15 an hour. Many well-known artists who paint large canvases, like Jules Olitski, have their stretchers made up here. Framemasters sells a wide-range of contemporary frames—natural wood, gilded, plexiglass, welded, etc.—both wholesale and retail. Retail customers get a discount of 20%. The entire operation is open Monday to Friday from 9:00 A.M. to 5:00 P.M., Saturday 9:00 A.M. to 11:30 A.M.

## Tuxedo Rental

**Starlight Tuxedo,** 606 Bloomfield Avenue, Bloomfield, N.J., 201-743-7566

It may be worth a trip to New Jersey to rent a tuxedo at Starlight. All its tuxedos rent for just under $30 (with the exception of Pierre Cardin, which was still cheaper than we had seen it anywhere else). The styles include all the popular names in tuxedos—e.g., Lord West and After Six—with a good selection of style and color. Open Monday to Saturday 10:00 A.M. to 5:00 P.M..

## Wine by Wire

**Tele-Wine,** 10 East 39th Street, between Fifth and Madison Avenues, 685-2100, 800-223-2660

You've probably wired flowers or candy to people on special occasions. Now you can also send them wine and champagne. Tele-Wine works just like FTD. It has a network of more than 21,000 participating shops throughout the United States and abroad that stock wine, champagne, spirits and related items. **Liquor Line,** another service (same phone numbers), sends liquors and liqueurs. Both services are worldwide (send a bottle to India if you like), and the selections are as wide-ranging as the inventory in the area you are sending to. You can order in any quantity, but the minimum order is $40, that price including attractively gift-wrapped merchandise, delivery, sales tax and service charge. Delivery is usually the same day in the United States (forty-eight hours at most); allow another day or two overseas. You can bill your order to a credit card. Tele-Wine takes orders weekdays only 9:00 A.M. to 5:30 P.M.

### Women's Sports Hot Line

**Sportsline,** 800-227-3988

The Women's Sports Foundation's Sportsline is a toll-free hot line that will answer questions you have about women's sports. If you want to know about scholarships, it'll send you a listing of more than 800 colleges that offer sports scholarships to women. It can direct you to different organizations for help with sports careers and to colleges that have outstanding programs in your field of interest. Don't call for game scores or results, and if you have a medical problem, it recommends you consult your doctor. Sportsline takes calls between noon and 8:00 P.M. weekdays.

## GETTING A JOB—EMPLOYMENT SERVICES AND COUNSELING

Most of us—as the ad says—make money the old-fashioned way: We earn it. But even with the best of intentions it's not always easy to get a job. The following individuals and organizations exist to help you find employment, determine the career you're suited for, and maybe even help you rise in it.

**American Woman's Economic Development Corp.,** 60 East 42nd Street, at Park Avenue, fourth floor, 692-9100

Women who are running their own businesses—or plan to be—can benefit from professional counseling offered by AWED. It'll match you up with a counselor who is an expert in your field and with whom you can discuss marketing and sales, banking and finance, accounting, personnel and all your other business concerns. Sessions average 1½ hours and cost $25. AWED also offers a year-long twenty-six session course called "Managing Your Own Business" ($350) for women who have been in business at least six months and are ready to achieve the next stage of growth and two nine-session seminars ($175) called "Starting Your Own Business" and "Building Your Own Business" for entrepreneurial women in the early stages of running a business.

**Council for Career Planning, Inc.,** 310 Madison Avenue, at 42nd Street, 687-9490

The council is a "nonprofit, educational organization concerned with providing services and support for women with college backgrounds as they work toward becoming assimilated profitably and productively in the business world." Its services include career counseling, job referral and job placement. The council also publishes three booklets on résumé writing and job hunting techniques as well as more than 200 fact sheets relating to specific careers. You must join the council ($10) to avail yourself of its placement and referral services. Two one-hour private counseling sessions cost $85, $75 if you're attending a college that is a member of the council. These sessions might include help with writing an effective résumé that will open doors, determining the kind of career you're suited for, learning how to mount a job campaign and referrals for additional information.

**Catalyst,** 14 East 60th Street, between Fifth and Madison Avenues, New York, N.Y. 10022 759-9700

Catalyst is a national nonprofit career resource and information center (basically for women, though men can use the service, too) that is affiliated with a national network of similar and related organizations. It helps job hunters and people reentering the career market, changing or expanding careers, trying to move upward or relocating. One of its facilities is a library of more than 4,000 books and periodicals crammed with career information; it's open to the public Monday 9:00 A.M. to 7:30 P.M., Tuesday to Friday to 5:00 P.M. Catalyst also puts out many of its own publications on dozens of career options (banking, restaurant management, fund raising, real estate, insurance, government, etc.), educational opportunities and general career topics. Write or call for free pamphlets on its available services and publications.

## FOR YOUNG ADULTS

**Youth Opportunity Center,** 45 West 36th Street, between Fifth and Sixth Avenues, 868-2850

This very valuable organization, a division of the New York State Department of Labor, specializes in helping young people (ages sixteen to twenty-two) find regular and summer employment from entry-level up. If you're in that age bracket, come in and fill out an application. It'll coach you on how to conduct yourself at an interview, how to talk to a prospective employer, how to dress, how to assess and project your most salable qualities and other job-procuring skills—and with luck it'll put you in touch with an employer who will give you a job. All the services of the Youth Opportunity Center are free, including job search workshops, vocational counseling, advice on where to train for particular fields and aptitude testing. Open weekdays 8:30 A.M. to 5:00 P.M.; just drop in, preferably before 3:00 P.M. so you have a chance to go out on an interview. For Manhattan residents only.

**New York State Job Service,** 485 Fifth Avenue, at 42nd Street, 599-3880

The New York State Job Service (a division of the Department of Labor) is looking for youngsters over eighteen who have completed at least one year of college to work as general and specialty camp counselors throughout the Northeast. It is also preferred that you have at least one summer of work in a camp, a good camping background and/or a well-developed specialty skill (e.g., can teach arts and crafts, canoeing, etc.). It has thousands of openings, but if you want your pick of the plums, apply as early as Christmas recess. No fee is charged. Call for an appointment.

This is just one of the many offices of the **New York State Job Service,** which functions throughout the state as an employment bureau for young people and adults. There are thirty-three offices in the five boroughs. All can help applicants with interview counseling, aptitude testing, résumé writing and other job-acquiring skills, but various branches specialize in particular fields—e.g., household, part-time and temporary, professional placement, sales and merchandising, industrial personnel, etc. Check your phone book (under "New York State Government Services—Labor, Department of") to find the office that will serve your needs.

**Anne Andrews Employment Agency,** 38 East 57th Street, 753-1244

High school and college students who are looking for summer work as mother's helpers will find plenty of openings at Anne Andrews, one of the top agencies in this field. It hires boys and girls, ages fourteen and up, to spend a month or two at the beach or a country house, usually taking care of children. Most of the jobs are on Long Island (including the Hamptons), in New Jersey and parts of New England. Depending on your age and experience, you'll earn between $55 and $150 a week, including room and board. Time off is generally one day a week. If you're interested, contact Anne Andrews during the spring. The agency charges a fee of 18% of one month's salary or 10% of the total earned, whichever is less.

## *FOR THE OVER-FORTY EXEC*

**40 Plus Club of New York, Inc.,** 15 Park Row, 233-6086

The 40 Plus Club is a self-help cooperative organization of unemployed executives and professionals over the age of forty. Its chief objective is to get everybody back on the job. Members make an initial contribution of $300 and pay $5 a week in dues after that. Once accepted, they're put through an in-depth examination of their career skills, achievements, goals and objectives. They're given detailed step-by-step job-search training, including a comprehensive course in interview techniques and pointers on how to use being over forty as an asset. A Marketing Committee solicits corporations to obtain jobs for members, and a Placement Committee screens résumés and sends them to appropriate employers. Members must donate 2½ days per week to the organization. The track record is good: On an average, one member leaves 40 Plus for a new position each working day.

# HEALTH

The most striking change in health care over the last decade has been the increasing shift of responsibility from doctor to patient. We've realized the importance of understanding our own illnesses, of considering alternative—often nonmedical—methods of treating them and of actively maintaining health through proper diet and exercise. This section is written with the person who takes responsibility for his or her own health in mind. In that regard, there are several listings that deal with losing weight and giving up smoking, both of which can considerably bolster your good health.

## DENTISTRY

**NYU College of Dentistry,** 345 East 24th Street, corner of First Avenue, 481-5900

If you need dental work and can't afford it, you don't have to let your teeth rot. The NYU College of Dentistry offers a low-cost alternative to high dental fees. At its clinic, treatments are done by students under very careful faculty supervision. Almost every dental service, including orthodontics for adults and children, is offered. An initial appointment is not required; just show up any weekday between 9:00 and 11:00 A.M. or 1:00 and 2:00 P.M. After the initial visit you can make appointments for specific times. The cost for initial registration, an oral examination, a full set of X rays and treatment planning is $20, payable in cash. Copies of your X rays are available at a modest fee. A cleaning is $15 to $25, depending on how long you've let it go. Special rates are available for senior citizens. There's limited evening service (in addition to regular clinic hours, which are weekdays from 9:50 A.M. to 12:45 P.M. and 1:25 P.M. to 4:15 P.M.) for root canal and periodontia performed by postdoctural students and faculty. The emergency service fee is $15. The clinic is closed during the summer.

## HEADACHES

Anyone who suffers from chronic headaches should know about two places that offer the most sophisticated diagnostic techniques and treatment available.

The **Montefiore Hospital Headache Unit,** 11 East 210th Street, Bronx, 920-4636, under the direction of Dr. Seymour Solomon, utilizes an eclectic approach. It considers both drug and nondrug therapies (e.g., biofeedback and psychological help) and takes all factors, organic and nonorganic, into consideration—dental, ophthalmologic, etc.

In Manhattan, try the **Mount Sinai Medical Center Headache Clinic,** 1 Gustave L. Levy Place (100th Street, at Fifth Avenue) 650-7691. It's under the direction of David R. Coddon, M.D., who pioneered the

"Coddon Cocktail" for migraine sufferers. A mixture of Compazine, Valium and Amytal, this "cocktail" puts headache victims to sleep for several hours and breaks the cycle so that intervals between attacks increase. Both clinics' fees are on a sliding scale.

## HEART TROUBLE

**Heart Information Service,** 661-5335

If you or someone in your family has heart trouble, you're likely to have more questions than your doctor has time to answer. That's when you should turn to the Heart Information Service of the New York Heart Association. It offers up-to-date information for the general public on the prevention and treatment of cardiovascular disease and stroke. Trained professionals can answer your questions on the phone and send you a variety of free pamphlets on subjects like coronary bypass surgery, exercise, stress, stroke, proper nutrition and diet, children's heart problems, high-blood pressure and smoking. They can also refer you to testing places, stop-smoking clinics, nursing homes and clubs for heart attack or surgery patients and other services. English- and Spanish-speaking personnel are available to help you. Weekdays between 8:30 A.M. to 4:30 P.M.

## HELP FOR STUTTERERS

**Communication Reconstruction Center,** 450 Park Avenue, between 56th and 57th Streets, 355-7111

The Communication Reconstruction Center is devoted to the remediation of the problem of stuttering. It offers a three-week intensive program (approximately 120 hours with a six-month follow-up) that treats stuttering in adults and children with a behavioral approach (physical rather than emotional behaviors), emphasizing control of respiration, articulation and phonation. The results have been excellent. At the end of the three weeks 93% of those who participated in the program achieved normal levels of speech fluency, and a long-term study (ten to forty-one months after therapy) showed that in 200 randomly selected cases, 75% retained fluency in the normal range and 15% retained substantial improvement over pretreatment levels. Contact the center for orientation, evaluation and to determine fees.

## LIFELINES AND EMERGENCY CARE

**EARS, The Metropolitan Jewish Geriatric Center,** 4915 Tenth Avenue, Brooklyn, N.Y. 11219, 946-1199

People with elderly parents or relatives living alone can't help worrying about their health and safety. Worrying won't help, but EARS (Emergency Alarm Response System) can. It works like this. Each subscriber wears an electronic transmitter that can send a signal to EARS headquarters. When the subscriber presses a button, someone at EARS hears the signal (it is staffed around the clock) and tries to phone the subscriber. If there's no answer, a prearranged "responder" (a nearby source of help that might be a friend, relative or community service) is called and immediately dispatched to the subscriber's home. Every case is closely monitored by EARS personnel until the situation is resolved. The service has saved lives in cases of heart attacks, falls, strokes and other emergencies, many of which occurred at night, when other help was not readily available. The cost is only about $20 a month—not much to pay for this kind of security. For details write or call the Metropolitan Jewish Geriatric Center.

**Medic Alert,** 697-7470 or 516-832-8140

Medic Alert could save your life if you have a heart condition, diabetes, penicillin allergy, hemophilia, epilepsy or any other condition that might render you unable to speak when it strikes or must be communicated in an emergency. Medic Alert speaks for you. It's an international organization that provides members with an Alert Emblem—a necklace or bracelet engraved with information on their condition and a phone number. All pertinent information about your condition can be retrieved at any time, twenty-four hours a day, by calling this phone number collect from anywhere in the world. Members also receive a wallet card with medical information and references. The cost is a mere $15 for a lifetime membership, and information can be updated at any time for a nominal fee.

**Bellevue Emergency Room,** 462 First Avenue, at 27th Street, 561-4141

When a medical emergency arises, it's often too late to figure out where to go. That's why you should know that Bellevue has the most complete emergency facilities in the city, treating 100,000 patients each year. It is second to no other hospital in providing round-the-clock vital services. Whatever the problem—asthma, broken bones, car accident, bashed skull, gunshot wound, rape, mental breakdown, DTs, drug overdose, poisoning, sick infant, etc.—this is the place to go when time is of the essence. The vehicular entrance to the Emergency Room is at 29th Street and First Avenue.

The one exception to the above has to do with serious burns. The only complete burn center in New York is at **New York Hospital,** 525 East 68th Street, 472-5132 (vehicular entrance on 70th Street, between York Avenue and the river), and this is where burn victims should be taken to receive optimum care. Among other things, it maintains a skin bank to provide life-sustaining grafts.

For poison information call **Poison Control,** 340-4494 or dial POISONS; it'll tell you the best course of action.

## LOSING WEIGHT AND LEARNING TO EAT CORRECTLY

The programs I've listed below are not the ones named for chic neighborhoods or the ones that require eating only bananas, only protein or only soup. They're the sensible kinds that emphasize slow weight loss and a change of eating habits. Weight Watchers is not listed here, only because everyone knows about it and knows it's good.

**Weight Control Unit,** Obesity Research Center, St. Luke's-Roosevelt Hospital Center, 411 West 114th Street, between Morningside and Amsterdam Avenues, 870-1743

Here a team of internists, psychiatrists, psychologists and nutritionists combines forces to help patients deal with the complex problems of obesity. The program begins with a full day of testing—a detailed physical, psychological and diagnostic examination that determines, among other things, the number and size of your fat cells, your basal metabolic rate and your allowable calorie intake. A slow rate of weight loss is encouraged. Gradual behavioral techniques are given primary emphasis and psychological, nutritional and medical aspects are also stressed. Dieters keep a record of every morsel eaten, as well as where, when, with whom and in what mood they ate it. The diagnostic phase of the program costs $400. After that treatment it's $35 a week for group sessions. During maintenance, once you've lost the weight, you attend groups less frequently. Some insurance plans are applicable especially when there's a health problem relating to obesity. Call for a brochure, application and fee schedule. You must be at least 20% over your ideal weight to qualify. Once every three weeks there's an orientation meeting explaining the program, which you attend for $10.

Another hospital weight-control program is **Mount Sinai's Nutrition Clinic,** 1 Gustave Levy Place (100th Street, at Fifth Avenue), 650-7201, for children. The program also involves behavior modification, but an individual diet and method of treatment are created for each patient, taking into account his or her medical history, life-style, etc. No drugs are used. Fees are on a sliding scale.

## MEDICAL AND HEALTH INFORMATION

**Center for Medical Consumers and Health Care Information,** 237 Thompson Street, south of Washington Square Park, 674-7105

Appropriate health care is not a simple matter. The Center for Medical Consumers exists to "encourage people to make a critical evaluation of all information received from health professionals, to use medical service more selectively and to understand the limitations of modern medicine." It maintains a free medical health library for laypeople where you can look up the effects of prescription drugs, check your doctor's credentials and evaluate the care you are receiving. It also has numerous telephone tapes of three- to five-minute duration on about 100 subjects, including cancer, arthritis/rheumatism, heart disease, children's illnesses, first aid, dental problems and many other subjects. Send a No. 10 stamped, self-addressed envelope to the above address for a full list of tapes. A subscription to their excellent monthly consumer newsletter, *Health Facts,* is $18 per year.

**Blue Cross and Blue Shield of Greater New York,** 3 Park Avenue, between 33rd and 34th Streets, 481-2323

Did you know that Blue Cross/Blue Shield offers free workshops to the public on more than fifty health and health-related issues? They cover quite a wide swath: holistic health, procrastination, lower-back pain, fire safety, planning for retirement, aching feet, death and dying, nutrition, high blood pressure, dental care, stress, insomnia, skin care, making relationships work, eye health, dieting and quitting smoking, among other subjects. The workshops take place at lunchtime and after office hours (6:00 to 7:00 P.M.). There are also free pamphlets available on numerous subjects. Call for details.

## *MEDICAL HELP ABROAD*

**The International Association for Medical Assistance to Travelers (IAMAT),** 736 Center Street, Lewiston, N.Y. 14092, 716-754-4883

It's frightening being ill in a foreign country—especially if you are being treated by a doctor with whom you have no language in common. But this need never happen to you if you join IAMAT, an organization that provides a complete listing of English-speaking, American-, British- or Canadian-trained physicians in 450 cities around the world whose fees are under $40 per visit. Such out-of-the-way places as Bangladesh, Botswana and New Guinea are listed. IAMAT also provides members with a World Climate Chart that includes information about dangers in drinking water and eating certain foods, a World Malaria Risk Chart, a World Immunization Chart and other warnings of dangerous medical conditions. In addition, IAMAT will give you a Traveler Clinical Record for information from your own physicians on drugs, prescriptions and emergency instructions. Membership in this very helpful association is free, though donations are appreciated. Don't leave home without it. To join, write IAMAT at the above address.

## *MEDICAL MASSAGE*

**Swedish Institute of Medical Massage,** 875 Avenue of the Americas, at 31st Street, 695-3964

Massage is one of the oldest techniques known to mankind, promoting improved muscle tone and circulation, relief of tissue congestion, elimination of toxins, stimulation of nervous, respiratory and digestive systems, balanced metabolism and stress management. At the Swedish Institute, one of the leading massage training institutes—and the only federally accredited one in the country—students provide massage therapy for various muscular-skeletal problems, including arthritis, stiff necks and scoliosis. They work under the close supervision of licensed massage therapists and teachers. You must get a massage prescription from your doctor to be eligible for their services. These include a profile evaluation of your entire body and six subsequent half hour treatments—all for just $35, payable on the first visit. Phone any Monday, Tuesday, or Wednesday between 1:00 and 4:00 P.M.

## STOP SMOKING

**The American Cancer Society,** 586-8700

The American Cancer Society runs an excellent—and inexpensive—smoke-quitting program with participating clinics all over the city and in Long Island and Westchester. Once- or twice-weekly sessions led by trained ex-smokers (all graduates of the course) offer support, guidance and a method of cutting down gradually. Prices are minimal. Once you quit, there's a special "I Quit" club for continued support. Call the above number any weekday between 9:00 A.M. and 5:00 P.M. for details and the location nearest you.

# HOUSEHOLD CLEANING AND HELP

They come to your home, wielding mops and pails, sponges and scrub brushes and make light work of your heavy cleaning. Aren't they wonderful?

## DISASTER SPECIALISTS

**Disaster Masters,** 126-13 101st Avenue, Queens, 847-5200, 441-1800

With luck, you'll never need Ron Alford's trouble-shooting service, but should you come home one day to find the ceiling on the floor, you'll be glad to know it's around. His one-of-a-kind company specializes in disaster management—cleaning up a mess fast and minimizing financial loss. Operating around the clock, Disaster Masters arrives on scenes of devastation and restores the premises to normal conditions—usually within three days. It can suction off water from flooding, remove spot and smoke stains, repaint or hang new wallpaper, sand and refinish floors, eliminate smells (even cat urine from rugs and fabrics) and wash windows if necessary. Carpentry, plumbing and electrical work are well within its scope, too. Disaster Masters has been called in by everyone from Brentano's (a pipe broke and 50,000 gallons of water flooded the store) to the police (to clean up messy murders) to a little old lady who left eggs boiling on the stove when she went away for a weekend (they exploded all over the ceiling and created a horrible odor). All Disaster Masters tradespeople are carefully selected for the high quality of their work. In addition to the abovementioned, they include air-conditioning mechanics, roofers, tree surgeons, landscapers, exterminators, alarm systems installers, cabinetmakers and chimney cleaners. And you don't have to have a disaster to hire one of them. As Alford points out, "If you hire a kid to sand your floors and he digs holes in them, then you will have a disaster." Yet another service is a licensed insurance broker on staff who can help clients deal with insurance companies (he speaks their language). And speaking of insurance companies, Disaster Masters can videotape your losses. Alford believes homeowners and businesses should do what they can to prevent disasters. With this in mind he offers risk-management and analysis inspections to advise people about potential problems and adequate insurance.

When you hire Disaster Masters to put things right, it'll give you an estimate in advance, stick to it within 10% and define, in a contract, words such as *clean.*

## FABRICS AND UPHOLSTERED FURNITURE

**Cleantex,** 2335 12th Avenue, 283-1200

When the staff at Gracie Mansion notices the mayoral drapes are looking less than radiant, where do they send them? To Cleantex, the specialty household cleaning company that has been servicing New York's finest homes, mansions and museums for more than half a century. It cleans anything made of fabric—not only drapes but rugs, tapestries, window shades, lampshades, slipcovers and furniture. It has special equipment for stretching, reshaping and squaring off your drapes and curtains, so they retain their original measurements. Everything is done with exquisite care; that is why clients trust Cleantex with precious Picasso wall hangings, Aubusson tapestries, silk wall coverings and Louis XIV furnishings. In addition to cleaning, this firm can flameproof your fabrics. Bonded, insured drivers do the pickups and deliveries, and they also rehang your drapes and relay your carpet. Call weekdays between 8:00 A.M. and 4:00 P.M.

## MIXED BAGS

**Lend-a-Hand,** 200 West 72nd Street, 362-8200
"Our houseboys love filthy apartments," is the boast of Donald Eggena, a former actor who for the last twelve years has turned his talents to providing New Yorkers with every imaginable service. His multifaceted staff consists of out-of-work performers who are waiting for the big break. They will wax floors, wash walls, polish silver, launder your clothes, scrub the kitchen tiles—do everything but windows. For parties Lend-a-Hand can provide bartenders, waiters, waitresses and coat checkers; it'll even prepare the hors d'oeuvres. In fact, it can cater anything from a cocktail party to an elaborate buffet complete with china, crystal, silver, linen and flowers—and, of course, it can provide entertainers. Office help? It has typists, proofreaders, receptionists and stenographers on hand. Not to mention fortunetellers, cat-sitters, babysitters, dog walkers, hairdressers, gardeners, painters, paperhangers, movers, plasterers, carpenters and probably anybody else you've got in mind. You pay a fee of $10 to $15 (up to a maximum of $60 a year) each time you hire a Lend-a-Hand employee plus a specified hourly rate. A four-hour minimum is usually required. Office hours are weekdays 9:00 A.M. to 5:30 P.M., Saturday (except July and August) to 1:00 P.M.

**Flatiron Services,** 230 East 93rd Street, 876-1000
Since 1893 Flatiron Services has been doing the kind of heavy cleaning chores I get tired just thinking about. For openers, reversing the cliché, it does do windows, a service which most New Yorkers are desperately in need of. Other services include carpet and rug shampooing (in your home or at its plant); washing walls, woodwork and ceilings; cleaning upholstered furniture, curtains, drapes and Venetian blinds; storage of carpets and rugs; floor finishing (sanding, staining and polyurethane and floor waxing). Flatiron can also provide you with regular maid service as well as waitresses, cooks, bartenders and other party helpers. Prices are reasonable. Office hours weekdays from 8:30 A.M. to 5:00 P.M.; after hours and on weekends you can leave messages on the answering machine.

## RUGS AND CARPETS—CLEANING AND REWEAVING

**Irwin Cohen,** 16-10 212th Street, Bayside, 224-9885

Rugs and carpets are so expensive these days I almost wish I could put plastic slipcovers on them or train my dog to respect them. Every rip, cigarette burn and stain is a trauma. Luckily Irwin Cohen (at WOR we call him the rug doctor) can cure sickly floor coverings and make them good as new. Equipped with skeins of yarn in every color, this expert rug weaver can repair any burn or tear, and even the most difficult stains disappear under his healing touch. Cohen makes house calls, little black bag in hand, with the average visit in the $50 to $75 range.

## WINDOW PLUS

**Sun Ray Window Cleaning,** 95 Nassau Street, 355-4030

Sun Ray does windows, and does them to sparkling perfection. Its motto: "Let the sun shine in." Owner Marty Koppel himself started out as a window cleaner and was the third generation in his family to wield the squeegee. Nowadays he oversees the operation, making sure that his window washers are thorough, courteous and careful with your property. Among other things, they can get hard-to-open windows working again. Window cleaning costs about $6 per window, depending on size, of course, with a $25 minimum. Sun Ray doesn't only do windows, by the way. It offers a full range of household cleaning services throughout the metropolitan area: floor washing and waxing; wall washing; cleaning Venetian blinds and light fixtures; furniture polishing; carpet, rug and furniture shampooing; and exterminating.

## INTERNATIONAL NEW YORK

New York is the international meeting ground for hundreds of different ethnic groups that have banded together to form neighborhoods that are replicas of those they left behind. So if you're interested in spending an afternoon in Russia, take a forty-minute trip outside Manhattan to Brighton Beach. Or would you prefer Japan? Or China? Or Italy? They're all here, as are German, Tibetan, South American, French, Irish, Thai and even Estonian neighborhoods.

In this section I have included five major areas (leaving out the most obvious like Chinatown and Little Italy) in or near Manhattan that have substantial ethnic populations.

## ARAB ATLANTIC AVENUE

At first glance, Atlantic Avenue, between Court and Henry Streets in Brooklyn, looks like any other major shopping thoroughfare. But upon slightly closer inspection, you'll notice the shop windows are filled with exotic tins, bags of dried fruits and nuts, belly dancing paraphernalia and decorative, distinctly not American-made, brassware. And looking up to catch the names of these shops, you will undoubtedly notice that they are written in Arabic as well as English, as are all the signs in this, the biggest Arab shopping area in New York. While a good majority of the 50,000 or so Arab residents in this part of Brooklyn are American-born, they keep close ties with their heritage and traditions, and the neighborhood maintains a definite ethnic flavor.

### Restaurants

The **Moroccan Star,** 205 Atlantic Avenue, between Court and Clinton Streets, 596-1919, serves French and Moroccan fare in a dimly lit stucco-walled dining room with small arched windows. Fresh flowers adorn the yellow-clothed tables. Owner-chef Ahmed Almontaser formerly plied his culinary skills at the Four Seasons, La Brasserie and Luchow's. A meal here might begin with an order of babaganouj (mashed eggplant in sesame butter), continue with a traditional Moroccan couscous or lamb tajine and wind up French with chocolate mousse pie. Entrées average about $8, and you can bring your own wine. On weekends there's belly dancing. Open daily from noon to 11:00 P.M.

The Almontaser family owns three other restaurants in the area—all, more or less, in the same price range. **Atlantic House,** 144 Atlantic Avenue, between Clinton and Henry Streets, 625-7888, is a cozy Yemenite eatery. A house specialty is Yemen fata—moistened pita in meat broth topped with chunks of lamb and garlic sauce. For dessert, apricot pudding (made from fresh apricots) is refreshing. Once again, bring your own wine. Open daily 11:00 A.M. to 11:00 P.M.

Another Almontaser establishment, **Adnan Restaurant,** 129 Atlantic Avenue, between Clinton and Henry Streets, 625-8697, has an intimate ambience created by a series of archways, brick and stone walls and lighting emanating from Tiffany-style lamps. The menu is similar to that of Atlantic House; bring your own wine. Open daily 11:00 A.M. to 11:00 P.M.

Last of this group is the **Near East Restaurant,** 137 Court Street, between Atlantic Avenue and Pacific Street, 522-4188. It's the most ornate of the lot, with brass chandeliers overhead and tables covered in white linen. Once again the menu is Middle Eastern/French with entrées running the gamut from couscous and kebabs to roast duckling à l'orange. A good bet here are the house special dinners (about $20 for two), which include appetizer, salad, entrée, rice and vegetables, dessert and coffee. Bring your own wine. Open daily 11:00 A.M. to 11:00 P.M.

The **Mediterranean Garden Restaurant,** 172 Atlantic Avenue, between Clinton and Court Streets, 624-9614, looks like a cheerful coffee shop—a fancy one with fresh flowers on the tables and Middle Eastern art on the walls. The extensive menu features eighty-three entrées, not to mention appetizers, soups and twenty-four desserts. Go for the more exotic items like an appetizer of moutabal (fried eggplant and squash mashed with tahini, yogurt, sesame paste, tomatoes, parsley and olive oil) and perhaps kharouf mehshi (lamb stuffed with rice, meat, green peas, raisins and mixed nuts, served with yogurt salad) for a main course. Entrées average about $7. You can bring your own wine, and on Friday and Saturday nights there's belly dancing. Open daily from noon to midnight.

**Son of the Sheik,** 165 Atlantic Avenue, between Clinton and Henry Streets, 625-4023, is the oldest Lebanese restaurant on the block. It's small and comfortable with minimal effort in the way of décor, but the food is homemade and delicious. Full dinners in the $6.50 to $8 range are the best bet. Such a one is the Sheik's special kafta, including a skewer of kafta kebab, rice pilaf, stuffed cabbage, sautéed mushrooms, stuffed grape leaves, string beans, baked eggplant and salad. Luncheon specials are about half the price of full dinners. Open Tuesday to Sundays noon to 10:00 P.M.

## Food Stores and Bakeries

**Sahadi Importing Co., Inc.,** 187 Atlantic Avenue, between Clinton and Court Streets, 624-4550, entices you in with a tantalizing array of Middle Eastern specialties. Oak containers are filled with dried beans and grains; there are barrels of olives and fresh peppers; dried fruits and nuts; tins of grape leaves, imported olive oils and vegetables; frozen dinners, like spinach and cheese in phyllo dough, and, of course, large rounds of halvah richly studded with pistachios, almonds and walnuts. Open Monday to Saturday 9:00 A.M. to 7:00 P.M.; a small adjoining shop is open only on Saturday.

**Malko Karkanni Brothers, Inc.,** 199 Atlantic Avenue, between Clinton and Court Streets, 834-0845, is well organized, its shelves neatly lined with tahini, couscous, pomegranate juice (used in flavoring meat dishes), grenadine molasses and other exotica. On the floor are enormous bags of dried okra, vats of olives and peppers, barrels of dried beans, rice, chickpeas and kasha. The brothers make sandwiches of felafel, grape leaves and babaganouj to eat on the spot or take out. Open daily 8:30 A.M. to 8:00 P.M.

Similar wares are at **Oriental Pastry and Grocery,** 170 Atlantic Avenue, between Clinton and Court Streets, 875-7687 (open daily 9:00 A.M. to 8:30 P.M.); **Shammas and Co.,** 197 Atlantic Avenue, between Clinton and Court Streets, 855-2455 (open daily 10:00 A.M. to 8:00 P.M.); and **Malko Importing Corp.,** 182 Atlantic Avenue, between Clinton and Court Streets, 624-2049 (open 9:00 A.M. to 9:00 P.M. daily).

You can try a new taste sensation—pumpernickel pita—at **Damascus Bakery,** 195 Atlantic Avenue, between Clinton and Court Streets, 855-1457. It also has baklava, bird's-nest pastry, date cookies, sesame cookies and other Middle Eastern pastries and will heat up a meat or spinach pie for immediate consumption. Open daily 7:00 A.M. to 9:00 P.M.

**Near East Bakery,** 183 Atlantic Avenue, between Clinton and Court Streets, 875-0016, has been baking bread from traditional recipes for more than eighty-five years at this location. In addition to pita, it sells Syrian bread, zathar (a flat bread spiced with oregano and thyme) and marook (a variation of pita). Then there are homemade pastries—nut-filled honey concoctions, fresh apricot tarts, pecan-filled cakes and cookies. Meat and spinach pies are also available. Open Tuesday to Saturday 7:30 A.M. to 4:30 P.M., Sunday 5:30 A.M. to 5:30 P.M.

You can relax over coffee and baklava at **Tripoli Pastry Co.,** 163 Atlantic Avenue, between Clinton and Henry Streets, 625-8094, a tiny coffee shop with ornately decorated sky blue walls. In addition to pastries, Tripoli offers homemade ice cream in American and Lebanese flavors (cashew, almond, fresh-squeezed juices, apricot, etc.) and even complete entrées like ma'ani Tripoli (lamb sausage with wine, pine nuts and special spices). Open daily 11:30 A.M. to 11:00 P.M.

## *A Book Store Plus...*

**Rashid Sales Co.,** 191 Atlantic Avenue, between Clinton and Court Streets, 852-3295, carries Middle Eastern books and periodicals as well as records and cassettes (Mr. Rashid claims if you can't find a particular Arab record here, you won't find it anywhere) and videocassettes of Arab movies. In addition, he has T-shirts, Islamic art prints, Yemeni postcards and Middle Eastern novelty items. Open Monday to Saturday 9:00 A.M. to 7:00 P.M., Sunday noon to 5:00 P.M.

## ATHENS IN ASTORIA

The most ethnic of all the neighborhoods here explored, by far, is the Greek community just twenty minutes from Manhattan in Astoria, Queens. You can actually spend the day here and not hear any English. With a Greek population of more than 150,000 in this area, that's understandable. Most of the action is between Broadway and 20th Avenue, from 31st Street to Steinway Street. Remember, many of the shopkeepers do not speak English (though everyone understands, "How much?"), so get your pointer finger ready.

## *Restaurants*

Most of the restaurants here look basically alike—like typical Greek taverns. When you finish a meal, you'll think you've spent the afternoon in a Greek city; it's rather surprising to find yourself in Queens.

Very typical of this Astoria genre is **Vedeta Restaurant,** 22-55 31st Street, near 41st Avenue, 728-9696. A steam table is at the entrance (since all food is on display, there's no problem ordering), and the dimly lit interior features clothed tables and Greek folk art murals on the walls. There are daily specials, always including lamb dishes, served with spaghetti, potatoes or vegetables, and regular items like moussaka and pastitsio (ground lamb, macaroni and cheese casserole). Open twenty-four hours.

**Nea Hellas,** 33-15 Ditmars Boulevard, between 32nd and 33rd Streets, 278-9728, is also fronted by a steam table. Souvlaki is the house specialty, and you can even purchase it from a window on the street. Inside, there are columns, statuary and hanging wine bottles and worry beads. No English is spoken or understood; it's a real neighborhood place. Open Sunday to Thursday 8:00 A.M. to 1:00 A.M., around the clock the rest of the week.

**Kalyva,** 36-15 Ditmars Boulevard, just off 36th Street, 932-9229, is a fish and meat market as well as a restaurant, replacing the ubiquitous steam table with a display counter. Farther along is a large dining room, its brick and stucco walls adorned with inlaid murals and works of a Greek artist. The Kalyva features many fresh fish and seafood items like lobster (from the tank), shrimp and scallops souvlaki and octopus salad in oil and vinegar. Entrées average $6 to $10, and in addition to baklava for dessert, you might opt for a fresh pear or yogurt with honey. Open daily noon to midnight.

Lots of ambience at the **Rumeli Taverna,** 33-04 Broadway, between 33rd and 34th Streets, 278-7533. The dimly lit dining area here is lightened up by white stucco and wood-paneled walls hung with oil paintings, hanging greenery and fresh flowers on every table. Greek music further enhances the setting. Try the lamb with orzo (a tiny pasta resembling rice) or the chicken with lemon and eggs. Beer and wine are served and prices are moderate. Open daily 11:00 A.M. to 2:00 A.M.

Finally, there's the **Neptune,** 31-05 Astoria Boulevard, corner of 31st Street, 278-4853, a classic Greek-American diner complete with foot-and-a-half-high four-page menu, proffering hundreds of items from Greek cuisine (moussaka, souvlaki, etc.) to wiener schnitzel, roast beef, franks and beans, stuffed lobster, even a bagel with Nova and cream cheese. Open twenty-four hours.

## Coffee and Pastry Shops

Hanging out over a cup of coffee is a Greek national pastime, and fabulous pastry shops abound.

The charming **Hilton Pastry Shop,** 22-06 31st Street, near Ditmars Boulevard, 274-6399, sells pastries downstairs and serves them upstairs. The latter area is mirrored and contains round marble tables and many plants. There's baklava, of course, among numerous Greek pastries like galactoburico (a custard-filled strudel). Open twenty-four hours Friday and Saturday, otherwise till 2:00 A.M.

Though more modest in appearance, **Omonia Pastry Shop,** 41-02 Broadway, between 32nd and 33rd Streets, 278-6165, has exceptional pastries; try the casstina (a dark chocolate-covered cake with butter cream and apricot filling). Open daily from 8:00 A.M. to midnight.

**Omonia II** is located at 32-20 Broadway, 274-6650. Open 8:00 A.M. to 2:00 A.M.

The **HBH Bakery,** 29-28 30th Avenue, between 27th and 28th Streets, 728-9082, is an enormous bakery with marble tables in the back. The specialty here is socolatina cake layers. HBH does special things on holidays: On New Year's there's a gold coin hidden in one loaf of bread, at Easter special breads are made with whole eggs baked into the tops and for Christmas the bakery does a huge business in cookies. Open Sunday to Friday 7:00 A.M. to midnight, Saturday till 1:00 A.M.

Another store full of good things to eat is **Kassos Bros.,** 32-22 30th Avenue, just off 32nd Street, 932-5479. Small, long and mouth-wateringly aromatic, Kassos specializes in Greek, Cypriot and Italian products. Large burlap sacks of grains and beans sit on the floor in front of shelves stocked with tins of olive oil, stuffed grape leaves, Greek coffees, sardines and other groceries. The counter features fresh stuffed grape leaves, Greek cheeses, cold cuts and olives. Open Monday to Saturday 8:30 A.M. to 9:00 P.M., Sunday 10:00 A.M. to 5:00 P.M.

And don't fail to explore **Kiryakos,** 29-29 23rd Avenue, near 31st Street, 545-3931, a tiny shop that utilizes every square inch to house delicious Greek specialties. Open Monday to Saturday 8:00 A.M. to 8:00 P.M.

All liquor stores in the area stock Greek wines and liqueurs, but **Grand Wine and Liquor,** 30-35 31st Street, seems to have the largest selection and best prices. Open Monday to Thursday 9:00 A.M. to 9:00 P.M., Friday and Saturday till 10:00 P.M.

## Gift Shops

Generally the food stores of Astoria are more exotic and interesting than the gift shops. One exception is the **Corfou Center,** 22-13 31st Street, just off Ditmars Boulevard, 728-7212. Amid cosmetics, perfumes and beauty aids, you'll notice Greek newspapers, magazines, candy and cigarettes, plus pottery, intricate icons and navy blue wool fishermen's caps. Lots of interesting little items to peruse, too. Open daily 6:00 A.M. to 1:00 A.M.

The **Hellenic Wedding and Gift Center,** 22-48 31st Street, off 23rd Avenue, 726-1996, specializes in Greek wedding accessories and decorations. It also carries ethnic costumes to be worn on various holidays, embroidered tablecloths, espresso sets, Greek books, greeting cards, records and dolls. Open 9:30 A.M. to 8:30 P.M. Monday to Saturday, 11:00 A.M. to 7:00 P.M. on Sunday.

## Churches

There are two local churches serving this enormous Greek community that you might want to look at. Especially if you attend a service, you'll get a glimpse into another vital aspect of community life here. These are Greek Orthodox, **St. Demitrios,** 30-11 30th Drive, corner of 31st Street, and **SS. Catherine and George,** 22-30 33rd Street, near Ditmars Boulevard.

## A Nightclub

Finally, if you'd like to stay on for the evening, why not catch the show at the **Grecian Cave,** 31-11 Broadway, between 31st and 32nd Streets, 545-7373. There are singers, musicians and belly dancers from Greece—all very authentic. The music begins at about 11:00 P.M. and goes till the wee hours.

# BROOKLYN'S LITTLE SCANDINAVIA

Scandinavian Bay Ridge, from Fifth to Eighth Avenue, between 54th and 60th Streets and again between 76th and 82nd Streets, has more Scandinavian businesses than it does ethnic residents. After reaching its peak between 1900 and 1920, this little ethnic enclave is today fighting for its existence. With every passing year, more local Scandinavian shops close. However, there still remains enough of Scandinavian culture to make a day in Bay Ridge a viable excursion in international New York.

## Restaurants

The **Atlantic Restaurant,** 5414 Eighth Avenue, between 54th and 55th Streets, 438-9348, is an old-fashioned luncheonette-diner with a long blue Formica counter and matching tables. It's homey, very friendly, and offers big portions of homemade fare at low prices. Try Mrs. Johnson's Norwegian pancakes, her traditional yellow pea soup, stuffed cabbage or karbonade (meat cakes with fried onions), but do leave room for home-baked Swedish apple cake. Try to avoid this smallish eatery on Sundays, when the after-church crowd creates long lines. Open daily from 9:00 A.M. to 8:00 P.M.

At the **Fredheim Café,** 476 50th Street, just off Fifth Avenue, 439-6131, you should never have to wait in line. The size of a small banquet hall, it nevertheless manages to evoke an old-fashioned hominess. There are comfortable booths, Scandinavian posters lining the walls and pink-flowered curtains flanking the windows. At breakfast you can have pancakes with lingonberries, at lunch sandwiches filled with egg and anchovy or Norwegian gjetost (a strong yellow goat cheese). À la carte meals (lunch or dinner) feature entrées like fish pudding with white gravy, Swedish meatballs and smoked Norwegian-style sausage, all homemade, priced at under $5 and served with potatoes, soup and vegetables. Open Tuesday to Sunday 10:00 A.M. to 7:00 P.M.

## Food Stores and Bakeries

Should you want to take home Scandinavian delicacies or purchase picnic fare, delicatessens abound. Stop in at **Petzinger's,** 7802 Fifth Avenue, corner of 78th Street, 745-0952, and fill your picnic basket with reindeer meatballs, fish dumplings and fish cakes from Norway, semisoft cheese with caraway seeds, a loaf of Swedish limpa (a mild rye) and some Scandinavian beer. For dessert there's Norwegian marzipan and chocolates. Open daily 8:00 A.M. to 10:00 P.M.

Filling up several shopping bags at **Hinrichsen's,** 7615 Fifth Avenue, between 76th and 77th Streets, 748-0940, is no problem. This tiny deli's shelves are lined with imported goods; its counters stocked with cheeses (try the spicy nokkelost), cold cuts and sausages. There are tins of fish dumplings, tubes (that's right, tubes) of smoked Swedish cod roe caviar paste, smoked herring pâtés, cans of red cabbage cooked with potato and apple, and red currant sauces to pour over rice pudding. Open Monday to Saturday 8:00 A.M. to 10:00 P.M., Sunday to 7:30 P.M.

**Heise Brothers,** 5417 Fifth Avenue, between 54th and 55th Streets, 439-8584, is run by Otto Peters and his wife. While Otto handles behind-the-counter business, selling Swedish wild flower honey, wild lingonberries in sugar, Swedish and Danish breads, fresh herring and such, the Mrs. is busy in the kitchen, cooking up fresh fiskekaker (fish cakes made from chopped cod fillets, stuffed into a dough and fried), meat cakes and potato dumplings. Open Monday to Saturday 8:00 A.M. to 8:00 P.M.

There are three superb bakeries in the area, featuring Scandinavian pastries and breads. Most renowned (you can buy its wares at Bloomingdale's) is **Lund's,** 8122 Fifth Avenue, between 81st and 82nd Streets, 745-7590. Lund's offers vortelimpa (rye flavored with anise and orange peel), Swedish limpa (rye with molasses) and cortakaker (rye with raisins and molasses). Or course, there are buttery Danishes (the real thing), along with krinkle (a coffee cake filled with almond paste, raisins and fruit jams), marzipan, almond cakes and pastries swimming in real whipped cream. Open Tuesday to Saturday 5:30 A.M. to 7:00 P.M.

Further goodies of this sort at **Leskes,** 7612 Fifth Avenue, between 76th and 77th Streets, 680-2323 (Tuesday to Friday 6:00 A.M. to 7:00 P.M., Saturday till 6:00 P.M., Sunday till 4:00 P.M.), and **Olsen's,** 5722 Eighth Avenue, between 57th and 58th Streets, 439-6673 (Monday to Saturday 6:00 A.M. to 8:00 P.M.).

**Fredricksen and Johannesen,** 7719 Fifth Avenue, between 77th and 78th Streets, 745-5980, is a small, bright meat shop that does 40% of its annual business from November through Christmas. At that time the ceiling is hung with sausages, dried mutton legs and hams that it ships throughout the country. Year round, however, you can sample a large choice of homemade sausages, cold cuts, fish pudding and homemade liver pâté. It also carries groceries—soups (note the Swedish blueberry), canned fish, crisp breads, mustard, jams, smoked salmon, mayonnaise, etc. Open Monday to Saturday 8:00 A.M. to 6:00 P.M.

## A Gift Shop

**Signe's Imports,** 5906 Eighth Avenue, between 59th and 60th Streets, 492-5004, carries everything from Danish straw Christmas decorations to Norwegian clogs. There are knitted sweaters, socks, hats and mittens from Norway (many of them handcrafted), hand-painted wooden bowls, Swedish crystal and Norwegian jewelry. Open Monday to Saturday 10:00 A.M. to 6:00 P.M.; closed Monday in summer.

## LITTLE INDIA

As you walk through the Indian shopping district (27th to 30th Streets, between Third and Madison Avenues, in Manhattan), the aromas of curry and coriander beckon you into the many colorful spice and grocery shops. That this is a flourishing Indian neighborhood is a relatively new phenomenon since Indians did not start coming here until the late sixties. Since that time they have flocked here in great numbers, bringing with them an entire culture and providing fortunate New Yorkers with yet another international area.

## Restaurants

**Shalimar,** 39 East 29th Street, between Madison and Park Avenues, 889-1977, is the oldest Indian restaurant in the neighborhood. Its interior is rather elegant, the white stucco walls embedded with pieces of mirror and colored glass and hung with Indian tapestries. This is a place for a long, relaxing meal—not a snack. I'm particularly partial to Shalimar's biryani and tandoori dishes, but everything is good. All bar drinks are available. Most entrées average $7 to $8. Open daily noon to midnight.

**Annapurna,** 108 Lexington Avenue, between 27th and 28th Streets, 679-1284, is one of the most attractive restaurants in the area. The dining room (past the bar as you enter) is lit by brass chandeliers and hung with colorful Indian paintings and rugs. Most popular entrée here is chicken tikka masala—boneless pieces of chicken marinated in yogurt and spices and cooked in the tandoori oven. Full lunches are in the $6 range; dinner entrées average about $8. Open Monday to Saturday 11:30 A.M. to 3:00 P.M. and 5:00 to 11:00 P.M., Sunday 4:00 to 11:00 P.M.

**Curry in a Hurry,** 130 East 29th Street, 683-0900, provides Indian fast food in a modernistic cafeteria setting. Nothing fancy here in the way of food or décor, but you can get a big platter of curries, rice, Indian bread and salad for about $3.50 to $4.50. Open Monday to Saturday, 11:30 A.M. to 9:00 P.M., Sunday to 7:00 P.M.

**Shaheen Sweets,** 99 Lexington Avenue, corner of 27th Street, 683-2139, is another cafeteria-style eatery (table service is available at dinner) with a heavy-on-the-Formica décor, but it is light and airy. The specialty here is Indian desserts; they may seem overly sweet at first but, like all things laden with calories, are an easily acquired taste. Take a few home or sample them on the premises; kheer mohan (fried cheese soaked in syrup with cream on top) and carrot halva (fresh puréed carrots with sugary syrup, cream, almonds, pistachio nuts and raisins) are both good bets. There's sometimes an all-you-can-eat luncheon buffet during the week from noon to 2:30 P.M. Open daily from noon to 9:00 P.M.

**Shamiana,** 119 Lexington Avenue, corner of 28th Street, 689-5150. Two stories high with a waterfall flowing from the second story, carpeted floors and modernistic chrome and cane furnishings, Shamiana is bright and airy with big picture windows overlooking the street. The entire menu here consists of a choice of eight price-fixed dinners (no à la carte) in the $5 to $7 range. Nizam, for example, includes kheema mutter (ground lamb cooked with peas and spices), chicken tikka (boneless chicken, marinated in yogurt and barbecued), a baked eggplant dish, vegetable pilaf, Indian bread and an Indian dessert. Open weekdays noon to 3:00 P.M. and 5:00 to 11:00 P.M., weekends noon to 11:00 P.M.

## *The Food Shops*

**Kalustyan's,** 123 Lexington Avenue, between 28th and 29th Streets, was recently renovated; it now looks like a hip Indian health-food store. Down the center are bins stuffed full of nuts and plump dried fruits, and the shelves are lined with Indian canned goods and condiments— pickles in ginger, chutneys, mango, lotus root, tikka paste, Indian chewing tobacco, even Monkey brand black tooth powder from Bombay.

Up front are fresh veggies, roots and spices, including chili peppers and coriander leaves. Open weekdays 10:00 A.M. to 8:00 P.M., weekends 11:00 A.M. to 7:00 P.M.

**India Food and Gourmet,** 110 Lexington Ave, between 27th and 28th Streets, 686-8955, carries a full line of Indian spices and teas, along with natural Indian snacks made of chickpeas and mung beans. Other items of interest to culinary adventurers are yams in brine, cans of green jackfruit, ghee (clarified butter) and packaged mixes for jalebis (a pretzel-shaped sweet), dosai (Indian pancakes) and vadai (lentil doughnuts). Open Monday to Saturday 10:30 A.M. to 7:30 P.M., Sunday 11:00 A.M. to 6:30 P.M.

One of the largest groceries in the area is **Food of India,** 120 Lexington Avenue, at 28th Street, 683-4419. Up a flight of stairs, this neatly stocked store carries vegetarian items—fresh vegetables, spices, condiments, nuts and dried fruits, canned goods, etc.—along with records and tapes, periodicals and incense. You might try the TimTom Thandai Syrup, a sweet drink base to be mixed with water, rose petals, almonds, pistachios, cloves, cinnamon and sugar. Better than Coke! Open Monday to Saturday 10:00 A.M. to 8:00 P.M., Sunday 11:00 A.M. to 5:00 P.M.

Also look in at the new **Little India Stores,** 128 East 28th Street, 683-1691, which, in addition to the usual groceries, carries stainless steel utensils, Indian records and videocassettes of Indian movies. Open Monday to Saturday 10:00 A.M. to 7:00 P.M., Sunday 11:00 A.M. to 6:00 P.M.

Want more? Continue on to **Spice and Sweet Mahal,** 135 Lexington Avenue, corner of 29th Street, 683-0900, and **Annapurna Indian Groceries,** 127 East 29th Street, 889-7540. The former is open Monday to Saturday 10:00 A.M. to 8:00 P.M., Sunday 11:00 A.M. to 6:00 P.M.; the latter, Monday to Saturday 9:30 A.M. to 7:00 P.M., Sunday 11:00 A.M. to 5:30 P.M.

## A Gift Shop

**The Annapurna Emporium,** 126 East 28th Street, between Park and Lexington Avenues, 696-4929, is a wholesale-retail operation offering an enormous variety of gift items in all price ranges. There are brass hand-wrought hanging fixtures; candlesticks, incense burners and pipes; inlaid boxes; wall hangings and paintings; musical instruments; antique statues of Hindu deities and a great deal more. Open daily 10:00 A.M. to 7:30 P.M.

### Sari Shops

There are sari shops throughout the area, most of them incongruously dealing in luggage, appliances, tapes and cosmetics as well as sari fabrics.

**Uma,** 30 East 30th Street, between Madison and Park Avenues, 532-1385, has a wide choice of fabrics from Japan, China, India, France and the United States as well as India. After you choose the fabric, the staff'll teach you how to wrap yourself properly and provide you with a step-by-step instruction sheet for home use. Uma also sells men's suiting. Open Monday to Saturday 11:00 A.M. to 7:00 P.M.

Continue your quest for sari fabrics at **Anita Sari Center,** 124 Lexington Avenue, between 28th and 29th Streets, 683-4518 (Monday to Saturday 10:00 A.M. to 7:00 P.M., Sunday noon to 6:00 P.M.); **India Sari Palace,** 102 Madison Avenue, corner of 29th Street, 725-5630 (Monday to Saturday 10:00 A.M. to 7:00 P.M.—a huge selection); and **Royal Saree House,** 262 Fifth Avenue, between 28th and 29th Streets, 679-0732 (weekdays 10:00 A.M. to 6:00 P.M., Saturday 11:00 A.M. to 6:00 P.M., Sunday noon to 5:00 P.M.).

## UKRAINIAN EAST VILLAGE

About 100 years before hippies put the East Village on the map, Ukrainian immigrants began settling in the area. Today, some 25,000 in number, the Ukrainian community is the most vital ethnic presence in the neighborhood. It's a smallish area bordered by East Sixth and East Tenth Streets, Avenue A and Third Avenue, but there's lots more to explore. Closest subway stop is the Astor Place station on the Lexington Avenue IRT.

### Restaurants

Though East Villagers have always patronized Ukrainian eateries for hearty, low-priced fare, it wasn't until 1975 that outsiders began flocking to the neighborhood for pirogis. That's when Michael Hyrenko, a young forward-looking Ukrainian, opened **The Ukrainian Restaurant,** 140 Second Avenue, between St. Marks Place and Ninth Street, 533-6765, in a space that previously served as a local social club. It's a large place, with a festive ethnic ambience and Ukrainian waiters and waitresses in national costume. The pirogis here are great; try them with bryndza sauce made from imported sheep milk cheese. There's a full bar, and prices are marvelously low; two can dine sumptuously for under $20. Open Sunday to Thursday noon to 11:00 P.M., Friday and Saturday noon to midnight.

Another Hyrenko creation is **Kiev,** 117 Second Avenue, corner of Seventh Street, 674-4040. A funky, twenty-four-hour eatery, it's extremely popular with the green-haired New Wave set, even though the music played here is mellow rock. The menu features all kinds of Ukrainian specialties—borscht, blintzes (best in New York), kielbasa (sausage), kasha with beef chunks, etc.—but it also offers such wide-ranging entrées as felafel, shish kebab, veal parmigiana and matzoh brei. Waitresses shout their orders to "Momma" in the kitchen. Big windows offer views of East Village street action, but the people watching inside is just as good.

**Odessa Coffee Shop,** 117 Avenue A, between Seventh Street and St. Marks Place, 473-8916, was the favorite hangout of the sixties hippies, though it has also always had a solid Ukrainian clientele. The attractions: big portions of low-priced homemade food served up by motherly waitresses and a casual attitude about hours of schmoozing over a cup of coffee. Today the Odessa is Greek-owned, but the atmosphere, food (Ukrainian and coffee shop fare) and prices are much the same. Best seats are up front in the large booths overlooking Tompkins Square Park. Beer and wine are served. Open Tuesday to Saturday 7:00 A.M. to 11:00 P.M., Sunday 6:00 A.M. to 11:00 P.M..

**Leshko's,** 111 Avenue A, corner of Seventh Street, 473-9208, offers a similar menu in a traditional coffee shop setting. Many booths lining the windows make for sunny dining, and, once again, views of the park. For under $3 you can enjoy a meal of two blintzes with sour cream or stuffed cabbage with potato and vegetable. Try the toasted babka topped with blueberries and ice cream for dessert. Open Monday to Saturday from 7:00 A.M. to 10:00 P.M.

**Veselka,** 144 Second Avenue, corner of Seventh Street, 228-9682, is really just a luncheonette serving ethnic specialities like beef stroganoff, goulash, pirogi and tripe stew. Soups are homemade, as are desserts. If you don't want to eat in such simple surroundings, you might consider taking home some kutia (a cake made with wheatberries, poppy seeds, walnuts and honey) or fresh-baked blueberry muffins. Open Sunday to Friday 7:00 A.M. to 1:00 A.M., Saturday till 2:00 A.M.

**Orchidia,** 145 Second Avenue, corner of Ninth Street, 473-8784, is dark and pubby. Probably the only restaurant of its genre anywhere, it features a combination of Italian and Ukrainian menus. The pizza here is spectacular; other items are better elsewhere. Except during summer, Ochidia serves a big prix fixe buffet brunch every Sunday which is especially popular with the after-church crowd; it includes appetizers, entrées, spiked punch, salads, Ukrainian pastries and more. Open Monday to Thursday 4:00 P.M. to 12:30 A.M., Friday to Sunday from noon to about 1:00 A.M.

## What to See, Do and Buy

First wander into **Surma,** 11 East Seventh Street, between Second and Third Avenues, 477-0729, where pysanky (decorated eggs) are featured along with other Eastern European handicrafts. Legend has it that pysanky conquer evil, and if not enough eggs are painted, evil will flow through the world and destroy it. If so, this neighborhood need not worry; fancy eggs abound. Most fun is to purchase your own egg-decorating kit.

You can also buy ready-made pysanky here, of course, as well as wooden eggs, intricate hand-embroidered blouses, banduras (the lute-like Ukrainian national musical instrument), paintings, embroidery patterns, greeting cards, Slavic books, records and sheet music, sequined velvet vests, traditional porcelain, imported ribbon and braid, dolls and much more. Mr. Surmach, who founded the store more than seventy years ago, has now retired to raise bees in New Jersey, while his son, Myron, tends the business. Jars of honey and pollen (said to be an energy booster) from the apiary are sold in the shop. Open weekdays 11:00 A.M. to 7:00 P.M., Saturday till 6:00 P.M., Sunday till 2:00 P.M.

Across the street is the beautiful domed **St. George's Ukrainian Catholic Church,** 674-1615, fronted by mosaic murals. The interior is also enhanced by exquisite mosaic tiling and stained-glass windows, sixteen of the latter right in the dome. The only way to see the inside is to go to a service—Monday to Saturday from 6:30 to 9:00 P.M., Sunday from 7:30 A.M. to 2:00 P.M. A special time to go is Easter Sunday, when, after 12 o'clock mass, there's Ukrainian dancing in the street. And every year, mid-May, the church sponsors a three-day Ukrainian street festival on East Seventh Street. Call the church for details.

**Norm Enamel Art Gallery,** 13 East Seventh Street, between Second and Third Avenues, 982-1600, is a showcase for the works of artist-owner Szonk Konstantin—framed copper enamel paintings, carved wood sculptures and silver and copper enamel jewelry. He also has a nice selection of coral and amber beads. Open Monday to Saturday 9:00 A.M. to 6:00 P.M.

There's really almost nothing you won't find at Surma, but if you'd like to poke around a few more gift shops, try the cluttery **Eko,** 145 Second Avenue, between Ninth and Tenth Streets, 254-0888. Open 9:00 A.M. to 6:00 P.M. Monday to Saturday, Sunday 11:00 A.M. to 2:00 P.M.

Finally, **Arka,** 48 East Seventh Street, between First and Second Avenues, 473-3550, has two tidy rooms filled with Ukrainian books and publications, fabrics, carved inlaid birch boxes, clocks, embroideries, icons, etc. Open 10:00 A.M. to 6:00 P.M. Monday to Saturday, Sunday 10:00 A.M. to 2:00 P.M.; closed Sunday in summer.

Lucky East Villagers have two superb sparkling clean Ukrainian meat markets purveying top-quality meats and sausages. Baked hams, a vast selection of cold cuts, every variety of kielbasa, pork and veal meat loaves, stuffed kishka and smoked bacon are just a few of the tasty treats that create such enticing aromas at **Kurowycky's,** 124 First Avenue, between Seventh Street and St. Marks Place, 477-0344 (open Monday to Saturday 7:00 A.M. to 6:00 P.M.; closed Mondays in July and August), and at the **East Village Meat Market,** 139 Second Avenue, between St. Marks Place and Ninth Street, 228-5590 (open Monday to Saturday 8:00 A.M. to 6:00 P.M.). Both stores also carry a full line of ethnic groceries—canned herrings, imported mustards, Hungarian paprika, marinated mushrooms, many soups and jams (including rose petal) from Yugoslavia, Poland and Germany, dumpling mixes, fresh black breads, Polish pickles, honey—and provide services like boning chickens—anything a quality butcher would do.

**A.V.D. International Foods,** 101 First Avenue, between Sixth and Seventh Streets, 982-7864, has more Ukrainian edibles—homemade meat-filled piroshki, caviars, halvah, smoked fish, frozen pirogi, bottles of black currants in syrup, strudel, etc. Open Monday 8:00 A.M. to 6:00 P.M., Tuesday to Saturday till 7:00 P.M.

A bit out of the basic area, the **Ukrainian Museum,** 203 Second Avenue, between 12th and 13th Streets, 228-0110, features folk art exhibits—native costumes, jewelry, embroideries (there are about 100 different stitches and techniques), woven textiles, metalwork, ceramics and, of course, pysanky. Most of the collections date from the nineteenth and early twentieth centuries. Museum hours are Wednesday to Sunday from 1:00 to 5:00 P.M. Admission is $1 for adults, 50¢ for students and senior citizens, free to children under six.

# MONEY

*New York* magazine tells us downward mobility has become a reality of American life. Each new generation no longer automatically surpasses its parents in affluence. As if we didn't know. What with taxes, inflation, the high cost of housing and schooling and the mass of baby boom kids coming of age and competing for jobs, we all feel the pinch. This section deals with getting your hands on more money—via grants, loans, investments, playing the stock market more intelligently—and, if all else fails, by working for it.

## BUYING ART FOR INVESTMENT

Barbara Berger of Confluence, Inc., a corporate art consulting firm, has provided these tips for novice art collectors.

Take a course in art collecting such as that offered at the adult education division of NYU or the New School of Social Research, and participate in gallery tours like those offered by Gallery Passport, 686-2244 (details in the vacation section of this book, pp.132-140).

Visit as many contemporary galleries as possible in Soho, on 57th Street and in the uptown area. Bring a notebook, and take notes on the art and artists that interest you. Introduce yourself to the staff of each gallery; find out what kind of art it represents, prices and biographies of the artists.

There is usually a standard pricing structure in the art market which you can learn by asking to see gallery price lists and attending auctions. Get on the mailing lists of art auction houses. When you have an idea of the pricing structure in commercial galleries, you can usually estimate a fair price for work bought in artists' studios by deducting 40% to 50% (standard gallery commission).

If you're a gambler with an adventurous spirit and want to locate artists before they're well known and their prices soar, visit alternative spaces that show the works of artists not affiliated with commercial galleries. These include **Artists Space,** 105 Hudson Street, corner of Franklin Street, 226-3970, **The New Museum,** 65 Fifth Avenue, between 13th and 14th Streets, 741-8962, **PS One,** 46-01 21st Street, Long Island City, 784-2084, and **The Drawing Center,** 137 Greene Street, between Houston and Prince Streets, 982-5266.

Get on gallery mailing lists and attend openings. Here you'll meet the artists in person and hear art world gossip—the best information is still word-of-mouth, and it's very easy for prospective buyers to secure invitations to artists' studios.

Once you have purchased a work of art, make sure you have all the necessary information for insurance.

Finally, if your small business or corporation is interested in starting a collection of fine art, give Barbara a call at 752-4774.

## CONTESTS

You may scoff at contest entering as a way to obtain money, but Selma Glasser, author of *The Complete Guide to Prize Contests, Sweepstakes, & How to Win Them* (Bantam), won't. She's won a Ford station wagon, vacations in Rome and Paris, a complete set of the *Encyclopaedia Britannica*, a date with Frank Sinatra, gas heat and hot-water systems for her home, a mink, a washing machine, several TV sets and hard cash...among other things. In addition to the book, Selma gives courses in contest winning. If you're interested in the course, write to her, including a stamped, self-addressed envelope, at 241 Dahill Road, Brooklyn, N.Y. 11218; to order the book, include $4.45 postpaid.

Contest aficionados also subscribe to publications like *Contest Newsletter* and *Golden Chances*. They describe all current contests and tell you how to enter, including the correct words to complete qualifying sentences, what's written on the label of such-and-such brand of scotch, etc. A subscription to either costs $12 a year. For *Contest Newsletter* write to Roger & Carolyn Tyndall, P.O. Box 1059, Fernandina Beach, Fla. 32034; for *Golden Chances* write to Tom Lindell, P.O. Box 655, S. Pasadena, Calif. 91030.

## THE DEBT DILEMMA

**Budget and Credit Counseling Service, Inc.,** 44 East 23rd Street, 677-3066

Inflation keeps spiraling upward faster than your income, credit is still pretty easy to come by and chances are very good you're in over your head financially. Don't panic. But do get yourself over to BCCS. It'll help you renegotiate with creditors (also landlords and employers), set up a plausible payment plan and create a sensible budget to avoid the recurrence of credit nightmares. It will inform you that credit cards are not a substitute for cash, merely a convenience to avoid carrying cash, and very likely it'll suggest you clip some—or all—of yours in half and file them in the circular file. Most of the people who come to BCSS for help are not social deadbeats. They're honorable, hardworking folks—often quite well educated—who never intended to work up debts they couldn't pay but never learned to budget either. If you're living above your income, it's time to visit BCSS now. Don't wait until you're hounded by creditors and the situation is dire. The cost for its services (one-on-one counseling) is $25 for as many visits as necessary. Call for an appointment.

## FOUNDATION GRANTS

**The Foundation Center,** 888 Seventh Avenue, New York, N.Y. 10106, 975-1120, 800-424-9836

Much money (more than $2.8 billion annually) is available for a multitude of projects from foundation grants. The Foundation Center's COMSEARCH printouts (computer-generated listings of more than 20,000 foundation grants) provide information about money available in about eighty different subject categories from hundreds of foundations. These include grants for projects in communications and media, education, health, humanities, work with population groups (women, minorities, etc.), sciences, social sciences, welfare and other areas. The printouts tell you each foundation's grant-making pattern in the past, and that's generally the best indicator of its future funding interests. Write or call to get a full list of COMSEARCH subject categories. Copies of printouts in any given subject cost $15; $5 for microfiche copies. Also ask about COMSEARCH Broad Topics—bound books of grants in eleven large subject areas with full indexing.

## FUND RAISING

**Luncheon Is Served,** 258 Degraw Avenue, Teaneck, N.J. 07666, 201-836-1438

If you're planning a fund raiser for any nonprofit organization, you will want to know about Luncheon Is Served. This is an interesting service with benefits for all involved. Luncheon Is Served represents leading food manufacturers who wish to call their products to the attention of the consumer. They will put together a large three-course lunch for you for a $100 service charge—enough food for 80 to 100 people. You sell the tickets and keep the profits for the organization. This is a painless way to get funds. The manufacturers often also give away coupons, recipe books and door prizes as a bonus.

## MEASURING THE RISK OF YOUR STOCK MARKET INVESTMENTS

**Paine, Webber, Jackson & Curtis,** 140 Broadway, New York, N.Y. 10005, 437-2121

Is your stock portfolio in line with your overall investment objectives? Is your entire stock picture high-risk or conservative? How are your stocks likely to perform if the market goes up or down 10%, 20% or 30%? Now you can easily have the answers to these and other vital questions about your securities.

Free of charge and obligation, Paine Webber will do a computer analysis of your portfolio and compare your holdings to the entire market. You'll get a printout with your stocks listed according to "volatility" ranking (high, medium or low) and "beta." High volatility means the stock has shown great fluctuation as compared to all other listed securities. The beta factor indicates your stock's sensitivity to market moves. You may find out that a portfolio you considered conservative is, in fact, quite speculative or that holdings you bought as speculative ventures have become conservative in recent years.

The whole process takes just twenty-four hours, and all you have to do is drop off or mail in a listing of your investments (including the name of each stock and the number of shares you hold) at any Paine Webber office. Or call the above number, and it'll send you a brochure explaining the service (it's called Portfolio Dynamics) in even greater detail. Thank you, Paine Webber!

## SETTING UP BUSINESS AFTER YOU RELOCATE

**Country Business Services, Inc.,** Box 824, Brattleboro, Vt. 05301, 802-254-4504 or 800-451-4251

Many people who want to leave urban life behind are overwhelmed at the prospect of setting up a livelihood in the country. That's where

Country Business Services comes in. A brokerage operation, it buys up businesses throughout New England, analyzes them completely and in great detail, packages the financing and helps the buyer prepare a five-year business plan. "We make a commitment to the success of someone who buys a business through us," says CBS president James Howard. His company can set you up in a variety of small manufacturing and retail operations as well as hotels and country inns. And the fee is paid by the seller, so the service is free to you. In addition, Country Business gives seminars on buying a business (it costs from $75 up to attend) and puts out three very helpful business manuals on valuation, acquisition and business planning. You can order any of these by sending $29.95 plus $1.55 for postage and handling to the above address. Country Business is in the process of franchising throughout the nation. Write or call for details.

**Service Corps of Retired Executives (SCORE),** 26 Federal Plaza, between Duane and Worth Streets, room 3130, 264-4507

If you are interested in setting up a small business in the metropolitan area, or already have your own business and need some advice, the Service Corps of Retired Executives can help. We all know that consultant fees can run into hundreds of dollars. SCORE will provide essentially the same services, free. Sponsored by the U.S. Small Business Administration, it is a volunteer group of retired executives who will provide management counseling to anyone who has or wants to start a small business of any kind. Open weekdays from 10:00 A.M. to 2:30 P.M.

## TRACING OLD STOCK CERTIFICATES

**Stock Market Information Service, Inc.,** P.O. Box 120, Station "K," Montreal, Canada HIN 3K9, 514-256-9487

There may be a fortune sitting in your garage or attic if, like thousands of people, you have musty old stock and bond certificates packed away and long forgotten. Sometimes unknown companies, left for dead, are, in fact, prosperous and active under different names (in North America alone more than 6,000 mergers take place annually). And sometimes when a company goes out of business, it leaves assets that can be claimed by unregistered stockholders as liquidating dividend from the trustees.

If you have old certificates around and want to find out their value, send them to the Stock Market Information Service, a stock sleuth company run by Micheline Masse in Montreal. Since she began her operations in 1969, she's recovered more than $1 million in stock money for clients. About 50% of stock certificates have some value, says Micheline, sometimes even as collectors' items because of engraving designs or historic values. If you'd like to have your stocks traced, send $30 per company along with a photocopy of each certificate. SMIS will undertake the necessary research in any country in the world in order to establish the exact value and present status of stocks and bonds issued since 1850.

# PARTIES

From the number of party-planning services available in this town, you'd think New Yorkers were in a constant state of celebration. Caterers, florists, entertainers, party consultants, special bakers, etc. number in the thousands.

The following is just a tiny sampling of what's available, but with this section alone, you have enough information for a lifetime of innovative parties.

## BARTENDERS

**Columbia Student Enterprises Bartending Agency,** 280-4536

For more than twenty-five years this very reliable agency has been sending out personable young Columbia and Barnard students to work as bartenders. They're all graduates of an eighteen-hour mixology course who have served an apprenticeship, and they can whip up anything from a martini to a mai tai in no time at all. The students come dressed in black trousers or skirts and white jackets. Their rates are most reasonable: $48 for the first four hours (the minimum charge), $12 an hour after that.

## ESPECIALLY FOR CHILDREN

**Jeremy's Place,** 905 Madison Avenue, between 72nd and 73rd Streets, 586-6300

The favorite entertainer of New York's under-seven set is not Kermit the Frog. It's Jeremy Sage, a children's party performer who tells jokes and stories, keeps up a nonstop patter, makes animals out of balloons, does magic tricks and much more. He recently opened Jeremy's Place, an innovative party space that has more fun frills per inch than Disneyland. There are carnival mirrors, toys and stuffed animals, a cave, costumes aplenty (with cardboard scenes for kids to stick their heads in) and a Polaroid camera for moms to take pictures, a 4½-foot electric robot, even a magic window out of which things are delivered by a strange hand. When it's time for the cake, the key to the magic window comes around on a miniature train. The birthday child takes it, unlocks the window, and out comes a cake with lit candles. There's much, much more from Jeremy's zany collection. He charges $65 for two hours' use of the room, plus $5 per child, $120 extra if you engage his services for entertainment. Included are the cake, ice cream, juice and other refreshments, plus special prizes for guests and birthday child. If you like, Jeremy can videotape the party for you.

He also performs in Manhattan homes. The fee is $145, including a balloon prize for each child and a 4½-foot-tall octopus balloon for the birthday child.

If you've got Jeremy, your child's party is an assured success. Book far in advance. He is outrageously popular.

**Magic Towne House,** 1026 Third Avenue, between 60th and 61st Streets, 752-1165

This center of hocus-pocus activity specializes in children's birthday parties. They're scheduled around the regular weekend shows for kids (at 1:00, 2:30 and 4:00 P.M.)—hour-long productions with live birds, comedy and magic in which the birthday child participates as an onstage assistant. After the show, guests go to a private room where clowns run the party. There are games, and a cake (baked fresh that day and topped with a rabbit coming out of a hat), fruit punch and ice cream sundaes are served. Each child gets a balloon animal made by a clown and a loot bag of fourteen party favors. Adults are served coffee and cake. Parents have nothing to do except send out invitations supplied by the Towne House. The cost is $135 for up to twelve people (adults or children), $10 for each extra person. Hot dogs are available at an extra fee.

**Teterboro Airport,** 201-288-6344

An expensive and novel solution for the what-should-we-do-for-junior's-birthday-this-year dilemma is to throw a party at Teterboro Airport.

Only six miles from the George Washington Bridge in New Jersey, the airport employs an old control tower for this purpose. The young guests can watch planes landing and taking off (the tower is glass), tune into communications and play with defunct equipment. They also get to tour the Aviation Hall of Fame and Museum and see an old movie of aerial circus stunts before cake and punch is served. The birthday child is given a Hall of Fame T-shirt and an honorary pilot's certificate; the guests get aviation souvenirs. And the price of these 1½-hour parties is about $30 for six, $1.25 for each additional child. They can take place any weekday between 10:00 A.M. and 4:00 P.M. Book far in advance.

**The USS *Ling*,** 201-487-9493

How about a birthday party aboard a restored World War II attack submarine? The USS *Ling* is moored in Hackensack, New Jersey (just a twenty-minute drive from Manhattan), at the Submarine Memorial Museum and is available as a party space on weekdays. Included in the deal are a nautically themed birthday cake with candles, a guided tour of the *Ling*, a captain's hat for the birthday child, tablecloth, napkins, glasses (and punch) and forks. The cost is about $30 for six children (they must be at least five years old), $2 for each adult and $1 for each additional child. If there are more than seven attending, there's an extra cake charge.

## THE FOOD

### Caterers, Picnics and Platters

**John Boyajy,** 877-1077

Specializing in nouvelle natural cuisine with a Middle Eastern slant, John Boyajy caters everything from little dinner parties to sit-down or buffet affairs for 200 people, cocktail parties for 400. He offers every imaginable catering service; in addition to food, he can arrange music (trust him, he's a Juilliard grad), other entertainers (mimes, psychics, palmists, you name it), staff, rentals, flowers, etc. His repertoire includes dishes like poached striped bass with ginger-scallion beurre blanc; Cornish hens stuffed with couscous, dates and pistachios; cold sea trout with green mayonnaise or walnut sauce; and delicious, but natural, desserts like strudel or dried fruits and nuts steeped in brandy. That's just a fraction of the possibilities. Complete vegetarian meals are a specialty. Prices begin at about $10 per person for a vegetarian cocktail party.

If the above-mentioned dishes sound like the kind you'd love to prepare yourself, consider enrolling in one of John's cooking classes at the **Natural Gourmet Cookery School,** 365 West End Avenue, between 77th and 78th Streets, 580-7121.

**Parties..."A La Cart,"** 490 Curry Avenue, Englewood, N.J., 201-568-7611.

The perfect caterer for garden and pool parties, sweet sixteens and other casual affairs, Parties... "A La Cart" serves buffet style from cheerful orange-and-white-striped umbrella carts staffed by youthful waiters and waitresses in matching orange and white getups—or in black tie if the occasion warrants it. You can choose from a variety of menus, including "Little Old New York" with hot dogs, coleslaw, potato salad, macaroni salad, rich egg creams and Italian ices for dessert. Other themes include "Country French," "Paradise Island Luau," "Festivale Italiano," "Fiesta Mexicana" and the "Wild West Bonanza." Frosted desserts—e.g., hot fudge sundaes prepared to order—are a speciality, and bar carts are an option. Prices begin at about $15 per person.

**Ruslan,** 1067 Madison Avenue, between 80th and 81st Streets, 371-3419 or 570-9160

Operating out of a small Upper East Side restaurant, Ruslan features "aristocratic Russian cuisine with a French accent." Owner Tania Hutchason is an émigrée, born of White Russian parents in China. Her catering credits include many Soho gallery openings, frequent parties for the Metropolitan Opera Guild, parties for the New York City Ballet and a bash for ballerina Natalia Makarova (at Xenon) among many others. She'll delight your guests with beautiful platters (decorated with fresh flowers) of caviar, kulibiaka (whitefish or salmon in a flaky pastry crust), chicken Kiev, roast duck with apples, piroshki, stuffed breast of veal, beef stroganoff, etc. There's also a choice of about sixty stunning hors d'oeuvres—saucisson en croûte, cucumbers with crab meat, mushrooms filled with eggplant caviar, seafood in aspic, etc.—and exquisite desserts such as peach mousse and orange Bavarian cream.

Ruslan provides full catering services—staff, rentals (tables, china, etc.), flower arrangements, music, liquor—according to your needs from $12 and up for cocktails, $25 and up for dinner.

**Hisae's,** 753-6555

Some of the most elegant parties in New York are given at Hisae's various restaurants: movie openings, the Carnegie Hall benefit for the Tappan Zee Playhouse (Liza Minnelli, Helen Hayes, etc.), the first-birthday party for the show *Woman of the Year* with Lauren Bacall and many, many others. Hisae's also caters parties at people's homes, reception halls, etc. and parties with a country-and-western theme at Swiss Chalet Barbecue, another Hisae venture. It does every aspect of catering for parties of up to 500, and the food can include any of the traditional fish and vegetable Hisae favorites or any other menu you might desire. Sushi is very popular these days. Specialty cakes such as a scale model of Yankee Stadium Hisae's did for a New York Yankees' bash are also featured. Cocktails are about $15 per head; dinner is at $20 to $30 per person.

**Second Avenue Deli,** 156 Second Avenue, at Tenth Street, 677-0606

Sometimes you want nouvelle cuisine; sometimes you want cocktail franks in blankets. Or as owner Abe Lebewohl puts it, "The French may have pâté, but New Yorkers have chopped liver." All the kosher deli favorites served in the restaurant are available for party fare—plus kosher Chinese dishes and Viennese desserts. Abe is a pro. He's been catering since 1954—for politicos like Carol Bellamy, for newspeople like Bill Boggs and Roger Grimsby, for weddings, bar mitzvahs, etc. You can order immense buffet platters of knishes, cold cuts, roast turkey (carved and put back on the frame), potato salad, chopped liver, deli sandwiches, gefilte fish, stuffed cabbage, etc... or have Abe cater a complete sit-down dinner—with hot entrées like stuffed roast chicken and Hungarian beef goulash—for any number of people. The deli offers full catering services, including traditional Jewish waiters. A buffet party for 100 can cost as little as $900. Go in and discuss your entertaining needs with Abe.

**Tea for Two,** 744-0001

Britisher Jennifer Lyons will deliver a traditional English afternoon tea to your home on a beautifully arranged doily-covered platter with a fresh flower. Her offerings include tea sandwiches cut in triangles and pinwheels (smoked salmon, cucumber and cream cheese, egg salad, chicken salad, red caviar, etc.), homemade scones with fresh whipped cream and strawberry jam and, of course, tea. The price for a single tea is between $10 and $12 per person, plus delivery charge; less for large groups (she does many cocktail parties). Jennifer supplies the Mayfair

Regent with its afternoon tea fare. It's a great party idea, also a lovely gift to send to a sick friend or someone who's just had a baby. Give Jennifer at least twenty-four hours' notice.

## *Chinese Banquets*

One of my most successful parties was given not at my home but at a Chinese restaurant where ten of us participated in a nonstop eating Chinese banquet. Take your pick from anyone of the following restaurants, whose facilities range from private rooms to comfortable large round tables. Prices start at about $12 per person and can go as high as $50 per head.

**Peng Teng,** 219 East 44th Street, between Second and Third Avenues, 682-8050

Ask for Jimmy I or II at this elegant restaurant which caters to New York's affluent Chinese community and is a favorite with visiting Washingtonians and UN delegates. Although there are two attractive dining rooms, try to reserve one of the private rooms which are perfect settings for a banquet or private party. Twenty-five dollars a person will bring you a twelve-course dinner, including sautéed lobster with hot spiced ginger sauce. At lunchtime it's $20. Monday through Sunday, noon to 10:30 P.M.

**The Canteen,** 45 Division Street, between Market Street and the Bowery, 226-9173

Eileen knows her Cantonese food and caters to an uptown crowd in this modern Chinese restaurant. Invite ten people or more; tell her your price limit (prices are about $150 per table). The tables are elegantly set with teal blue linen and lovely blue and white pattern china, and seating is in wicker and chrome blue-cushioned chairs. The seafood dishes are especially good, and if crabs are in season, see if the chef will do a casserole with black bean sauce. Tuesday through Sunday 11:30 A.M. to 10:00 P.M.

**Jumbo,** 9, Elizabeth Street, between Canal and Bayard Streets, 966-2090

This one is a rather unimpressive-looking Chinese restaurant that specializes in authentic Chinese banquet foods. For about $150 about ten people can feast on shrimp, chicken, abalone and steak. I never let the fact that few, if any, of the waiters speak English bother me. Just be brave and order away. You might not know what you ordered but it's bound to taste good. Monday through Sunday, 9:00 A.M. to 10:30 P.M.

## *Gourmet Shops*

Most of the city's gourmet food markets do some form of catering—from sending out exquisite mouth-watering platters to providing full catering services. And almost all offer attractively packaged picnic meals, which are detailed here.

**Washington Market,** 162 Duane Street, at Hudson Street, 233-0250, in Tribeca, offers full catering services from buffet platters of cheeses, pâtés and smoked fish to the likes of braised port stuffed with prunes and bourbon, cold poached chicken breast à la russe and mousseline of trout with pistachios. Its sumptuous picnic boxes are priced from $5 to $11 per person. Open Monday through Saturday, 6:00 A.M. to 9:00 P.M., Sunday till 5:00 P.M.

Nothing could be more wonderful than serving platters of heavenly food from **Dean & DeLuca,** 121 Prince Street, between Wooster and Greene Streets, 254-7774, Soho's famed culinary temple. You can order anything that is sold here—rabbit pâtés, roast suckling pig, extraordinary breads and cheeses, Ligurian olives, dried tomatoes in oil, saucisson in cornbread, leek pie, a salad of conch, octopus and squid, chicken salad with sorrel and perhaps strawberry mousse cake for dessert. I mean, roast quails are Dean & DeLuca's idea of finger foods. If you've ever visited the store, no further explanation is necessary; if you haven't, you're missing one of New York's most awesome attractions. Open Monday through Saturday, 10:00 A.M. to 7:00 P.M., Sunday to 6:00 P.M.

Picnic boxes with utensils and napkins begin at $30 for two and, like catering platters, are made to order only.

**Zabar's,** Broadway at 80th Street, 787-2000, also does platters only—but what platters! Priced from about $6.50 per person (minimum of ten people) they're piled high with cold cuts—Black Forest ham, smoked turkey, Italian salami, etc., smoked fish, herrings, cheeses, lobster, shrimp and crab-meat salads and much more. You can get caviar, chopped chicken liver molds, whole turkeys carved and replaced on the frame, a whole smoked whitefish boned, filleted and served on a marble board or a whole poached salmon garnished with lemon slices and capers. Or how about French smoked duck, or roasted Cornish game hens, or trays of hors d'oeuvres—everything from miniature quiches to cocktail franks in blankets?

Zabar's picnics in a box—including cutlery and napkins—are priced at $15.75 for two eaters. An example: the "West Side Picnic," with stuffed grape leaves, roast Cornish hens, three-bean salad, French rolls, fruit, cheese and cookies. Many other choices.

You can't go wrong with platters of gourmet goodies from **Balducci's**, 424 Sixth Avenue, between Ninth and Tenth Streets, 673-2600. It has no set platter menus, so you can just select anything from the store: stuffed shrimp, spinach and cheese strudel, stuffed squab with fresh raspberry sauce, Szechuan chicken, cheeses and cold cuts, tortellini salad, beautiful cakes and pastries, etc.

You can also choose items for inclusion in picnics; they're packed in stained mushroom baskets for two people, in wicker baskets for four, and prices begin at about $15 per person.

Parties catered from **Country Host,** 1435 Lexington Avenue, between 93rd and 94th Streets, 876-6525, Lexington Avenue's only country English kitchen, can include any of Rona Deme's delicious creations. How original to serve up potted kipper pâté, sweetbreads and oyster pie, Scotch eggs, Cornish pasties, savory ducks, bubble and squeak, Stilton cheese soufflé and perhaps seed cake or treacle tart for dessert. Or offer your guests a complete European cuisine. Party rates begin at about $12 per person. Country Host can cater for up to 100 people, supply waiters and waitresses, bartenders, etc.

It also does lovely picnics wrapped in pie boxes and tied with pretty colored ribbons. Prices begin at about $8.50 a box; that might include fried chicken, salad, a buttered scone, crudités with dip, cheese, fruit and hard candies, plus forks, napkins and plates.

**Word of Mouth,** 1012 Lexington Avenue, between 72nd and 73rd Streets, 734-9483

Word of Mouth specializes in hearty home-style cooking. Walking into the shop is like walking into your grandmother's pantry. We love its fresh vegetable and chicken salads, its pasta and rice dishes. Don't miss its hearty soups in the winter—split pea and bean, cream of tomato, corn and clam chowder. Baking is done on the premises. Prices are upper moderate to expensive.

The **Silver Palate,** 274 Columbus Avenue, between 72nd and 73rd Streets, 799-6340, is a one-stop gourmet shop where you can purchase a full-scale dinner party ready to heat and serve. There are hundreds of choices, the likes of pâté de campagne with walnuts, curried chicken salad with red grapes, country-baked ham with apricot sauce, whole poached salmon, fresh-baked breads and croissants and desserts like tartetatin. Or leave it all to the staff. Silver Palate offers full catering services. It also does some of the most exquisite picnic baskets in town. You can get them in a pretty Silver Palate shopping bag, a cloth-insulated hamper or a traditional picnic basket—it'll even include fresh flowers. Prices vary. Twenty-four hours' notice is appreciated if you want something elaborate.

**In a Basket,** 226 East 83rd Street, between Second and Third Avenues, 472-9787, is a delightful French country kitchen with baskets on the walls. You can take out party food or have owners Renée and Gary Frase handle all your catering needs. They do scrumptuous hors d'oeuvres—assorted quiches, stuffed mushrooms, dates wrapped in bacon, new baby potatoes stuffed with sour cream and chives, etc.—and entrées like salmon or veal in pastry, roast pork stuffed with port-soaked fruit, veal stuffed with sausage and chicken breast with tarragon and Dijon mustard. Marvelous homemade breads and desserts, too. An average In a Basket dinner party is in the $20 to $40 per person range.

As for picnics, they come in mushroom baskets with all necessary utensils, etc. An $18 picnic for two might contain herb-roasted chicken, salad, Brie, crackers, fruit and the brownies that Gael Greene said were "worth a crosstown detour." Monday through Friday 9:00 A.M. to 6:00 P.M.

### Picnics Only

**The Brasserie,** 100 East 53rd Street, 751-4840, open around the clock, is renowned for its classic French-style picnics. They're packed in traditional wicker baskets (you leave a deposit) with real (not plastic) silverware, glassware, linen tablecloth and napkins. Priced from about $6.50 to $11.50 per person, one of these provincial picnics might include marinated mushrooms and artichokes, roast duckling, orange salad with red onions, crudités, a French roll, Camembert cheese and a fruit tart. A few hours' advance notice is all that's needed.

### Where to Get the Cake

**Patticakes and Baked Ideas,** 925-9097

Patti Paige's baked creations have been called gastronomic art. She sculpts and designs them to order, and no two are the same. When Jacob Javits was senator, she made a cake in the shape of New York State with a marzipan bust of him on top. And for the opening of the movie *King*

*Kong* she fashioned an immense ape cake with a nude marzipan Fay Wray in his palm. Though it almost seems Philistine to eat them, her butter and chocolate cakes are absolutely delicious.

**Pie in the Sky,** 173 Third Avenue, between 16th and 17th Streets, 228-2790

Unbelievable melt-in-your-mouth desserts are alluringly displayed at Pie in the Sky. You can purchase its fresh-baked pecan chocolate, key lime, lemon chess, sweet potato and ginger pear pies and cakes like the very rich chocolate with chocolate icing, wet walnut, pineapple upside down, banana whipped cream, etc. Or have cakes made to order for special occasions. They begin at just $8 for a cake that amply serves six. Pie in the Sky offers full catering by the way—not just desserts, but charcuterie, salads and hot entrées; Andy Warhol and Ed Koch are among its clients. You can also enjoy all Pie in the Sky culinary creations on the premises; it is primarily a restaurant open Tuesday to Saturday 11:30 A.M. to 11:00 P.M., Sunday and Monday 11:00 A.M. to 10:00 P.M.

**Flying Birthday Cakes,** 865 First Avenue, between 48th and 49th Streets, 838-5115

Sending a cake to kids away at school or camp is a great idea, but how can you be sure that after post office handling it doesn't arrive as a box of crumbs? By leaving it all to Robert D. Grimm, who has perfected baking and packing methods that ensure perfect delivery. His cakes are made with light golden batter and topped with butter-cream frosting. They go out frozen and arrive thawed and bakery fresh. Included with the cake are a dozen plates and forks, a knife, candles and a gift card with your message. The cost: $23.95 for a cake that serves 12, plus $5 for shipping, handling and insurance in the United States and to military addresses. For additional postage, Grimm can send cakes anywhere in the world.

## *PARTY ENTERTAINERS*

**Le Menage,** 567-4607, 362-2546

I always love weddings that dispense with the band—at least for part of the affair—and in its place offer chamber music. An elegant enhancement to any entertainment, Le Menage is a delightful classical trio (oboe, violin and bassoon) of three charming young Oberlin Conservatory graduates who play regularly at parties, weddings, gallery openings and other events throughout the metropolitan area. Their repertoire consists primarily of music from the Renaissance, Baroque, and classical eras. Fee is $150 an hour (plus a minimal travel charge where applicable). A cassette tape is available for audition purposes.

**Garth's Original Rent-a-Clown,** 242-4034

This group consists of six professional clowns (male and female). Members of this talented troupe are adept at mime, juggling, fire eating, magic, stilt walking, musical acts, slapstick and tightrope walking— all the clown arts, in fact. They can also turn children into clowns, ghouls, tramps, vampires, werewolves or the Wizard of Oz clan— actually into anything you can think of—using stage make-up. You might even hire them to create a knockout Halloween or costume-party getup. Rates range from $100 to $250 per clown, depending on the size of the group to be entertained and travel distance.

**Music at Home,** 165 West 91st Street, 362-7365

Imagine your next dinner party with a string quartet in white tie and tails performing in the background... or everyone retiring after the meal for chamber music in the salon. Music at Home director Alice Weaver has selected the city's finest professional chamber music groups and soloists to enhance any occasion with music of any style or period. Her performers range from cocktail and classical pianists, harpists, flute players and classical guitarists to string, woodwind, brass and jazz ensembles. She can provide a group to play Renaissance music on authentic period instruments, perform minioperas and operettas, or do eighteenth-century dances—anything, in fact, from Scarlatti to New Wave. She'll help you design a musical program suitable for the occasion and work to suit your musical tastes and budgetary requirements. Alice has personally auditioned any group she sends out. Call her as far in advance as possible.

**Rent-a-Witch,** 349-1956, 201-873-3093

This "coven" of thirteen witches will enchant your guests with all kinds of occult entertainment—divination, palmistry, tarot readings, astrology, crystal gazing, psychic caricatures (they draw who you were in a significant past life!), numerology, handwriting analysis, etc. The witches—psychics—all arrive at your party in pointy hats and black capes, broomsticks in hand. They never give bad forecasts or say anything negative, but they might use their spiritual powers to absorb bad energies and change a guest's aura from gray to white. What more could you ask of a host? Witch rental costs $200 for two hours (the minimum), $75 an hour after that.

Under the same auspices is **Make-Believe Children's Parties,** offering a variety of entertainments for tots—fairy godmothers who transform children into clowns, monkey faces, etc. with stage make-up; costumed Minnie and Mickey mice and Miss Piggys who sing, organize games, give out gifts, perform magic and put on marionette shows. Charges are about $100 per character for the first hour, $50 an hour after that, including balloons and gifts.

All services are available throughout the metropolitan area.

## PARTY PLACES/PARTY IDEAS

Want to know where to throw a party? The most complete source is a book called *Places: A Directory of Public Places for Private Events & Private Places for Public Functions* (Tenth House Enterprises, Inc.). It contains more than 1,000 entries, mostly in New York but with a section on nationwide choices. They include a plethora of places—armories, auditoriums, ballrooms, discos, boats, mansions, churches, hotels, meeting rooms, lofts, etc.—and party ideas ranging from a wedding aboard a mule-drawn barge to a champagne party in a hot-air balloon. It makes good reading even if you never get around to entertaining. To order, send $16.95 to Tenth House Enterprises, P.O. Box 810, Gracie Station, New York, N.Y. 10028. Or call 737-7536; there's a free information service to help you find a party space to suit your needs.

**The Morris-Jumel Mansion,** West 160th Street and Edgecombe Avenue, 923-8008

The fact that you don't have a garden doesn't mean you can't give a garden party—and in the garden of a stately eighteenth-century Georgian mansion no less. The Morris-Jumel Mansion caters light luncheons for corporations and special interest groups only—they'll serve up to sixty people for $6 to $10 a person. With prices like that you can afford to hire a chamber music ensemble, too. The fare is light—wine punch, salad, quiche or sandwiches, homemade carrot or rum sponge cake and tea or coffee. Guests also get to tour the mansion, which is the oldest extant private dwelling in Manhattan. George Washington was headquartered here for a short time during 1776, and Aaron Burr was married in the front parlor. There are many beautiful antiques and things of interest to see inside, including Napoleon's bed.

**World Yacht Enterprises,** 14 West 55th Street, 246-4811

Want to impress your friends? Throw a party aboard a luxury yacht. World Yacht Enterprises has a fleet of yachts available for anything from a cocktail party for six to a wedding party of 250 to an extended party-*cum*-cruise around the world! These floating functions can be as casual or lavish as you wish. Possible frills include flowers, music, cabaret shows, open-bar service, special lighting and décor, black-tie service, photography, invitations, just about anything you like. It'll even supply a rabbi or minister for on-board weddings. There are many luncheons, dinner, buffet and cocktail party menus to choose from. The average figure for a four-hour party with food and drink is about $50 per person. A lovely idea is an evening cruise with dinner and dancing on board or at a waterside restaurant. There are almost infinite possibilities. Most boats are available from April to November only. Reserve as far in advance as possible to ensure the widest selection of boats and dates.

**Chateau Animal Stables,** 608 West 48th Street, near 11th Avenue, 246-0520

Sleigh rides, hay rides and horse-and-buggy rigs are just the tip of the iceberg of Chateau's offerings. It rents performing animals (anything from a flea to an elephant) and horse-drawn vehicles. It even supplied an elephant to Ronald Reagan for a Republican event. A two-hour hayride (usually through Central Park) is about $200 for a dozen children or ten adults; most people pack lunches and cake for a picnic in the park. A ride with a horse and buggy in Manhattan is about $50 an hour. Chateau has a marvelous choice of vehicles—old-fashioned stagecoaches, carriages, hansom cabs, Oklahoma surreys, buggies, delivery wagons, chuckwagons, farm wagons, peddlers' wagons, donkey carts, pedicabs, royal chariots, even an antique hearse. As for animals, it can supply you with white doves, a pony or donkey for children to ride, performing dogs, farm animals, you name it. Sleigh rides are an option only when there's considerable snow, of course. Chateau serves the entire metropolitan area.

## PARTY PLANNERS

**All About Parties,** 341 East 33rd Street, 686-3296

If you're planning a large party—or one that has a complicated theme—you couldn't do better than to leave everything to All About Parties' Myra Sincoff. She has hundreds of party facilities at her fingertips, and her services cost you absolutely nothing; she works on commission from restaurants, caterers, etc. Myra's a stickler for quality, so you can be sure all her sources are up to snuff. She can arrange for caterers, florists, entertainers, musicians, recorded music, invitations, thematic settings, costumes, photographers, liquor—anything at all. She's done every kind of party—not just weddings, birthdays and bar mitzvahs—but such oddities as a divorce party and a party for a travel agent where guests went through a time tunnel that began in an 1880s setting and led into the future. Myra will work within your proposed budget. She's an expert on corporate functions. For the best results, call early so you can have the widest choice of places and services.

**Linda Kaye's Birthdaybakers...Partymakers,** 195 East 76th Street, 288-7112

These professional partymakers can supply and plan any kind of party for adults and children.

Linda has created many original themed parties for kids. One of her concepts is to let the kids bake their own birthday cake under the supervision of a chef—in your home or Birthdaybakers' party room at the above address. Each guest gets to wear a chef's hat and apron and is given a cooking diploma. Linda can also supply entertainers—story-tellers, clowns, magicians, puppeteers, etc.—or plan a party in a skating rink, roller disco or bowling alley. And she can provide a cake in any shape or design, including a portrait of the birthday child. The bake-your-own-cake parties cost $135 for a dozen children if you do it at your house, $100 extra if you do it at Birthdaybakers' party room; hats and aprons are additional.

That's not the half of this very creative organization's offerings. It can handle every element of adult parties, providing caterers, invitations, flowers, entertainers, the works. It even does edible four-foot cakes out of which pops a belly dancer, show girl or whatever you like.

## PARTY POEMS

**Rhymes for Any Reason,** 427-3913 or 516-764-7405
Gladys Phillips creates personal tributes in rhyme—biographical, sentimental and humorous poems—for any occasion. She's done it for birthdays, anniversaries, roasts, bar mitzvahs, thank-yous, weddings, get-well messages, even divorces. Through in-depth interviewing Gladys gets to know the subject's likes and dislikes. The reading of her poems at parties creates a very warm feeling, evoking tears and laughter. Give her at least two weeks' advance notice (more if you want the poem calligraphed and illustrated on parchment—suitable for framing). Customers are given a reading before the date of the event, and if necessary, Gladys will make changes in the text. Prices begin at $35 for a poem of about twenty-eight lines. For calligraphy and artwork add another $40.

## PARTY SUPPLIES AND FAVORS

**Rainbow Party Supply,** 280 Midland Avenue, Saddle Brook, N.J. 201-791-1850
If you're giving a party—anything from a child's birthday celebration to an elaborate wedding—you can save money, and get all kinds of inspiration, at Rainbow Party Supply. Here are 5,000 square feet of party goods, including top brand names, at 20% to 25% off retail prices—up to 40% if you buy the case. In addition to the year-round choice of every kind of themed paper and plastic tableware, invitations, wrapping papers, party hats, balloons, decorations and party favors, there are vast seasonal offerings: Halloween costumes, masks, wigs and candy; Easter baskets, egg dye, stuffed bunnies and gourmet jelly beans; Christmas tinsel, tree lights, ornaments, Santa suits, you name it—they go all out—New Year's Eve hats, horns, noisemakers, streamers, confetti, etc.; and so on for St. Patrick's Day, Mother's Day, Father's Day and whatever else anyone celebrates. There's also a huge wedding department, selling invitations, name matchbooks, personalized wedding favors, garters, ring pillows, bridal albums, wedding cake tops—everything. It's fascinating and it's fun.
Rainbow is just ten minutes from the George Washington Bridge.

Hours are Tuesday to Saturday 9:00 A.M. to 5:30 P.M., till 9:00 P.M. on Wednesday to Friday. During Halloween, Christmas and Easter seasons, hours are 9:00 A.M. to 9:00 P.M. weekdays and to 5:30 P.M. on Saturday.

**Knight Toy & Novelty Company,** 57 Hanse Avenue, Freeport, L.I. 11520, 516-378-4360

Want to delight your children and their friends with a cornucopia of party favors? Knight is a wholesaler of little toys, stuffed animals and novelties that are available to individuals—as long as you buy by the gross. But that means you can get 144 bug rings for $2, the same number of crawly creatures for $7.20, squirt guns for $3, Freddie the jumping frog for $6, clip-on sheriff's badges for $2 or crystal pets for $7.20. Some things can be bought in lesser quantities: twenty-five high-bouncing little balls are $2, little fur dogs are 75 cents each, football or baseball banks 70 cents apiece, clip-on raccoons and bears 90 cents each. And 100 of those little capsules kids get from vending machines at about 25 cents each are $10. Call for an appointment or send a postpaid, self-addressed envelope to the attention of Helen Bee at the above address and ask for a free catalog.

## TEEN PARTY IDEAS

**Stagelight Cosmetics,** 757-4851

This one's sure to be a hit with young teenage girls. Stagelight Cosmetics will send one of its artists to your home (anywhere in the metropolitan area), laden with eye shadows, brushes, lipsticks, blushes, mascaras and all the rest to give a complimentary make-up lesson to each of your party guests. A low-key practical-for-every-day look is stressed, but after the actual lesson the artist will also do fun stuff like painting glitter hearts and flowers and glueing rhinestones on the girls' faces. There's no selling to mar the fun. An artist for a party of twenty girls costs $35 an hour (figure about two hours of face painting). For an additional cost, Stagelight can also arrange cosmetic favors, the obvious cream on the cake for such a party.

## WHITE HOUSE GREETINGS

If you know someone over eighty, he or she is eligible for personal birthday greetings from the White House—a birthday card signed by the president. Over one hundred, the person gets a personal letter. Similarly, anyone who has been married between fifty and fifty-nine years can receive a presidential anniversary card, over sixty years a personal letter. There's no charge. All you need do is send your request a month in advance to White House Greetings Office, Washington, D.C. 20500.

## PHOTOGRAPHIC SERVICES

Rent it, use it, print it, enlarge it—everything for your picture-taking pleasure.

### CAMERA RENTAL

**Olden Rentals, Inc.,** 1265 Broadway, at 32nd Street, second floor, 725-1234

Before you need a darkroom (see below), you need a camera. Olden rents top-of-the-line photographic equipment at reasonable prices and will provide instruction where necessary. If you're thinking of buying an expensive camera but want to try it out first, a rental might be just the ticket. If you're going to China and want a better camera than you take when you go to Disneyland, once again, an Olden rental is the economical answer. It's also a handy service for those items for which you need a special lens or camera—e.g., for underwater photography. All equipment is carefully checked before you leave the store, and you can insure the equipment on the premises. Olden carries just about every kind of camera and lens you can think of, as well as studio lighting and accessories, strobes, tripods, slide projectors, motion picture cameras and projectors. It's best to discuss your needs with a knowledgeable Olden employee on the phone, then come in and pick up your camera. Of course, you can also visit the shop and peruse the equipment, but the camera you want may not be available the same day. Olden also offers good buys on new and used equipment. Open Monday to Saturday 9:00 A.M. to 6:00 P.M., Thursday until 8:00 P.M., Sunday 10:00 A.M. to 5:00 P.M.

## COLOR PRINTING AND DEVELOPING

**Best-Color Photographic Laboratory,** 425 Park Avenue South, at 29th Street, 689-5325

I've discovered a terrific place for color printing and developing. Best-Color is a professional lab open to the amateur (about half its work is for professional photographers), but because all the work is done right on the premises, prices are reasonable. If you're interested, you can tour the plant and see how it's done. Among the services it offers is enlargement of favorite shots for wall decoration (up to 20 by 24 inches). Bring in your film, or call Best-Color for free postage-paid mailers. Your photos will be ready in eight hours, and you'll get a free little photo album (kids love them) with every roll developed. Open weekdays 8:00 A.M. to 6:00 P.M.

## DAMAGED MOVIE FILM REPAIR

**Filmlife, Inc.,** 141 Moonachie Road, Moonachie, N.J. 07074, 201-440-8500

If your favorite home movies have deteriorated with age and improper storage, here is a place that will restore them for you. If you want your film restored, rejuvenated and preserved, call Filmlife. It has restored such big-name films as *Snow White* and *Robin Hood*. Owner Marvin Bernard has been in the business for more than twenty years. He would not reveal his process to me, but his nine steps restore the actual film. He does not simply make a copy. Charges are quite reasonable—under $20 for a fifty-foot roll. No charge if he cannot repair your film.

## DARKROOM RENTAL

**Photographics Unlimited Dial-a-Darkroom,** 43 West 22nd Street, between Fifth and Sixth Avenues, 255-9678

This complete photo resource center is suitably situated in Chelsea,

New York's photo district. For openers, you can rent a fully equipped black-and-white or color darkroom here, along with specialized equipment—a Omega 8 by 10 enlarger, print dryers, dry-mount facilities, etc. Bring your own supplies, or purchase them on the premises. There are several advantages to darkroom rental. For one thing, if your at-home darkroom space (i.e., the kitchen sink) is makeshift, at a rented studio you don't have the hassle of putting away everything each time you use it. You can use more expensive and sophisticated equipment than might otherwise be available to you. Beginners will get a lot of help from qualified staffers, and more experienced photographers will enjoy the camaraderie and the opportunity to exchange methods and ideas with other professionals. Photographics Unlimited also offers learn-by-doing workshops in color and black-and-white printing and studio lighting techniques. Enrollment is limited so that you get personalized, individual instruction. It rents cameras, too, for on-premises use. Call for rates and details.

## PSYCHE AND SPIRIT

New Yorkers do not live by quiche alone. To be a New Yorker is to introspect, be it via shrinks, workshops, Eastern mysticism or California philosophies. This section presents a variety (only a fraction of what's available; the full range would fill another whole book) of options for self-discovery and self-transformation.

**Dialogue House,** 80 East 11th Street, corner of Broadway, 673-5880
   Keeping a journal has always been a tool for introspection and enhancing self-awareness. Dr. Ira Progoff's method of intensive journal keeping involves the recording of silent dialogues with your inner self. It's like putting a magnifying glass on your life and seeing from a clearer perspective where you've been, where you are and where you are going. Participants receive a loose-leaf notebook with sections for recording various entries and insights. They deal with your relationships to yourself, other people, social issues, your work, your body and your personal destiny. Unlike most self-help programs that are done in groups, journal workshops encourage privacy. The basic premise is that the answers to all your life problems are in yourself; the journal is simply a method of tapping into that inner wisdom. You don't need any experience or facility as a writer to learn the method or to use it as an everyday tool for self-integration and enlargement of your creative ca-

pacities. The course is given in a three-hour evening session, usually on Friday night, followed by a twelve-hour session the next day. Tuition is $75, including the notebook.

**Tranquility Tanks,** 141 Fifth Avenue, near 21st Street, 475-5225

Sensory reduction is the name of the game. Floating in total darkness and silence in a saturated solution of Epsom salts and water heated to exactly skin temperature, you're completely free of distractions and alone with your inner self. The tanks are like those seen in the movie *Altered States*, though your experiences in them are not likely to mirror those of William Hurt (he turned simian and then some). Most people talk about experiencing a meditative state, profound relaxation and release from tension. And of course, in New York, total absence of noise itself amounts to a luxury. There is a brief orientation before your first tank experience, and if once inside you should panic, you can always just get out. However, people almost never die. An hour float is $25; you can also sign up for less expensive series of six or twelve sessions, even a midnight to 8:00 A.M. float for $70.

**Dream Workshop,** 30 Waterside Plaza, suite 13E, 889-7956

Every night we receive messages from our unconscious via dreams, but most of us toss them away as if they were junk mail. Psychotherapist Kay C. Greene's Dream Workshop teaches a series of creative techniques for exploring and interpreting your dream imagery. Her methods involve art, meditation, writing, Gestalt dialogue and free association. "Any dream," says Kay, "can be used to transform your life and solve specific problems." She particularly recommends the workshop to people who can't remember teir dreams or are plagued by nightmares. It's an eight-week course, meeting once a week for a two- to three-hour session. Cost is $120. You can also take a shorter six-hour one-day seminar for $50. Kay, who has a B.A. in music in addition to her Ph.D. in clinical psychology, also gives workshops in music therapy for emotional and physical problems.

**Serenity Natural Healing Center,** 74 West 69th Street, between Columbus Avenue and Central Park West, 496-0354

We all hear a lot about holistic health these days. Serenity is its state-of-the-art center in New York, dedicated to helping people develop a sense of responsibility for their own health. It offers excellent yoga classes as well as workshops and lectures on everything from massage techniques to color and sound therapy. It even has an occasional "sprout day"—an entire day devoted to creating your own food supply from sprouts. The Herb & Spice Shop on the premises carries a complete line of oils, natural vitamins, herbal and flower essences, Edgar Cayce products, etc.—everything that might be used in healing, plus the books that explain how and why it works. Hours, Monday through Friday 11:00 A.M. to 8:00 P.M., Saturday 10:00 A.M. to 8:00 P.M., Sunday 11:00 A.M. to 6:00 P.M.

**Biofeedback Study Center of New York,** 55 West Ninth Street, between Broadway and University Place, 673-4710

Biofeedback has been proved an effective therapeutic technique for relieving stress and stress-related problems—migraines, bruxism (teeth grinding), insomnia, alcoholism, hypertension, asthma, anxiety and other such disabilities. It has also been helpful to hyperactive children and those with learning disabilities. It's a method in which the mind heals the body, naturally, without the use of drugs. And unlike traditional medicine, it puts the responsibility for healing on the person who is ill, not on a doctor or therapist. Even if you have no physical manifestations of tension, the process is helpful in increasing awareness of stress and dealing with it, hence preventing future illness. Biofeedback can really teach you to relax deeply, no matter how much tougher—as one headache remedy darkly warns—life has become. Generally ten to twelve seventy-five-minute sessions are required (they cost $65 each), and there's a $165 fee for a two-session obligatory intake evaluation. A consultation is only $35, refundable upon completion of the program. To read up on the subject first, pick up a copy of Barbara Brown's *Stress and the Art of Biofeedback* (Harper & Row); it is the authoritative text on the subject.

**American Center for the Alexander Technique,** 142 West End Avenue, at 66th Street, 799-0468

People in otherwise good health often complain of back pain, fatigue, physical tension and poor posture. And in fact, most people stand, sit (are you slouching as you read this?) and move in an improper manner. The Alexander Technique is a method of restoring your innate awareness of muscular constriction and relaxation so that you can learn to recognize when you are storing tension and use your body with ease, grace, flexibility and freedom from strain. When the technique is applied, the body alignment changes, making for an effortlessly improved relationship of head, neck and torso. The method is very popular with dancers, actors, singers and athletes—those who are most conscious of bodily ease or its lack. And the theory is that a change in physical structure is linked to the psychological structure, so that the Alexander Technique effects include improved emotional as well as physical health. If you're interested, the center refers people to teachers for lessons; these generally cost $20 to $35 per session, and the average student requires twenty to thirty lessons.

**The Shiatsu Education Center of America,** 52 West 55th Street, between Fifth and Sixth Avenues, 582-3424

Shiatsu, or finger-pressure massage, was developed in China and brought to Japan in the sixth century. Practitioners claim it can cure chronic ailments, improve the functioning of organs, reduce tension and maintain health of mind and body, not to mention rejuvenating same. It works in much the same way as acupuncture, but without needles, by balancing energy flow. Wataru Ohashi, author of *Do-It-Yourself Shiatsu* (E. P. Dutton) has worked with the American Ballet Theater company and Martha Graham. His methods combine the traditional shiatsu with exercise, meditation and other techniques. The center offers an ongoing series of classes, workshops, intensives and retreats at beginner through advanced levels. A typical beginner's course meets for eleven three-hour sessions and costs about $230. Call for a class schedule. You can also have a shiatsu massage session here; it costs $35 an hour with a qualified shiatsu instructor, $65 with Ohashi himself.

**Integral Yoga Institute,** 227 West 13th Street, between Seventh and Eighth Avenues, 929-0585

The goal of Integral Yoga, according to founder Swami Satchidananda (he's the Woodstock Swami), is a "body of perfect health and strength, [a] mind with all clarity and control, [an] intellect as sharp as a razor, [a] will of steel, [a] heart full of love and mercy, a life dedicated to the common welfare, and realization of true self," and though you may not achieve all that through IYI classes, you will get very limber if you attend them with any degree of regularity and will probably feel a lot more relaxed and peaceful. The 1¼-hour beginners' classes include all basic asanas (or postures), some breathing techniques, meditation and chanting. They cost just $4, and there's an open class schedule, which means you can attend at your convenience; you're not tied down to the same day and hour every week. Of course, more advanced classes in other aspects of yoga and related disciplines are also offered here. The same options are available at the IYI's other location at 500 West End Avenue, corner of 84th Street, 874-7500.

**Don Ahn's Tai Chi Studio,** 81 Spring Street, between Broadway and Lafayette Street, 226-6664

Tai chi is an ancient Chinese exercise invented by a twelfth-century Taoist priest, but it is more than that. It is an esoteric art form, a means of self-defense, a physical therapy and a way of life. Courses in every aspect of tai chi are given at Don Ahn's, a Taoist health center dedicated to helping people improve their health and happiness through Taoist disciplines. There's even an occasional workshop in Taoist weight loss. A beginners' tai chi class meets twice weekly and costs $49 a month. Call for a class schedule.

**Frederick Davies,** 757-6300

English psychic astrologer Frederick Davies is consulted by Liza Minnelli, Valerie Perrine, Goldie Hawn, Arthur Ashe, Debbie Reynolds and numerous other celebrities both here and abroad. He even numbers U.S. senators and congressmen among his clients. Davies uses an astrology chart plus his psychic abilities. If you'd like a reading from the stargazer to the stars, astrological sessions begin at $200 (that includes a personal consultation or cassette tape); psychic sessions, at $100.

**Martha Wheelock,** 477-3702

Martha Wheelock, an astrologer, also has star clients—Elizabeth Ashley and stage actress Jessica James, among them—and she works with many therapists who have charts done for their patients (Carl Jung initiated this practice, by the way). An initial consultation is $45. It includes a natal reading (your inherent propensities and energies, where you are, and where you're going in the year ahead) that is discussed in a two-hour session with the client. Her emphasis is on how to manifest most effectively who you are astrologically.

## *CHOOSE A THERAPIST*

**Psychotherapies Selection Service,** 3 East 80th Street, between Fifth and Madison Avenues, 679-0700

How do you go about choosing a therapist? The decision could drive you crazy. There are hundreds of schools of therapy (probably more) represented in New York, and the personal rapport between therapist and client is also a vital factor. The Psychotherapies Selection Service is a three-step program designed to help you make an informed and intelligent decision without spending a fortune shopping around. Step 1 is an orientation—a 2½-hour lecture and film presentation that provides an overview of major therapies. Traditional psychoanalytic, Gestalt, primal, bioenergetic, behavior therapy, sex therapy, etc. are discussed in detail. The orientations are done in small groups (three to seven persons), and ample time is allotted for questions. Step 2 is a consultation in which you discuss your needs, problems, goals, expectations and previous experience with therapy; this information helps the service in advising you on the types of therapy to explore. Step 3 is exploration—an opportunity for the client to see three different therapists for one or two forty-five-minute sessions. This is a shopping-around period. All affiliated therapists are New York State-licensed or -certified in the professions of psychology, psychiatry or social work, and all work on a sliding-fee scale based on income. PSS also has a free telephone information number with taped advice on the subjects of choosing a therapy and therapist; 679-0701.

**The William Alanson White Institute,** 20 West 74th Street, between Central Park West and Columbus Avenue, 873-7070

Feel the need of therapy, but find the usual costs mind-boggling? The William Alanson White Institute might be your answer. It offers treatment by candidates in analytic training under supervision of more senior people at the institute. Call up for an application which you fill out and return. When it's processed, you'll be called for an appointment and assigned to a therapist or analyst on the basis of your perceived needs. Depending on your income, fees for psychoanalysis (which requires three visits each week) range from $8 to $35 per session; fees for psychotherapy (once or twice a week) are $16 to $35. There's also a $35 fee for processing the application and your interview. Group and family therapy are available, and the institute can provide Spanish-speaking therapists for Hispanic clients.

**The Phobia Clinic,** Long Island Jewish-Hillside Medical Center, Glen Oaks, 470-4556

If you suffer from phobias—irrational fears of heights, open spaces, closed spaces, social situations, flying, driving, death, whatever—you are not alone. These fears affect approximately 10 million Americans. Traditional psychotherapeutic methods, while often providing insights into a patient's phobias, seldom remove them. But help is at hand. The Phobia Clinic offers treatment in homogeneous group sessions with fees on a sliding scale based on your income. Its methods include desensitization in real-life phobic situations and assertiveness training, and its success rate is over 80%. Length of treatment will vary. If phobias are hampering your enjoyment of life, give the clinic a call.

**The Phobia Resource Center,** 1430 Second Avenue, between 74th and 75th Streets, 288-3400

Another organization offering help to phobics at very reasonable fees, The Phobia Resource Center works with groups on desensitization in the context in which the person has a fearful reaction. In addition to groups, it offers individual and outreach therapy, the latter of special benefit to agoraphobics. It means a therapist will come to your home if your phobia prevents you from coming to the center. The outreach program serves the entire metropolitan area.

**Fly Without Fear,** 310 Madison Avenue, between 41st and 42nd Streets, 697-7666

Fear of flying can mean anxiety around vacation time and arguments with a nonfearful spouse who resents always taking trains and boats; it can limit your job advancement. Face it—we live in the jet age. Fly Without Fear is a self-help program that meets Thursdays from 8:00 to 10 P.M. at various terminals of JFK Airport. Members get to speak to pilots, flight attendants, airtraffic controllers and safety experts. They become acquainted with the facts, and these do support the safety of air travel. Members do relaxation exercises aboard actual stationary aircraft and visit a flight simulator wherein they can experience flight— the sights, sounds and sensations of it—without ever leaving the ground. The cost for all this is a $5 membership and $20 per weekly meeting. American, TWA, United and Eastern are among the many participatory airlines. Every three months Fly Without Fear sponsors a short conditioning flight to Washington or Boston on which you fly with other members, and once or twice a year there are long weekend flights to Bermuda or Nassau. These conditioning flights are, of course, extra. More than 90% of the FWF members who attended a dozen consecutive meetings reported flying afterward with a great reduction of anxiety.

**The Cult Hot-Line and Clinic,** 1651 Third Avenue, between 92nd and 93rd Streets, 860-8533

The Jewish Board of Family and Children's Services, who operate The Cult Hot-Line and Clinic, estimate that between 2 and 3 million people belong to the 2,500 or so cult groups operating in the United States today. The organization was set up to offer assistance to the often-distressed families and friends of cult followers as well as to individuals who are in or have left a cult. Staffed by trained mental health professionals, the program includes a twenty-four-hour hot line for crisis intervention; provides information about specific cults, their beliefs, practices and methods of recruitment and conversion; offers guidance as to possible courses of action; counsels former cult members and helps them readjust to life outside the cult group; and counsels families of cult members to help them deal with the "loss" of an estranged child, feelings of failure as a parent, etc.

## *HANDWRITING ANALYSIS*

**A New Slant, Inc.,** 595-6076

"Your personality comes through on a piece of paper," says certified master graphanalyst Sheila Kurtz. Just by examining a page of your handwriting, she can discover some 300 personality traits, including your thought patterns, your goals, what holds you back, your unused potential, your fears and defenses and your cultural, scientific and business aptitudes. These traits help Sheila counsel clients on career choices. She can also look at the writing of your prospective mate or business partner to determine compatibility. And many of her clients are corporations that screen potential personnel via handwriting analysis. If you'd like to have her analyze your writing, her fees begin at $85.

# REPAIRERS, RESTYLERS AND RESTORERS

If it's broken, they can fix it. If it's old, they can renew it. If it's ugly, they can restyle it. Many of the people listed in this category also do unique custom designs and sell or rent the kinds of items they work on.

## ANTIQUES

**Thorp Brothers,** 410 East 62nd Street, room 706, between First and York Avenues, 752-4232

People in the antiques trade—dealers, decorators, museums, etc.—all know about Thorp Brothers. It's been restoring valuable antique furniture since 1935. Skilled Thorp Brothers craftsmen are adept in replacing veneers, missing parts and marquetry inlays, reproducing carvings, gold leafing and lacquerwork. Open weekdays 8:00 A.M. to 4:00 P.M.

## APPLIANCES, HOUSEHOLD

**All City Appliance Service,** 1 East 36th Street, between Fifth and Madison Avenues, New York, N.Y. 10016, 689-7180

If you've lost the top to your blender, broken the handle of your iron or have a blower that's on the fritz, you need All City Appliance Center. This reliable, reasonably priced company replaces parts of and repairs more than fifty major brands (there aren't many more) of small appliances—toasters, vacuums, pressure cookers, humidifiers, electric knives, shavers and suchlike. It'll examine your appliance free of charge and tell you how much repairing it will cost; all work is guaranteed for three months. It's a good idea to bring your iron in every once in a while to have the bottom cleaned and buffed, and if you've got frayed cords around, come in and replace them immediately—they're dangerous. All City accepts repair work in the mail and ships worldwide; it gets a lot of requests for parts and repairs from overseas. Open Monday to Thursday 8:30 A.M. to 5:30 P.M., Friday till 5:00 P.M., Saturday 10:00 A.M. to 2:00 P.M. (closed Saturday in July and August).

## BRASS RENEWAL

**Michael Dotzel and Son, Inc.,** 402 East 63rd Street, between First and York Avenues, 838-2890

If you need to replace any brass hardware or need that old brass chandelier or wall sconce polished or rewired, call Michael Dotzel. He will reproduce missing brass hardware, repair and refinish antiques and polish brass in your home at $35 an hour ($100 minimum). He also lacquers brass, helping prevent tarnish. Bring in your brass for an estimate; if it is an unusually large item, he will come to your home.

## CAMPING WEAR AND GEAR AND OUTDOOR EQUIPMENT

**Greenman's Down East Service Center,** 93 Spring Street, between Broadway and Mercer Street, New York, N.Y. 10012, 925-2632

Leon Greenman promises "housewifely care" to all your outdoor-related garments. That means that if an item brought in for dry cleaning needs patching or mending, the center will do it at no extra charge—just like Mom. An author of trail guides with more than fifty years' experience as a hiker, camper and climber, Leon offers a wide range of services and considerable expertise to outdoor enthusiasts. He specializes in dry cleaning down garments, quilts, comforters and sleeping bags, using the fluff-restoring Stoddard Process, a pure petroleum solvent method with no chemical additives that can damage your down. The way down costs are skyrocketing, don't risk having your down items cleaned elsewhere. Nor should you entrust your hiking boots to the local shoe repair shop. They need special treatment. Leon replaces worn scree collars, resoles with Vibram (a rubber sole with a super-heavy tread) and otherwise revitalizes them. He can also clean, repair and make alterations (windows and doors) on your nylon tents; replace broken zippers, grommets and snaps on any piece of equipment; make your sleeping bag longer; take any garment and shorten, lengthen or modify it, add pockets, hoods, fur trim or whatever; waterproof your tents, raincoats, boots; custom-create or repair any kind of bag... and much more. You can mail in garments for servicing and repair, or have him arrange for UPS pickup; he'll return them COD. Just make sure you explain clearly what you want done. There's much to buy at the center, too. Among other things, Leon sells down items at discounted prices; outdoor-related books and maps; a large variety of fabrics from parachute-weight nylon to heavyweight Cordura (a texturized nylon used in soft luggage) and a special line of soft luggage and travel packs. Open weekdays noon to 6:00 P.M., Thursday till 7:00 P.M., Saturday (except July and August) 11:00 A.M. to 2:00 P.M.

## CANE AND WICKER FURNITURE

**Veteran's Caning Shop,** 550 West 35th Street, between Tenth and Eleventh Avenues, 868-3244
 Is your beautiful wicker furniture in a state of disrepair? Don't despair. Veteran's, the city's oldest caning shop, can revitalize anything from 1 Chinese Chippendale to 1,000 bentwoods. Veteran's is able to offer reasonable prices because of the high volume of work it does, which includes providing exclusive service to the Museum of Modern Art. It gives free estimates and can arrange pickup and delivery. Machine caning starts at about $20 per seat; handwork at about $50. Open weekdays 7:30 A.M. to 4:00 P.M., Saturday (except June, July and August) 9:00 A.M. to 1:00 P.M.

## CHINA, CRYSTAL AND GLASSWARE

**Gem Monogram and Cut Glass Corp.,** 623 Broadway, between Bleecker and Houston Streets, fifth floor, 674-8960
 If a beautiful crystal chandelier has a missing or chipped crystal part or prism, it can change the effect from one of luxury and elegance to that bargain-from-a-flea-market look. Fortunately your missing pieces can be replaced, your broken parts repaired, at Gem Monogram. For more than half a century it has been amassing an extraordinary collection of old and antique chandelier components from all over the world. And its craftspeople can do just about anything in the way of glass repair. In addition to chandelier repair, they can fix chipped glassware of all kinds, but this is worthwhile only if the piece is rather valuable; otherwise it will be cheaper to buy a new one. Gem also does excellent custom lighting, sells museum-quality stemware and features a large retail collection of sparkling chandeliers. Open weekdays 9:00 A.M. to 5:00 P.M.
 A similar service is offered by **Art Cut Glass,** 79 East Tenth Street, between Third and Fourth Avenues, 982-9580.It can repair chipped glasses and any kind of art glass from figurines to cherished mementos. Prices are quite fair. Open Monday to Friday 8:00 A.M. to 5:00 P.M.

**Hess Repairs,** 200 Park Avenue South, at 17th Street, New York, N.Y. 10003, 260-2255

Someone from the Metropolitan Museum of Art once said, "If Hess can't fix it, nobody can." It restores porcelains, china, ivory, glass, silver, alabaster, crystal, jade, pewter, wood, mirrors and much more. It grinds chips off glasses, fills in chips on china, replaces the blue glass liners of silver salt dishes, restores brushes on old dresser sets, polishes and lacquers tarnished silver, makes new velvet linings for fine boxes...and that's not the half of it. If it's broken, don't throw it out until you've tried Hess. You can bring in items weekdays 10:30 A.M. to 4:00 P.M. for a free estimate, or pack them carefully and send them by parcel post (insured). Upon receipt of mailed items Hess examines them and sends you an estimate of the cost of restoration. Oh, and did I mention it can also repair wrought iron, vases, pottery, screens, lamps, onyx, handbags, brass...?

## *How to Find Discontinued Patterns— China, Crystal and Silver*

What do you do if your china pattern is discontinued, and you have broken the serving platter and five saucers? Or if you inherit your grandmother's discontinued silver and wish to add to the set? I have compiled a list of pattern finders—those businesses involved in the network of pattern swapping and recording. More often than not, given a short amount of time, they can complete the set of the most elusive pattern. Write to any of the below-listed, tell them what pattern you are interested in and, if they do not have information immediately, they will keep you on file and start searching for your pattern.

**Jean's Silversmith**
16 West 45th Street
New York, N.Y. 10036
212-575-0723

**Replacements, Ltd.**
1510 Holbrook Street
Greensboro, N.C. 27403-2785
919-275-7224

**Patterns Unlimited**
Box 15238
Seattle, Wash. 98115

**Pattern Finders**
Box 206
Port Jefferson Station,
N.Y. 11776
516-928-5158

## DOLLS

**New York Doll Hospital,** 787 Lexington Avenue, between 61st and 62nd Streets, second floor, 838-7527

How can you mend a broken heart? In some cases by mending a broken doll. Though the New York Doll Hospital's *raison d'être* is repairing antique dolls, it does a fair amount of sentimental trade as well. In most cases, however, it would be cheaper to buy a new doll. Just about every kind of "surgery" can be done here—eye, finger, hand, arm and leg transplants, nose jobs, repairing chips and replacing hair and eyelashes—and the staff has never lost a patient. The Doll Hospital also cares for teddy bears and stuffed animals; appraises, buys and sells antique dolls; makes doll clothes to order and sells doll parts. It's worth coming in just to look at the thousands of dolls on display—both antique and contemporary collectibles—but it's also possible to mail in a doll for repair. The Doll Hospital will send you an estimate, and if you approve, it'll fix the doll and ship it back to you. Open Monday to Saturday 10:00 A.M. to 6:00 P.M.; closed in July and Saturdays in August.

## FURNITURE STRIPPING AND RESTYLING

**Capability Brown,** 130 West 28th Street, 242-5112

Before you throw out any piece of furniture, be sure you're not getting rid of something beautiful that's hidden beneath coats of ugly stain, varnish or paint. Enid Dent of Capability Brown will strip your coated furniture to the raw wood. (She doesn't dip it—she sprays on the remover; it's a gentler method, which doesn't warp wood or play havoc with veneers.) Then she'll refinish it for you or teach you to do it yourself. The cost of stripping varies with the item; a small dining room table, for instance, will run between about $60 to $80, 25% to 50% more if it's been painted. Enid can also rescue furniture that is ugly or out of date, changing the style of upholstered furnishings, upholstering unupholstered pieces, applying silver or gold leaf and using carpentry to change the design. It's often cheaper than buying new furniture, and I've seen her transform boring old couches and chairs into Art Deco masterpieces. Open Tuesday to Friday from 9:00 A.M. to 6:00 P.M., Saturday from 10:00 A.M. to 2:00 P.M.

## HANDBAGS

**Artbag Creations,** 735 Madison Avenue, at 64th Street, New York, N.Y. 10021, 744-2720

Most women have at least five exhausted-looking handbags moldering on closet shelves. If you do, pull them out and bring them into Artbag. It can clean, restore and repair your worn-out bags and return them to you for another incarnation. Whatever the problem, Artbag can fix it. With infinite skill, it dyes and refinishes frayed edges, repairs reptile and beaded bags, "lusterizes" dull leather, relines, hand-cleans suede and fixes broken zippers. It even offers a nine-month guarantee on workmanship. In addition to repair work, Artbag can turn your needlepoint creations into attractive handbags or design anything you have in mind, not only bags but belts and wallets. If you can't stop by, Artbag accepts items for repair through the mail. Open weekdays 9:00 A.M. to 5:45 P.M., Saturday (except July and August) to 4:00 P.M.

The same services are offered at **Rima Boutique,** 888 Ninth Avenue, near 58th Street, 489-8470. It'll tackle any dilapidated handbag or piece of luggage, regardless of the condition—and the price is right. Ask for Mr. Chamoun.

## JEWELRY

**Rissin's Jewelry Clinic,** 4 West 47th Street, between Fifth and Sixth Avenues, 575-1098

Whether your jewelry is precious, or precious only to you, Joe Rissin will give it his utmost attention. "I can repair just about anything," says Joe. "The impossible takes a little longer." A qualified gemologist of considerable acclaim (*Times* write-ups, TV appearances, etc.), Joe does work for the British Museum, jewelers and dealers. In addition to repair work, he does alterations and appraisals and designs custom jewelry. The clinic can also handle emergencies—like a ring stuck on your finger; Joe cuts the ring off and, of course, repairs it. Open Monday, Tuesday and Thursday 9:00 A.M. to 4:30 P.M.

## LAMPS

**Louis Mattia,** 980 Second Avenue, between 51st and 52nd Streets, 753-2176

Louis Mattia loves lamps. He makes them (almost every found object from a brass shoeshine stand to an old fire extinguisher suggests a lamp to Louis), repairs them, buys, sells and rents them. "I can repair any lamp, no matter what's wrong with it, electrical or structural," boasts Louis. His shop is cluttered with lamps and lamp parts (including chandelier crystals), wall sconces and candelabra, and there's more of the same in the basement. Open weekdays 9:00 A.M. to 5:30 P.M.

## LEATHER GOODS

**Superior Repair Centre,** 2 West 32nd Street, between Fifth and Sixth Avenues, 564-2267

"We can repair anything but a broken heart," boasts Superior's owner Marvin Rosen. Anything made of leather, that is. For more than fifty years Superior has been mending New Yorkers' broken luggage, handbags, jackets, boots, camera and instrument cases, attaché cases, chairs, sporting and camping goods. It can make your boots wider or shorter, redo the stitching or put a new zipper in. In fact, it can put a new zipper in anything, leather or not. Prices are moderate, estimates are free and the work is guaranteed. Open weekdays 8:00 A.M. to 5:30 P.M., Saturday 9:00 A.M. to 1:00 P.M.

**Fordham Repair Center,** 10 East 33rd Street, between Fifth and Sixth Avenues, 889-4553

Fordham will do most anything when it comes to leather and luggage repair. Its prices are not bad, and its work is very good. Open Monday to Friday 8:30 A.M. to 5:00 P.M.

**Kay Leather Goods Service,** 10 West 32nd Street, between Fifth and Sixth Avenues, 564-1769

Kay Leather Goods will not hesitate when you bring in your most worn leather bag or luggage. Its prices are very reasonable. Monday to Friday 8:00 A.M. to 6:00 P.M.

**Lee Fordin,** 19 West 44th Street, between Fifth and Sixth Avenues, 840-7797
   Lee Fordin sells luggage at a discount, besides specializing in leather suitcase and pocketbook repair. While you are getting your old suitcase fixed, don't browse around too much or chances are you will leave the store with two suitcases! Monday to Friday 9:00 A.M. to 5:45 P.M.

## *PIANOS*

**Detrich Pianos,** 211 West 58th Street, between Seventh Avenue and Broadway, 246-1766
   Anything to do with pianos, Detrich Pianos does. It designs pianos, using chrome, Lucite, brass, mirror, etc. It restores old pianos, tunes pianos, rebuilds pianos, removes bad finishes and refinishes properly. It also rents pianos, buys old pianos and sells secondhand, antique and Victorian pianos as well as miniature pianos, figurines and piano-shaped music boxes. Owner Kalman Detrich teaches a 100-hour course in piano tuning and repair in a studio above the shop. It costs $2,200, the price including all necessary tools (which account for about $600). Both children and adults can also take lessons here (beginners to advanced) from piano teachers who have master's degrees in music education. And if you are a pianist looking for a place to practice, Detrich rents out a soundproof practice room at $5 an hour. Open Monday to Saturday from 10:00 A.M. to 6:00 P.M.

**Rom Kovalsky,** 261 Lafayette Street, between Prince and Spring Streets, 925-2647
   Third generation in a family of piano tuners, beginning with his grandfather in Russia, Rom Kavalsky was already tinkering with pianos when other children were still playing with blocks. He offers a complete—and innovative—range of reasonably priced piano-related services. Beginning with the more prosaic, Rom does expert stripping and relacquering as well as tuning, piano repair and restoration. He buys old pianos, restores and restrings them and sells them at low prices. He also rents out pianos, but most interesting is Rom's custom piano work. For a rock musician he created a piano with an attached bucket seat

that could be driven onstage. His skilled artists can paint anything on your instrument, from stenciled airbrush designs to romantic pastoral scenes. He can create pianos of any shape and cover them in just about any material—mirror, chrome, marquetry, fiber optics under Lucite, whatever. And he can make a piano that plays itself or one with a video component that translates music into color. The only limit is your imagination.

**La Piana Piano Sales Ltd.,** 147 West 24th Street, 243-5762

Owner Frank La Piana says that no one believes La Piana is his real name, but it is! He will tune, rebuild and repair your old piano. He specializes in Steinway and Knabe's pianos that were built from 1880 to 1930. He can also help you find a special older piano if you are looking for one, and he builds new pianos to order. He will build uprights, consoles or three sizes in grand. Frank taught Debbie Reynolds how to tune a piano for the musical *Irene*...her role—a piano tuner. Open Monday to Saturday 9:30 A.M. to 6:30 P.M.

## SEWING MACHINES

**Metro Sewing Machines, Inc.,** 100 Lexington Avenue, at 27th Street, 725-4770

Not only does Metro stock all major sewing machine brands, but it also does expert repairs on any household machine you bring in. Open weekdays 10:00 A.M. to 6:00 P.M., Saturday to 5:00 P.M.

## SHOES AND BOOTS

**Occhicone,** 425 North Main Street, Portchester, N.Y., 914-937-6237

There's nothing in the way of shoe and boot repair and maintenance that's beyond Occhicone's expertise. He can fix dry cracked leather, remove dirt and water stains, deodorize, clean hopelessly dirty-looking suede, widen boots or make them narrower, dye them another color, replace a broken zipper, raise or lower a heel or do a total restyling. He can even make an open-toed slingback out of a shoe with a closed heel and toe. Open weekdays 9:00 A.M. to 5:30 P.M., Saturday to 5:00 P.M.; closed the first two weeks of August.

**Jim's Shoe Repair,** 50 East 59th Street, between Madison and Park Avenues, 355-8259

Jim Rocco offers all the above-described services and is listed second only because when you list two things, one of them has to be second. Both shops do excellent work. Open weekdays 8:00 A.M. to 6:00 P.M., Saturday 9:00 A.M. to 4:00 P.M.

**Schwab's Second Wind,** 101B Main Street, Port Jefferson, N.Y. 11777, 516-473-2302

Running shoes these days can cost as much as a pair of Charles Jourdan sandals, so it makes sense to consider repairing your run-down Adidas before parting with a bundle for a new pair. Any kind of athletic shoes (not just running, but basketball, tennis, etc.) can be repaired, resoled, retreaded and otherwise renovated by world-ranked runner Harold Shwab and his dad, Ray. Just send them your out-of-shape shoes at the above address, and they'll return them to you within a week, looking fit. The charge is about $15 to $16 plus $1.50 for shipping.

## TIN AND COPPERWARE

**Retinning and Copper Repair, Inc.,** 525 West 26th Street, between Tenth and Eleventh Avenues, New York, N.Y. 10001, 244-4896

In the city's oldest (since 1916)—and probably only—tinsmithery, amid burning fires, caldrons of caustic soda and monstrous machines (one is ominously called the banger), Mary Ann Miles performs wonders, restoring anything of copper, tin, steel, cast iron or brass. Along with a staff of skilled artisans she buffs and cleans your copper pots and makes your pitted teapots and tarnished samovars gleam again; she'll even tackle a brass bed. Though bakeries, restaurants, schools and institutions make up the majority of her clientele, she'll take any order, no matter how small. You can mail in your pieces (she'll repair them and ship anywhere), or visit the shop weekdays between 9:30 A.M. and 6:00 P.M. Retinning costs about $1.25 an inch. To figure out the price, hook a tape measure on the top lip of the pot or bowl you want repaired; run it down across the side and up the other side (like a U); translate the inches into dollars.

## UPHOLSTERERS

**Sutton Place Studio,** 942 Fifth Avenue, between 51st and 52nd Streets, 758-0394

Sick of your sofa? Before you spend a lot of hard-earned cash on a new one, consider reupholstering and/or restyling the one you have. The Sutton Place Studio can overhaul your old furniture, restyling it to your concept or its own designs. It can also design new furniture or implement your ideas; work up matching bedspreads, drapes, dust ruffles, cushions and pillows; and upholster new seats for otherwise irreparable wicker chairs. Workmanship is always first-rate. The studio has a vast selection of upholstery fabrics from every major house in the country. If you do needlepoint, bring it in to upholster your chairs with. The studio offers pickup and delivery service as well as free estimates and designer consultations at your home. Open weekdays 8:30 A.M. to 5:30 P.M.

**GNJ van Dam, Inc., Upholstery Company,** 3414 Church Avenue, between New York and Brooklyn Avenues, Brooklyn, 327-4907 or 469-7216

Mr. van Dam, Jr., is the eighth generation of van Dams, descended from a long line of European craftsmen in the custom upholstery business. His family still runs the original shop in Antwerp. He will come to your home and give a free estimate (slight charge if you live outside Manhattan, Brooklyn or Queens) and show sample books of fabrics. Or you can visit the Brooklyn showroom, where thousands of fabrics are on display along with local (made in Brooklyn) good-quality brands of mattresses, high-risers, headboards, etc. GNJ van Dam also restyles your upholstered furniture and creates matching drapes, bedspreads or cushions. Pickups and deliveries are done by its own trusted truckers, always accompanied by a principal of the company to make sure your furniture is treated with the utmost care. The Brooklyn showroom is open Monday to Saturday from 8:00 A.M. to 8:00 P.M.

## ANYTHING MISSING?

If there's a service I've failed to list, call...

**Cityphone,** 675-0900
You can find just about anything in New York. The question is where. Cityphone, a free service offered by New York Yellow Pages' Bluebooks knows, and if it doesn't have the information ready at hand, it'll find out and get back to you. Among the items and services it's located for callers are an organ grinder with a monkey, a special oil that attracts sharks, a camel saddle, rattlesnake meat, sterile dirt for mud wrestling, a place where you can rent a coffin and chocolate-covered fortune cookies that are big enough to hold a check. It can also provide more mundane information about shops, services and restaurants (e.g., "Is there a Japanese restaurant near Lincoln Center?), and if you're trying to find something in the Yellow Pages and don't know what heading to look under, it'll tell you. Cityphone makes referrals, but it doesn't rate or recommend anyone. Call any weekday between 10:00 A.M. and 6:00 P.M. Cityphone loves a challenge.

## SHOPPING FOR A NEIGHBORHOOD YOU CAN AFFORD—RENAISSANCE NEIGHBORHOODS

There was a time—and not so very long ago—when ardent Manhattanites never considered living elsewhere. The other boroughs, and even the less convenient sections of the city, amounted to a virtual exile.

But all that has changed. With Manhattan rents continuing to soar, increasing numbers of New Yorkers are exploring alternative places to live.

The following neighborhoods (two are actually in Manhattan) are all in the process of revitalization. The Office of Neighborhood Economic Development is involved in the upgrading of most of them. Parks and storefronts on major shopping streets are being given face-lifts, and in some cases, low-interest home-improvement loans are available.

People in these up-and-coming areas are active, too, in civic groups and local development associations; increased community involvement is, indeed, an advantage of living outside Manhattan. There's a feeling of neighborhood.

Except for Avenues B and C, all the below-described neighborhoods are safe, family-oriented environments.

## AVENUES B AND C: THE FAR EAST

If you think there's no scope left for pioneering in the 1980s, hop into your covered wagon and go east, young man. The currently depressed area from Avenues B and C between 14th and Houston Streets is struggling to rise from the rubble and may be as gentrified as Columbus Avenue in ten years.

A little farther west, Avenue A, First and Second Avenues are already prime real estate. On streets traversing these avenues it's a stroke of luck nowadays to get a one-year lease on a $550 tenement studio.

On and between B and C, however, there are still bargains for the brave. Crime and drugs are a problem here, and the available housing is mostly in run-down tenements. But investors and speculators are quietly starting to buy up buildings in the area. Sixteen abandoned or burned-out buildings on East Eighth between B and C have been relegated to artists (shades of Soho?) for development as live-in working space. Revitalization funds are pouring in, and the OED is working with Avenue C merchants, providing economic assistance for upgrading storefronts. As for the tenements, growing numbers have become terrific living spaces following a process known as gut rehab.

The area around Tompkins Square, a really lovely park, is the prime focus for investors. Those who claim the neighborhood will eventually be upgraded point to the obvious: It is one of the last plausible areas of Manhattan to escape gentrification. Unlike any of the other neighborhoods mentioned in this section—including Inwood—it offers all the traditional advantages of Manhattan living, including easy access to Soho, Greenwich Village, Chinatown and excellent First Avenue shopping.

## BROOKLYN BROWNSTONING—SUNSET PARK AND GREENPOINT

This multiethnic family-oriented residential community may be the coming decades' Park Slope—the next Brooklyn neighborhood due for a turnaround. It does contain an actual park called Sunset Park, and Prospect Park is within convenient distance.

There are hundreds of brownstone and limestone row houses in the "brownstone belt" between 41st and 63rd Streets from Fourth to Sixth Avenues (the full area of Sunset Park extends from the waterfront to Eighth Avenue between 17th and 65th Streets). Brownstones such as those that line Park Slope streets, with three living floors and a basement, beautiful woodwork, fireplaces and parquet floors, are still available here for $50,000 to $75,000. Less ornate post-World War I brick and wood-frame houses are even more modestly priced. And there are good buys for apartment dwellers, on both rentals and coops, the latter often available for under $15,000 with very affordable maintenance charges. There are even some loft spaces. Best of all, it's just thirty minutes from midtown Manhattan by subway, less by car.

Fifth Avenue is the main shopping drag, made more interesting by the presence of Polish, Chinese, Italian, Greek and Hispanic food shops and ethnic restaurants like Fredheim, where Norwegian homestyle cooking is served. More shopping along Eighth Avenue, including a number of antiques stores.

For details contact the Sunset Park Restoration Committee, P.O. Box 288, Bay Ridge Station, Brooklyn, N.Y. 11220, 492-4697 or 871-0775.

Greenpoint, home to New York's largest Polish community, is directly across the East River from Manhattan's East Side. It is a working-class family neighborhood, and its assets include one of the lowest crime rates in New York and the city's fourth-largest park, McCarren Park, which is currently getting a $1 million upgrading. The district is bordered by Newtown Creek to the north and the east, the East River to the west and the BQE to the south. It's a tightly knit ethnic community with restaurants like the Polka and the Little Europe and many shops vending kielbasa and homemade pirogi. Artists (there are very inexpensive loft spaces) and professionals are beginning to come into the area, however. It's just twenty minutes from midtown by subway, ten minutes by car.

Most important, there are brownstones at $70,000, wood-frame dwellings at $45,000, two-bedroom apartments and lofts at $400 a month. Cooping and condominum development are beginning.

For details contact the North Brooklyn Development Corporation, 861 Manhattan Avenue, Brooklyn, N.Y. 11222, 389-9044.

Anyone interested in Brooklyn brownstoning should know about the **Brooklyn Brownstone Conference,** 325 State Street, Brooklyn, N.Y. 11217, 858-7760. It puts on the annual fall Brownstone Fair, in which all aspects of Brooklyn brownstoning—buying, renovating, etc.—are explored in more than fifty exhibits, and it conducts ongoing workshops and coordinates tours throughout the year.

## THE FIFTH OUTER BOROUGH: WASHINGTON HEIGHTS-INWOOD

Washington Heights-Inwood encompasses all Manhattan above 155th Street, between the Harlem and Hudson Rivers. The area has more public parkland (600.5 acres) than any other section of Manhattan, including Fort Tryon Park (home of the Cloisters).

Though it's only a twenty-five minute subway ride from midtown, this quiet middle- and working-class neighborhood is removed by at least a decade in terms of rent. West of Broadway, spacious Upper West Side-style apartments in well-maintained buildings predominate. River views, parquet floors, high ceilings and Art Deco lobbies are not uncommon. The housing east of Broadway tends more to tenements, but many buildings here are being rehabilitated. The amazing news: You can still get a two-bedroom apartment in a decent building up here for $400 to $500. Cooping is tentatively beginning in the area, with people investing mostly between 165th and 168th Streets, and mostly on the West Side. A two-bedroom coop for under $65,000 (equivalent to a $265,000 coop downtown) is not an unusual find.

For shopping, restaurants, etc., 181st Street is the main commercial drag; other major activity centers on Broadway, 207th Street, Dyckman Street, and St. Nicholas Avenue. Residents with cars often take advantage of the Bronx's famed Arthur Avenue and New Jersey shopping. A $1.4 million revitalization of 181st Street was recently completed, and one of the most exciting plans for the area involves a proposed redevelopment of the marina along the Hudson River south of Dyckman Street.

In summary, this neighborhood is definitely on the upswing, and very likely within a decade many people will be kicking themselves for having failed to invest in it.

For details contact the Washington Heights-Inwood Development Corporation, 656 West 181st Street, New York, N.Y. 10033, 795-1600.

## THE KOSHER BRONX—PELHAM PARKWAY

If your idea of the Bronx was gleaned from *Wolfen*, you'll be amazed at Pelham Parkway, a middle-class, largely Jewish community (there's also a sizable Italian population) with one of the city's lowest crime rates. Neighbors stroll the parkway late into the evening, and a general feeling of security prevails. Its advantages are numerous. Subways and express buses can whisk you to midtown Manhattan in forty-five minutes. The area is sandwiched between Pelham Bay Park and Bronx Park, the latter containing the Bronx Zoo and Botanical Gardens. City Island and Long Island Sound beaches are just ten minutes by car—and the famous Arthur Avenue shopping area is a bus ride away.

Pelham Parkway is large, bounded by White Plains Road, its main shopping artery (a semimall and sidewalk improvement have just been completed here), Gun Hill Road, the Hutchinson River Parkway and East Tremont Avenue.

Though people tend to think of the Bronx in terms of apartments, Pelham Parkway offers a wide range of private homes from modest one- and two-family houses to suburban Westchester-style dwellings. You can easily find a home for $60,000. Of course, many buildings do have low-rent apartments. A two bedroom in a modern building with good services and maintenance at $450 is not at all uncommon, not to mention meticulously kept rent-controlled apartments recently vacated by Florida-bound little old ladies. And two-bedroom coop apartments can go for as little as $5,000.

For details contact the Jewish Community Council of Pelham Parkway, 990 Pelham Parkway South, Bronx, N.Y. 10561, 792-4744.

## RIDGEWOOD—LIVING IN TWO BOROUGHS

Straddling the Brooklyn-Queens border, and only twenty minutes from Manhattan by car or subway, the Ridgewood area is a pentagon sided by Myrtle Avenue, Knickerbocker Avenue, Starr Street, Metropolitan Avenue and Fresh Pond Road. About half the community's residents are German-born or of German descent. Italians and many Eastern European ethnic groups are also represented. Hence the many Bavarian restaurants on Myrtle Avenue, ethnic delis and meat stores, konditoreis and shops selling Hummel figures and German records.

More than $2.7 million has been secured for the revitalization of Myrtle Avenue, Ridgewood's major twelve-block-long shopping street. It will have two pedestrian plazas, new trees, outdoor cafés, improved store façades and more quality shops. Nearby Forest Park is also an asset. Another local shopping street, Brooklyn's Knickerbocker Avenue, is also being upgraded.

The tree-lined streets contain mostly late turn-of-the-century brick row houses (many are as attractive as Park Slope brownstones) with small gardens in back. Two- and three-family houses begin as low as $55,000 to $60,000, with apartments going for much less than Manhattan equivalents.

·For details contact The Myrtle Avenue Local Development Corporation, 57-14 Myrtle Avenue, Ridgewood, N.Y. 11385, 366-3806.

## *STATEN ISLAND: THE FORGOTTEN BOROUGH—ST. GEORGE, TOMPKINSVILLE AND STAPLETON*

These three adjoining Staten Island communities are just a half-hour's ferry ride from Manhattan. Step off the boat and you're home—or within easy walking distance of it. And many of these homes are glorious Victorian harbor-view properties.

Although Staten Island still feels a bit like Middle America, many Manhattan singles and couples have already made the move, and there's bound to be a great influx of Gothamites seeking modestly priced housing in coming years. Manhattan-style restaurants have begun to appear in these communities.

St. George (closest to the ferry terminal) contained many elegant homes in the nineteenth century. Today this tranquil residential community, more or less a triangle framed by Bay Street, Victory Boulevard and Jersey Street, offers great housing bargains. Bay Street is its main commercial artery.

Tompkinsville is wedged between St. George and Stapleton. At this writing, the Bay Street landing development on the St. George—Tompkinsville border is nearing the second stages of completion, many units with waterfront views, and they're selling for half the price of their Manhattan equivalents. A 450-boat marina is part of the plan.

Stapleton, some areas of which are in the process of landmark districting, offers a half mile of unobstructed waterfront and a burgeoning artists' community. It extends from the harbor west to about Howard Avenue between Ward and Vanderbilt Avenues (at least that's one definition; no two experts agree). Stapleton's hub is Tappen Park, a "village green" complete with a village hall built in 1889 and a gazebo for events and festivals. The park is currently being restored for events and festivals to the tune of $2.5 million. It will have a Victorian theme appropriate to the area's architecture, new trees and foliage are being planted, sidewalks are being widened, new streetlights are being installed and Canal Street shops are getting a face-lift. Other highlights are Pier 13, a public recreation pier, and Bay Street between Broad and Canal—the antiques center of Staten Island with about two dozen dealers.

There are great housing bargains—many with backyards—in all three areas: one- and two-bedroom apartments renting at $350 and $450 a month, respectively, one-family houses that sell for under $45,000, two-family houses for under $55,000 and gracious Victorian and post-Victorian mansions for under $90,000—even less if you're willing to do extensive renovation. In Stapleton there are small cottagelike houses for under $30,000, though mansions on the hill can get pretty pricey.

For information contact the St. George Civic Association, 14 St. Mark's Place, Staten Island, N.Y. 10301, 720-8181; 79 Monroe Avenue, Staten Island, N.Y. 10301, 448-2479; and for Stapleton the Mud Lane Society, 239 St. Paul's Avenue, Staten Island, N.Y. 10304, 981-3986. For leads on properties in all three areas the *Staten Island Advance* is a good bet.

## SHOPPING FOR SPORTS

Keeping fit is a national obsession—so much so that I sometimes wonder if the body snatchers have arrived and are jocks. You can hit New York's parks at 6:30 A.M. on a Sunday and find joggers out and about. There are hundreds of health clubs, sports facilities and exercise gurus in town, each touting his or her system as the most effective way to stay in shape. The following is a smorgasbord of New York's exercise options, with something for everyone, including the folks who find any and every kind of physical activity a chore.

### *BELLY DANCING*

**Serena Studios,** 243 West 55th Street, between Broadway and Eighth Avenue, 245-9603

Belly dancing is great exercise, and if you don't tip the scales at 200 pounds or anything, it can be sexy. One of the best places to study this Near Eastern art is at Serena Wilson's. Her students dance in top clubs throughout the nation (looking for a career change?) and on cruise ships, and every June her company presents a free outdoor Middle East dance fantasy at Lincoln Center which is attended by thousands of people. She also features occasional cabaret nights at the studio with live music, dance, Middle Eastern food and wine. Four levels of belly dancing (beginner through advanced) are taught at Serena Studios, and you don't have to sign up for any specific time or number of classes. Just get a schedule of classes, and come at your convenience. Serena's book, *The Belly Dance Book, the New Serena Technique*, is a McGraw-Hill paperback.

## DANCING, ROLLER SKATING AND DANCING ON SKATES

**Lezly Dance & Skate School,** 939 Eighth Avenue, between 55th and 56th Streets, 245-6033 or 477-6839

Ever envy those wonders on wheels breezing gracefully along the avenues—not to mention the park and roller disco performers. If you'd like to join their ranks, Lezly and his staff of champion skaters can teach you. He claims they can get anyone—of any age or level of klutziness—skating confidently in just four lessons! For outdoor skating the emphasis is on safety. Indoor skating classes teach you to skate to music and cover every aspect of dancing on skates—both disco and figure skating. If you're really nervous about your ability, sign up for private lessons (about $20 an hour) with an instructor at your elbow. Rates are lower for semiprivate and group lessons. Once you've learned the basics, you can proceed to the fancy stuff, like lifts and spins at competitive prices. The school is also an excellent place to learn the latest dance steps off skates—disco, Latin, New Wave, etc.—and it sponsors many social events and studio parties.

## GYMNASTICS

**Manhattan Gymnastics Center,** 405 East 73rd Street, between First and York Avenues, 737-2016

Nadia Comanici totally captivated America in the 1976 Olympics and sparked a gymnastics craze that is still going strong. A great place to study it is at the Manhattan Gymnastics Center, a spiffy modern facility with 12,500 square feet of mat-covered floor under a 33-foot dome. Head coach Sylvia Cazacu coached the Rumanian Olympic team for twenty years. The center utilizes the most sophisticated gymnastics equipment and has a pro shop, locker rooms and showers on the premises. Classes for children six months old to sixteen are given in eighteen-week September to June semesters; kids can enter at any time. If they are under two and a half, they take parent-participation classes, ages three to four and a half learn basic gymnastic skills and after that, through adulthood, the program is based on Olympic events with twelve levels of skills to accomplish. Some students participate in gymnastics competitions. Adult classes in gymnastics, aerobic dance and physical fitness are also available here, and do inquire about One to One Center on the premises which offers private exercise programs using Nautilus equipment.

**Sports Training Institute,** 239 East 49th Street, between Second and Third Avenues, 752-7111

Sports Training Institute is a no-nonsense facility where many professional athletes—both men and women—engage in rigorous training. There are no pools, Jacuzzis, steam baths, saunas or massage rooms. "If you want to have a good time, go to a bar," says an institute representative. "We're here to work you." Facilities include a large exercise floor with the most extensive line of Nautilus equipment in the city as well as the most sophisticated aerobic training equipment available. Though you may find yourself exercising next to Arthur Ashe or Billie Jean King, your personal exercise programs will be geared to your own level of ability. In order that you get the most out of each session, you always work one to one with a trainer (the same each time) who makes sure you are exercising correctly, safely and effectively... and will push you to the edge of your limit! A series of thirty one-hour sessions (the minimum you can opt for) costs $450, and unlike other clubs, there are no special rates and come-ons. In addition, you're required to undergo an initial physical evaluation ($75) to assess your fitness level. The club is serious, but it's not a Marine Corps boot camp. Trainers are friendly and encouraging, and the clientele (40% female) includes models, actors and actresses, dancers and people from all walks of life—not just jocks. STI is also set up to devise rehabilitation programs for people with injuries. The club is open weekdays from 6:00 A.M. to 8:30 P.M., Saturday 9:00 A.M. to 1:00 P.M..

## RUNNING

**New York Road Runners Club,** 9 East 89th Street, between Fifth and Madison Avenues, 860-4455

If you're seriously into running, this is one club you'll want to join. As a member you have access to the club library, a terrific resource that can supply answers to questions about running techniques, good places to run, equipment, etc. The NYRRC sponsors more than 150 races each year—breakfast and lunch runs, corporate runs, couple runs and, of course, the New York City Marathon—and offers reduced entry fees to members. Members also get *New York Running News* magazine seven times a year, are kept abreast of the club's many clinics and classes, get discounts on merchandise, can attend post race refreshments and award ceremonies and use locker facilities in Central Park. All that for only $15 annually.

# THEATER

New York is the theater capital of the world, with hundreds of ongoing productions at all times both on and off Broadway, in major and minor houses, in lofts, community centers and cabarets. No other city can match the number, diversity and high quality of our theatrical offerings. Much has been written lately about escalating theater costs, excluding the average person from attending. But if you know how to go about obtaining tickets, you'll find that prices—even for major Broadway shows—are still affordable and sometimes actually free. The following listings will clue you in.

### TKTS

Run by the Theatre Development Fund, TKTS has been the greatest boon to theatergoers since Shakespeare. TKTS offices offer half-price tickets on the day of performance to major shows on Broadway, off Broadway, City Center, Lincoln Center and other performing arts houses.

There are two TKTS locations in Manhattan: at Father Duffy Square (Broadway at 47th Street), 354-5800, and downtown at Two World Trade Center, 354-5800. The Times Square theater center is open seven days a week with tickets for evening performances sold from

3:00 to 8:00 P.M. Monday to Saturday, noon to 2:00 P.M. for Wednesday and Saturday matinees. Tickets for Sunday matinees and evening performances are sold from noon to just before curtain time. The World Trade Center location (lower Manhattan theater center) is open weekdays from 11:30 A.M. to 5:30 P.M. and Saturday for evening performances only 11:00 A.M. to 3:00 P.M.

Lines begin forming at both locations hours before the service opens, so come early. The lines are, of course, longer at Times Square; go downtown, and you'll avoid the mob. You must pay for your tickets with cash or traveler's checks.

In Brooklyn, there's a TKTS office at Fulton Street and De Kalb Avenue, 625-5015, open 11:00 A.M. to 5:00 P.M. Monday to Saturday.

**New York Shakespeare Festival Public Theater,** 425 Lafayette Street, off Eighth Street, 598-7150

Under the leadership of Joseph Papp, the New York Shakespeare Festival has presented numerous free productions in city parks and produced hundreds of plays in Lincoln Center, on and off Broadway and in its own permanent off Broadway home, the Public Theater. James Earl Jones, Raul Julia, Meryl Streep, George C. Scott, and Colleen Dewhurst are among the many actors whose careers began with the festival and whose talents have enhanced many of its productions.

Half-price tickets ($7.50 week nights, $9 weekends) are available for all regular Public Theater attractions. These are called Quiktix, and they account for at least 25% of all tickets sold—even for shows otherwise sold out at full price. They go on sale at 6:00 P.M. (1:00 P.M. for matinees) on the day of the performance only. Arrive as early as possible (the advance time you need to be assured of a ticket depends on the popularity of the show), get a number and take a seat. When Quiktix go on sale, number holders are called in order of arrival. You can purchase only two tickets with each number.

For New York Shakespeare Festival Central Park productions, tickets are distributed at the Delacorte Theater (entrances at 81st Street and Central Park West or Fifth Avenue and 79th Street). Distribution begins at 6:15 P.M. the night of the performance; lines often begin forming late in the morning. For details call 598-7100.

If you're not fully cognizant of bargains offered by this marvelous institution, you should know that *A Chorus Line* opened at the Public, where you could have seen it for $7.

**Audience Extras,** 163 West 23rd Street, New York, N.Y. 10011, 989-9550

Audiences Extras is essentially a program to provide actors and actresses, playwrights, aspiring directors—and others to whom theater is of major interest—with affordable theater tickets. If you're actively involved in some aspect of the theater, membership is especially inexpensive, but the general public can also join. There's a limited membership which lasts for a year in order to provide opportunities for other people. Once you join, you're eligible for unlimited *free* show tickets to Broadway and off-Broadway previews, classical concerts, dance events, and private film screenings, though you do pay a few dollars' handling charge. It costs $35 for the general public, $25 for people affiliated with the theater. There's a twenty-four-hour number, 741-7317, that informs members of the shows and performances they can get tickets for.

**Hit Shows,** 300 West 43rd Street, at Eighth Avenue, room 602, New York, N.Y. 10036, 581-4211

Hit Shows distributes discount coupons for major Broadway and off-Broadway shows like *Evita, A Chorus Line, Dream Girls*, etc. They're good for one or two tickets on certain dates (usually more than one coupon is sent for each show, however, so that larger parties can avail themselves); all relevant information is on the coupon. You exchange the coupons at the box office—as far in advance as possible to make sure you get seats—and pay the prices indicated. A $35 orchestra seat on a Friday evening might be just $22 with your coupon; a $16 balcony seat on a weeknight as little as $9. To get on Hit Shows' mailing list, send a stamped, self-addressed envelope to the above address. You'll receive coupons in the mail. You can also stop by the office any weekday between 9:30 A.M. and 3:30 P.M. to pick up coupons. If you call the above number, you'll hear a recording of what shows are available.

# Index

Aaron's Fifth Avenue, 29
ABC Carpet Company, 110
ABC Trading Company, 4
Adnan Restaurant, 179
Adrien Arpel, 129
adult education, 121–125
Adventure on a Shoestring, 139
Ahn's (Don) Tai Chi Studio, 221
Alexander Butcher Block & Supply
    Corp., 85
Alexander Technique, 219
Alexander's Hardware Company, 66
Alkit Camera Shop, 108
All About Parties, 212
All City Appliance Service, 225
Alternative Heat Company, 156
Altman, A., 25
Altman, Azriel, 25
Aly's Hut, Inc., 53
American Cancer Society, 174
American Center for the Alexander
    Technique, 219
American Society of Journalists and
    Authors, Inc., 152
American Surplus, 62

American Woman's Economic
    Development Corp., 164
Anbar Shoes, 52
Andrews (Anne) Employment Agency,
    167
Anelra Lingerie, 40
Animal Hospital of Brooklyn, 105
animals, 105–108
Anita Sari Center, 190
Anjou Violanti, Ltd., 20
Annapurna, 187
Annapurna Emporium, 189
Annapurna Indian Groceries, 189
Antiquarian Booksellers' Center, 17
antique clothing, 20
antiques:
    appraisals, 146
    restoration, 225
antiquities, 112
Antzis Live Poultry Market, 80
Aphrodisia, 79
appliances, 4
    Lower East Side, 4
    by phone, 5
    repairing, 225

appraisals, 146
Arab Atlantic Avenue, 178–181
   food stores and bakeries, 180–181
   restaurants, 178–179
architectural salvage, 84
Ardsley Musical Instruments, 100
Arka, 193
art buying, 194
Art Cut Glass, 227
art prints and posters, 5
art supplies, 6, 7
art tours, 132
Artbag Creations, 230
Artists Space, 194
Ashanti, 31
Ashil Fabrics, 64
Ashley, Laura, 58
ASPCA, 107
Astor Wines and Spirits, 83
astrology, 221
At Home Abroad, 138
Atchison, John, 126
Athlete's Foot, 54
athletic equipment, 53–55
   shoes, 50
Atlantic Avenue. See Arab Atlantic Avenue
Atlantic City, 133
Atlantic House, 178
Atlantic Restaurant, 185
auctions, 11–12
   of unclaimed merchandise, 12–13
Audience Extras, 247
A.V.D. International Foods, 193
Avenue I Flea Market, 68
Avenues B and C neighborhood, 237

baby furniture, 88
baby-sitters, 153
Balducci's, 76, 206
bartenders, 199
Basior-Schwartz, 82
bathroom accessories, 13
beads, 6
Bear Essentials, 150
Beauty Checkers, at Henri Bendel, 130
beauty services, 125–132

days of beauty, 127
electrolysis, 125
facials and waxing, 125
hair salons, 126
make-overs, 129
nail salons, 131
bed and breakfast, 133–134
Bed & Breakfast League, 133
beds and bedding, 96–98
beer- and wine-making supplies, 14
Bell Yarn, 9
Bellevue Emergency Room, 170
belly dancing, 242–243
Bendheim (S.A.) Company, Inc., 10
Benny's Import & Export, 4
Ben's Babyland, 86
Ben's Cheese Shop, 78
Ber-Sel Handbags, 35
Best-Color Photographic Laboratory, 216
Better Made Coat and Suit Company, 26
Bettinger's Luggage Shop, 98
bicycles, 14
Bide-A-Wee Home, 108
billiards and gaming tables, 55
Biofeedback Study Center of New York, 219
birthday parties, children's 199–201
Biss Tours, 134
Black's Furniture, 87
Blatt Bowling and Billiard Corp., 55
blinds, 102–103
Bloomcrest Fabrics, 64
Blue Cross and Blue Shield of Greater New York, 172
boating gear, 56
Bogie's Antique Furs and Clothing, 21
Bondy Export Corporation, 4
Bonsai Dynasty Co., Inc., 141
bookstores, 15–17
boot repair, 233–234
bottles, 17
Bottles Unlimited, 17
bowling equipment, 55
Boyajy, John, 201
brass:
   furniture, 84–85
   housewares, 91

INDEX 251

renewal, 225
Brass Bed Factory, 85
Brass Loft, 91
Brasserie, 207
Bridge Kitchenware Corp., 93
Brill's Liquor Mart, Inc., 83
Broadway Panhandler, 93
Bronx, 240
Bronx Terminal Market, 82
Brooklyn neighborhoods, 237–239
Brooklyn Brownstone Conference, 238
Brothers II, 34
Budget and Credit Counseling Service, Inc., 195
bus tours, 134
business counseling, 164–167
business relocation, 197–198
Buss (I.), 38
butcher blocks, 85
buttons, 6, 18; see also notions

cakes, 207–208
California Hot Tubs & Spas, 89
camera rentals, 215
camping wear and gear, care and repair, 226
Canal Jean Company, 37–38
Canal Street Flea Market, 67
candles, 19–20
caning, 227
Canteen, The, 204
canvas, 85–86
Capability Brown, 229
Capezio Dance-Theater Shop, 55
Capitol Fishing Tackle Co., 56
Cardarelli Fine Furniture, 84
career counseling, 164–167
Carlsen Import Shoe Co., 50
carpets, 110–111
  cleaning and reweaving, 177
Casa Moneo, 81
Caswell-Massey Company Ltd., 60
Catalyst, 165
Catcare, 106
caterers, 201–204
caviar, 71
Caviarteria, 71

Center for Medical Consumers and Health Care Information, 172
Center for Speech Arts, 122
Central Carpet, 110
Central Electronics, 4
Century 21, 46
ceramic supplies, 7
Ceramic Supply of New York and New Jersey, 7
Ceramica Mia, 113
Chateau Animal Stables, 211
cheese, 71–72
Cheese of All Nations, 71
Cheese Shed, 74
Chef Chow Food Company, 72
children's clothing, 22–25
  shoes, 50
Children's Factory Warehouse, 48
china, 89–91
  patterns, discontinued, 228
  repair, 227–228
Chinatown food shops, 72–73
Chinatown Ice Cream Factory, 72
Chinese banquets, 204–205
chocolates, 73–74
Chor Bazaar, 41
Christie's, 11, 147
Christmas tree cutting, 135
Church of the Resurrection Episcopal, 134
churches, 184, 192
cigars, 20
Cinderella Flower & Feather Co., 65
Citipostal, 160
City Dump, 60, 104
Cityphone, 236
Clairol Test Center and Consumer Research Center, 127
Clark & Wilkins, 67
classes, 121–125
cleaning, household, 174–177
Cleantex, 175
closeout stores, 59–60
clothing and accessories, 20–53
  antique, 20–22
  children's 22–25
  costumes, 32–33

custom-made, 33
dancewear, 55
extra-small and extra-large sizes, 30–32
furs, 34–35
handbags, hats and gloves, 35–36
hip chic, 37–39
lingerie and hosiery, 39–41
maternity, 41–42
men, women and children's, 45–48
men's, 42–45
resale and thrift shops, 48–50
shoes, 50–53
sporting, 53–55
wedding dresses, 58–59
western wear, 56–57
women's 25–30
coffee and tea, 74
Cohen, Ezra, 96
Cohen, Irwin, 177
Cohen's Fashion Optical, 62
coins, 112
Coleman Bartick, 91
color printing and developing, 216
Columbia Student Enterprises Bartending Agency, 199
Columbus Farmers' Market, 69
Communication Reconstruction Center, 169
Consumer News, Inc., 149
contact lenses, 62
contests, 195
contractors, 147
cookware, 90–91
copperware repair, 234
Corfou Center, 183
costumes, 32–33
Council for Career Planning Inc., 165
Country Business Service, Inc., 197
Country Dance and Song Society of America, 135
Country Host, 206
courses, 121–125
crafts, 6
Creative Resources, 149
crystal:
   patterns, discontinued, 228
   repair, 227–228
Cult Hot-Line and Clinic, 224
Curry in a Hurry, 188
custom-made shirts, 33
Custom Shops, Shirtmakers, 33
cutlery and kitchenware, 93–94

D. & A., 40
D & D Creative Designs, 65
Daines, David, 126
Damascus Bakery, 180
dancewear, 55
dancing, 135
darkroom rental, 216–217
dating service, 154
David, Jean-Louis, at Henri Bendel, 126, 128
Davies, Frederick, 221
De Santis Brothers, 81
Deals, 46
Dean & Deluca, 75, 205
Decorators Contracting Service, 147
debt counseling, 195–196
Delbon Cutlery, 94, 158
Dembitzer Bros. Export Company, 4
Dempsey & Carroll, 63
dentistry, 168
Designer Shoes for Men & Women, 51
Detrich Pianos, 232
Dialogue House, 217
diet food delivery, 154–155
Disaster Masters, 174
divorce kits, 155
Divorce Yourself, 155
doll repair, 229
dolls and dollhouses, 8
Dotzel (Michael) and Son, Inc., 225
Doyle (William) Galleries, Inc., 11
Drawing Center, 194
Dream Workshop, 218
driving courses, 124
drugstores, 60–62
dry-cleaning, 143–144
Duane Reade Drug Stores, 61
dyers, 144–145
dyes, 7

## INDEX

EARS, The Metropolitan Jewish Geriatric Center, 170
East Village Meat Market, 80, 193
Eastern Onion Singing Telegrams, 162
Eastern Silver Company, 89
Economy Foam Center, 97
Edmund Scientific, 111
education, 121–125
Eeyore's Books for Children, 16
EKO, 193
electrolysis, 125
electronics equipment, 62
Elizabeth Arden, 128
Ellen, Rennie, 92
emergency care, 170–171
Emotional Outlet, 27
employment services, 164–167
Encore Resale Dress Shop, 49
entertainment, party, 208–210
Essential Products, 105
Essex Camera & Electronics, 4
ethnic neighborhoods, 177–198
Exchange Unlimited, 49
experts and consultants, 146–164
eyeglasses, 62–63

Fabric Warehouse, 64
fabrics, 63–65
   cleaning, 175
face-lifts, 129
Factory Outlet, 29
Factory Warehouse, 48
Fae-Mart, 90
Farm and Garden Nursery, 141
farmer's markets, 75
fashion courses, 123
feathers, 65–66
Feilbusch (A) Zippers, 18–19
Feltly Hats, 36
Filmlife, Inc., 216
Fine & Klein, 35
fireplace accessories, 66–67
fireplace and heating stoves, installation and renovation, 156
firewood, 67
First Nighter Formals, 44
fishing gear, 56

Fishkin, 25
Fishkin Knitwear, 26
flagmakers, 156
Flatiron Services, 176
flea markets, 67–70
florists, 157
flowers, 70
   artificial, 65–66
Fly Without Fear, 223
Flying Birthday Cakes, 208
foam, 97
folk dancing, 135
Folklorica, 91
Fonda's, 21
food, 70–83
   Arab, 178–181
   caterers, picnics and platters, 201–204
   caviar, 71
   cheese, 71–72
   Chinatown shopping, 72–73
   Chinese banquets, 204–205
   chocolates, 73–74
   coffee and tea, 74
   diet, delivery, 154
   dried fruits and nuts, 74–75
   farmers' markets, 75
   gourmet emporia, 75–76
   gourmet shops, 205–207
   Greek, 181–183
   Indian, 187–189
   meats, 79–80
   pasta, 80
   pick your own fruits and vegetables, 138–139
   poultry, 80
   sausages, 81
   Scandinavian, 81, 185–186
   Spanish, 81–82
   Ukranian, 190–192, 193
   wholesale markets, 82–83
   wine and liquor, 83
Food of India, 189
For Your Information, 153
Fordham Repair Center, 231
Fordin, Lee, 232
Fortunoff, 92

40 Plus Club of New York, Inc., 167
fossil tours, 136
Foto-Electric Supply Company, 4
Foundation Center, 196
Frame It Yourself, 109
Framemasters, 163
framing, 6, 109–110
Frankel's Discount Store, 57
Fredheim Café, 185
Fredericksen and Johannsen, 186
French Fashion Academy, 123
Frugal Frog, 23
fruits:
    dried, 74–75
    pick your own, 138–139
Fulop (John) Associates, 148
fund raising, 196–197
furniture, 84–88
    architectural salvage, 84
    baby, 88
    butcher blocks, 85
    canvas, 85–86
    children's, 86
    cleaning, 175
    by phone, 86
    pillow, 87
    plastic, 87–88
    stripping and restyling, 229
Furniture Distributors of America, 86
furs, 34–35

G & G Projections, 43
Gabay's Outlet, 60
Gabrielle's Fine Chocolates, 73
Gallery Passport, Ltd., 132
gaming tables, 55
gardening, city, 140–143
Garnet Wines and Liquors, 83
Garth's Original Rent-a-Clown, 209
Geiger, Maggy, 141
Geller, Abe, 27
Gem Monogram and Cut Glass Corp., 227
General Post Office Auctions, 12
Gene's Bicycle Shop, 14
Georgette Klinger, 128
Gettinger Feather Corp., 65

gift brokers, 149–150
Gift Brokers, Inc., 150
giftware, 89–91
Gimme Seltzer, 161
Gingerbread House, 114
glassware, 90–91
    repair, 227–228
Glemby International, 126
Gloria Umbrellas, 116
gloves, 35–36
GNJ van Dam, Inc., Upholstery
    Company, 235
Go Fly a Kite, Inc., 115
Goldberg's Marine, 56
Goldman & Cohen, 39
Goody's, Sam, 110
Gordon Buttons Company, Inc., 18
Gothic Color Company, Inc., 7, 145
gourmet emporia, 75–76, 205–207
Grand and Liberty, 43
Grand St. Bootery, 52
Grand Wine and Liquor, 183
grants, foundation, 196
Grecian Cave, 184
Greek community in Astoria, 181–184
    coffee and pastry shops, 182
    gift shops, 183
    restaurants, 181
Green Guerillas, 142
Greenman's Down East Service Center, 226
Greenpoint, Brooklyn, 238
Greenwich Village Emporium, 68
Grow Truck, 142
Gusenburger Pick-up and Delivery, 143
gymnastics, 243–244

hair salons, 126–127, 131–132
haircare, 131–132
handbags, 35–36
    repair, 230
handicrafts, international, 91–92
handwriting analysis, 224
hardware, 66
Harmer Rooke Numismatics, 112
hats, 36
HBH Bakery, 183

# INDEX 255

headaches, 168
health, 167–174
   emergency care, 170–171
   information, 172–173
heart trouble, 169
Heart Information Service, 169
Heise Brothers, 186
Hellenic Wedding and Gift Center, 184
Hendel's, 26
Henri Bendel, 126, 128, 130
Herman's, 53
Hess Repairs, 227
Hilton Manufacturing Company, 44
Hilton Pastry Shop, 182
Hinrichsens, 185
hip chic clothing, 37–39
Hired Hand, 64
Hirsch Photo, 108
Hisae's, 203
hit shows, 247
hobby supplies, 8
holistic health, 218
home exchange vacations, 136
Homework Help, 157
Homework Hotline, 157
Horenstein, Sidney, 136
Hornmann (Flosso) Magic Shop, 98
hosiery, 39–41
Hotaling's, 101
hotline, women's sports, 164
hot tubs, 89
House of Candles & Talismans, 20
House of Flaubert, 104
House of Talisman, Inc., 19
household cleaning, 174–177
housewares, 89–91
Hudson's, 53

I Do I Do Bridal Salon, 58
image consultants, 147–148
In a Basket, 207
India. *See* Little India
India Food and Gourmet, 189
India Sari Palace, 190
interior designers, 148
Integral Yoga Institute, 220
International Association for Medical Assistance to Travelers (IAMAT), 173
international handicrats, 91–92
International Solgo, 5
Isabel Brass Furniture, 84

J. & R. Tobacco, 20
Jackson (William H.) Company, 66
James Roy, 87
Janovic/Plaza, 124
Jay Bee Magazines, 101
Jay Kay, 25
Jay's Advance Garments, 27
JBZ, 26
Jeans Shop, 26
Jean's Silversmiths, 89
Jeeves of Belgravia, 144
Jensen-Lewis, 85–86
Jeremy's Place, 199
jewelry, 92–93, 230
Jim's Shoe Repair, 234
job counseling, 164–167
Job Lot Trading Company, 59
Joey's Infants and Children's Wear, 24
Jonas Department Store, 52
Josef, Jerry, 109
journals, 217
Just Bulbs, 94
Just Shades, 95
Jumbo, 204

Kahn (Jack) Music, 100
Kalustyan's, 188
Kalyva, 182
Kam Man Food Products, Inc., 72
Kane Enterprises, 92
Kassos Bros., 183
Kauffman (H.) & Son Saddlery Co., 56
Kaufman, A. W., 40
Kaufman Pharmacy, 61
Kaufman Surplus, 38
Kay Leather Goods Service, 231
Kaye (Linda), Birthdaybakers...Party makers, 212
Kennelworth, 107

**256** JOAN HAMBURG'S MOST-FOR-YOUR-MONEY NEW YORK

Kiehl Pharmacy, Inc., 61
Kiev, 191
Kingsley (Philip), Trichologist/Hair Care, 131
Kirshner (Harry) & Son, 34
Kiryakos, 183
kitchenware and cutlery, 93–94
Klein's of Monticello, 23
Kleinsleep/Clearance, 97
knife sharpening, 158
Knight Toy & Novelty Company, 214
Knowhow Workshops, 123
Kovalsky, Rom, 232
Kree International, 125
Krieger (Bernard) & Son, Inc., 36
Krön Chocolatier, 73
Kunst Sales Corporation, 4
Kurowycky's, 80, 193

La Piana Piano Sales, Ltd., 100, 232
Lady Madonna Maternity Boutique, 42
lamps and lighting, 94–95, 231
Last Wound-Up, 115
laundering, 145
Lazars Stationers, 32–33
LBC Clothing, Inc., 43
leather and suede, 47
 cleaning, repairing and restoring, 145, 231–232
Leathercraft Process of America, 145
Lekvar-by-the Barrel, 78
Lend-a-Hand, 151, 176
Leshko's, 186
Leskes, 186
Leslie Bootery for Men and Women, 51
Let Millie Do It!, 151
Levy, Harris, 96
Lewi Supply Company, 4
Lezly Dance & Skate School, 243
Lido Cleaners, 145
Limited Editions, 49–50
Lincoln Cener tours, 137
linens, 96–98
Ling, USS, 201
lingerie, 39–41
liquor, 83

Liquor Line, 163
Little India, 187–190
 food shops, 188–189
 restaurants, 187–188
 sari shops, 190
Little India Stores, 189
Loehmann's, 28–29
Loft, The, 27
London Majesty, 32
London (Gene) Productions, 22
Lord & Taylor Clearance Center, 47
Louis-Guy D, 130
Love, Diane, 65
Love, Harriet, 22
Lower East Side, 3, 4
L. S. Men's Clothing, 44
Lubin Galleries, 12
Lugene Opticians, 63
luggage, 98
Lunch Is Served, 196
Lund's, 186
Luxor Costume Jewelry, Inc., 92

M. M. Shoe Center, 51
Macy's, 30–31
magazines, 101
magic, 98
Magic Menders, 146
Magic Towne House, 200
Make A Frame, 109
Make-Believe Children's Parties, 210
make-overs, 129–131
Malko Importing Corp., 180
Malko Karkanni Brothers, Inc., 180
Manhattan Gardener, 142
Manhattan Gymnastics Center, 243
Manhattan Sales Company, 95
Manny's Millinery, 99
Marble Modes, 113
marriage counseling, 158
Marshe InfoService, Inc., 152
Martin's (Billy) Western Wear, 57
massage, 159
 medical, 173
maternity clothing, 41–42
math, 122

## INDEX    257

Mattia, Louis, 231
mattresses, 97–98
McNulty's Tea & Coffee Company, 74
meats, 79–80
Medic Alert, 170
medical information, 172–173
Mediterranean Garden Restaurant, 179
Melnikoff's, 24
Menage, Le, 208
mending, 146
men's clothing:
    extra-small and large sizes, 31–32
    hats and gloves, 35–36
    hip chic, 37–39
    resale and thrift shop, 48–50
    shoes, 50–51
Menzel Brothers Farm and Farm Market, 138
Merit-Kaplan, 103
Metro Sewing Machines, Inc., 233
Metropolitan Safety Services Institute, 124
Michael (I.), Resale, Inc., 48
Michael's Children's Haircutting Salon 132
military surplus, 38–39
millinery supplies, 99
Mind over Math, 122
miniatures, 8
Minishop Boutique, 30
models, 8
Modern Hatters, 36
Moi Cosmetology Ltd., 131
Moishe's Home Made Bakery, 78
Montefiore Hospital Headache Unit, 168
Moroccan Star, 178
Morris-Jumel Mansion, 210
Mount Sinai Medical Center:
    Headache Clinic, 168
    Nutrition Clinic, 172
Mouthpiece, 150
M.O.V.E. (Moves Organized Very Easily), 148
moving consultants, 148–149
Mr. Apples, 139
Mr. Ned, 47
Ms., Miss or Mrs., A Division of Ben Farber, Inc., 27
Municipal Art Society, 140
Murder, Ink, 15
museums, 193
Music at Home, 209
music boxes, 99
musical instruments, 100–101
Mutual Dried Fruit, 75

nail salons, 131
Natan Borlam, 24
Natural Gourmet Cookery School, 202
Nea Hellas, 182
Near East Bakery, 180
Near East Restaurant, 179
needlework supplies, 9–10
neighborhoods, 236–242
    ethnic, 177–193
Neptune, 182
New Image, 147
New Museum, 194
New School, 152
New Slant, Inc., A, 224
New York Academy of Dog Training, 106
New York Doll Hospital, 229
New York Gas Lighting Company, 95
New York Hospital, 171
New York Road Runners Club, 245
New York Sailing Center, 124
New York School of Dog Grooming, 106
New York Shakespeare Festival Public Theater, 246
New York State Job Service, 166
New York University Student Employment Office, 154
New York Yarn Center, 9–10
newspapers, 101
nightclubs, 184
Norm Enamel Art Gallery, 192
notions, 6
    feathers and flowers, 65–66
    see also buttons; zippers
nutrition, 172
nuts, 74–75
Nyborg and Nelson, 81
NYU College of Dentistry, 168

Occhicone, 233
Odd Job Trading Corp., 59, 104
Odessa Coffee Shop, 191
Oestreicher's Prints, 5–6
office and office personnel rental, 159
office equipment, 102
Offshore Sailing School, Ltd., 123
Olden Rentals, Inc., 215
Omonoia Pastry Shop, 183
Omonoia II, 183
Orchard Bootery, 52
Orchard Toy and Stationery Co., 114
Orchidia, 192
organizers, 151–152
Oriental Pastry and Grocery, 180

Paine, Webber, Jackson & Curtis, 197
painting and paperhanging courses, 124
paints:
    artist's, 6
    theatrical, 7
paints, wallpaper and windowshades, 102–104
Pan Am, 42
Paprikas Weiss, 78
Paragon Sporting Goods, 54
Paris Fashion, 27
parties, 199–215
    bartenders, 199
    children's, 199–201
    entertainment, 208–210
    food, 201–208
    places/ideas, 210–211
    planners, 212
    poems for, 213
    supplies and favors, 213–214
    teen, 214
    White House greetings for, 215
Parties... "A La Cart," 202
pasta, 80
Patticakes and Baked Ideas, 207
Paul's Veil & Net, 58
Pearl Paint Co., 6, 103
Pelham Parkway, 240
Peng Teng, 204
Peninsula Buying Service, 5
Penn Garden, 43

People Resources, Inc., 154
perfumes, 104–105
Pet Clinicare, 105
Pet Club of America, 107
Pet Med, 105
Petfinders, 107
pets, 105–108
Petzinger's, 185
pharmacies, 60–62
Phillips, 11, 147
Phobia Clinic, 222
Phobia Resource Center, 223
photo portraits, 160
photographic equipment, 108
photographic services, 215–217
Photographics Unlimited Dial-a-Darkroom, 216
Piaffe, 30
pianos, repair, 232–233
picnics, 206, 207
picture framing, 109–110
Pie in the Sky, 208
Piemonte Ravioli Company, 80
Pinchpenny Miniatures, 8
Pintchik Inc., 102
Plant Watcher, 143
Plastic Supermarket, 87
Play It Again, 116
Plexi-Craft Quality Products Corp., 88
poems, 213
Poison Control, 171
Police Department Public Auctions, 12–13
Polk's Hobby, 8
portrait photography, 160
postal service, 160
posters, 5–6
Pottery Barn, 90
poultry, 80
Pricewatchers, 5
Prince Fashions, 33
prints, art, 5–6
PS One, 194
psyche and spirit, 217–224
Psychotherapies Selection Service, 221
P/T Child Care, Inc., 153

## INDEX

Quarry, The, 113

Rafal (Jeanne), The French Boutique, 31
Rainbow China Import Company, 90
Rainbow Party Supply, 32, 213
Rashid Sales Co., 181
Reborn Maternity, 41–42
records and tapes, 110
Reminiscence, 38
Renaissance Art Gallery, 19
Rennert Manufacturing Company, 97
Rent-a-Witch, 209
repairers, restylers and restorers, 224–236
resale and thrift shops, 48–50
researchers, 152–153
restaurants:
    Arab, 178–180
    Greek, 181–182
    Indian, 187–188
    Scandinavian, 185
    Ukranian, 190–192
restoration, 224–236
Retinning and Copper Repair, Inc., 234
Rhymes for Any Reason 213
Rialto Florists, Inc., 157
Rice & Breskin, 22
Rice's Sale & Country Market, 69
Richie's Shoes, 50
Ridgewood, 240–241
riding gear and wear, 56–57
Rima Boutique, 230
Rissin's Jewelry Clinic, 230
Rita Ford Inc. Music Boxes, 99
Ritz Thrift Shop, 34–35
Riverside Animal Hospital, 105
Robotorium, 114
roller skating, 243
Roosevelt Raceway Flea Market, 69
Rosenthal, A., 39–40
Royal Saree House, 190
Royal Silk, Ltd., 29
rubbings, brass, 134
Rug Warehouse, 111
rugs, 110–111
    cleaning and reweaving, 177
Rumell Taverna, 182

running, 245
Ruslan, 202
Russ and Daughters, 77

Sac's Costume Jewelry, 93
Saffon, M. J., 129
Sahadi Importing Co., Inc., 180
sailing, 123
St. Demitrios, church, 184
St. George, Staten Island, 241, 242
St. George's Ukranian Catholic Church, 192
SS. Catherine and George, church, 184
San Michel Leather & Suede, 47
sanding machines, 161
sari shops, 190
sausages, 81
Save a Marriage, Inc., 158
Scandinavian community in Brooklyn, 184–187
    food stores and bakeries, 185–186
    restaurants, 185
Scandinavian foods, 81
Schachter's, J., 96
Schacter's Babyland, 86
Schaller & Weber, 79
Schneider's Juvenile Furniture, 86
School Products Company, 9
Schwab's Second Wind, 234
Schwartz Candies, 73
Schwarz (F.A.O.) Warehouse, 113
scientific equipment, 111–112
Scribner's (Charles) Sons, 17
Sculpture House, 7
sculpture supplies, 7
Second Avenue Deli, 203
seashells, 112
Seashells Unlimited, Inc., 112
Second Act Childrenswear, Inc., 23
Second Cousin, 23
seltzer delivery, 161
sensory reduction, 218
Serena Studios, 242
Serenity Natural Healing Center, 218
Service Corps of Retired Executives (SCORE), 198
sewing machine repair, 233

Schackman (B.) and Company, 8
Shaheen Sweets, 188
Shalimar, 187
Shamiana, 188
Shammas and Co., 180
Sheila's Wall Styles, 103
Shelgo, 28
shells, 112
Sherman Shoes, 50–51
Sheru Enterprises, 6
Shiatsu Education Center of America, 220
shirts, custom-made, 33
Shoe Steal, 52
shoes, 50–53
  repair of, 233–234
shoppers, 149–150
silver, 89–90
  patterns, discontinued, 229
Silver Palate, 206
Signe's Imports, 187
Singing Experience, 122
Sizes Unlimited, A Division of Roaman's, 31–32
skating, 243
Skinny Dip, 154
smoking, quitting, 174
Soho Canal Antique Market, 68
Son of the Sheik, 179
Sosinsky (S.) and Son, 43
Sotheby Parke Bernet, 11, 147
Southflower Market, 70
Space Makers for Living, 87
Spanish foods, 81–82
speech arts, 122
Spice and Sweet Mahal, 189
Spice Market, 94
sporting goods and clothing, 53–55
Sporting Woman, 54–55
sports, 242–245
Sports Training Institute, 244
Sportsline, 164
Stagelight Cosmetics, 214
stained-glass supplies, 10
stamps, 112
Stapleton, Staten Island, 241–242
Starlight Tuxedo, 163

Staten Island, 241–242
stationers, 63
Stencil Magic, 10–11
stencil supplies, 10–11
stone and tile, 113
Stonehenge Mill Store, 63
stock market, investments, 197
Stock Market Information Service, Inc., 198
stove installation and renovation, 156
Strand Bookstore, 15
Stretcher Company, 163
stuttering, 169
Suit Yourself, 44–45
Sun Ray Window Cleaning, 177
Sunset Park, Brooklyn, 237–238
Superior Repair Center, 231
Surma, 192
Surrey Liquors, 83
Sutton Place Studio, 235
Sweater Outlet, 47–48
Swedish Institute of Medical Massage, 173
Syms, 45

tai chi, 221
tailors, 146
talismans, 19–20
tapes and records, 110
tea and coffee, 74
Tea for Two, 203
Tele-Wine, 163
telegrams, 162
Tender Buttons, 18
Terminal Music, 101
Teterboro Airport, 200
theater, 245–247
theatrical paints, 7
therapists, 221–224
Thorp Brothers, 225
thrift shops, 48–50
tile, 113
tinware repair, 234
TKTS, 245
tobacco, 20
Tomo n Tomo, 131
Tompkinsville, Staten Island, 241, 242

# INDEX 261

tours:
  art, 132–133
  fossil, 136
  Lincoln Center, 137
  walking, 140
Toy Balloon, 115
toys, 113–116
Tranquility Tanks, 218
trichologists/hair care, 131, 132
trimmings, 6
  feathers and flowers, 65–66
Tripoli Pastry Co., 181
Tuli-Latus Perfumes, 104
tuxedo rental, 163
Typex Business Machines, 102

Ukranian community in East Village, 190–193
  restaurants, 190–192
Ukraninan Museum, 193
Ukranian Restaurant, 190
Ultra Smart, 41
Uma, 190
umbrellas, 116
unclaimed merchandise, 12–13
Unique Clothing Warehouse, 37
United Van Lines' Bette Malone Consumer Services Center, 148
upholsterers, 235
Urban Archaeology Ltd., 84
U. S. Customs Auctions, 13
Us on a Bus, 133

Vacation Exchange Club, 136
vacations, 132–140
  abroad, 138
  art tours, 132
  bed and breakfast, 133
  bus tours, 133–134
  home exchange, 136
  learning, 137
Valley Forge Flag Company, 156
Valmy (Christine) International School, 125
Vartali Salon, 130

Vedeta Restaurant, 181
vegetables, pick your own, 138–139
Veselka, 191
Veteran's Caning Shop, 227
Victory Shirt Company, 46
Vidal Sassoon, 126
videocassettes and dics, 116–117
Video Shack, Inc., 116
Video to Go, 117
Villas International, 138

Wagner (Sherle) International, Inc., 13–14
walking tours, 140
wallpaper, 102–103
Washington Heights-Inwood, 239
Washington Market, 77, 205
Watson, Jill, 160
wedding dresses, 58–59
weight control, 171–172
Weight Control, St. Luke's-Roosevelt Hospital Center, 171
Weiser (Samuel E.), Inc., 15
Weiss (Charles) & Sons, 39
Welles Fireplace Company, 156
western gear and wear, 56–57
Wheelock, Martha, 221
White House Greetings Office, 215
White (William Alanson) Institute, 222
wholesale food markets, 82–83
wicker, 88
  repair, 227
Wicker Garden, 88
Wicker Garden's Baby, 88
will kits, 155
window cleaning, 177
window shades, 102–103
Window Works, 103
wine and liquor, 83
wine by wire, 163–164
wine making supplies, 14
Wingdale Hosiery Co., 40–41
Winston, Stephanie, 151
Wolsk (J.) & Company, 74
Womanbooks, 16
women's clothing, 25–30

extra-small and large sizes, 31–32
handbags, hats and gloves, 35–36
hip chic, 37–39
lingerie and hosiery, 39–41
maternity, 41–42
resale and thrift shops, 48–50
shoes 50–53
Woodside Wood Cutter, 67
Word of Mouth, 206
World-Wide Business Centres, Inc., 159
World Yacht Enterprises, 211
writers, 152–153
Wynnewood Pharmacy, 104

Yale Picture Frame & Molding Corp., 109
yarn, 9–10
Yentagram, 162
yoga, 220
Young's Hats, 36
Youth Opportunity Center, 166

Zabar's, 76, 205
Zamart Discount Yarns and Fabrics, 10
Zelf Tool & Die Works, 161
Zetina, Armando, 159
zippers, 18–19
Zotta, Alice, 146